Volume 91 Number 3 September 2019

T0341502

The Plantation, the Postplantation, and the Afterlives of Slavery

Edited by Gwen Bergner and Zita Cristina Nunes

Contents

American Literature

Book Reviews

Gwen Bergner

Introduction:
The Plantation, the Postplantation,
and the Afterlives of Slavery

This special issue focuses on the plantation, the postplantation, and the afterlives of slavery to consider how we have inherited and continue to be structured by the plantation form. The essays here rethink the biopolitics of plantation slavery and its legacies to interrogate the plantation as a form, logic, and technology by which inequalities of power, personhood, and value are realized. They consider the plantation from a variety of points across the geographic and temporal ranges of American literary studies, including the spaces of the Caribbean, Latin America, and the United States and the periods of plantation slavery proper in the eighteenth and nineteenth centuries, to its subsequent iterations in the Jim Crow and civil rights eras, and up to the neoliberal present in which the carceral state props up fantasies of postracialism. This is not to say that we can simply map the plantation's form onto all contemporary forms of racial injustice or that the slave past wholly determines our present, the meaning of blackness, or the grounds for political affiliation. Rather, there is something to be gleaned from interrogating this structure and resistances to it, not perhaps for liberal humanism's heretofore failed project of human rights and racial equality but to change the ground (sometimes literally) of the discussion, to approach the archive aslant, and to imagine different possibilities of relation.

This reconsideration of the plantation heeds recent calls to challenge the omission of race in much current theory of biopolitics and bare life. As Alexander G. Weheliye (2014: 32–36) and Zakiyyah Iman Jackson (2013: 670) note, Michel Foucault's biopolitics and Giorgio

American Literature, Volume 91, Number 3, September 2019
DOI 10.1215/00029831-7722078 © 2019 by Duke University Press

Agamben's state of exception and bare life—arguably the predominant critical frameworks for analyzing state violence and inequality as constituent aspects of democratic formation—neglect the history and legacy of racialization, colonialism, and slavery. Foucault's biopower and Agamben's state of exception helped shift the conception of modern political sovereignty away from the belief in a democratic community ordered by rational subjects and toward a view of the state as defined by its power to organize and regulate populations. This power includes the right to kill, let live, or expose to death certain subgroups. Although Foucault (2003) names "racism" the mechanism through which the state demarcates these subgroups and Agamben (1995, 2005) chooses "the camp" as the exemplary state of exception for those who are divested of political status and reduced to bare life, Achille Mbembe (2003: 21) notes that slavery "could be considered one of the first instances of biopolitical experimentation" and "the plantation system and its aftermath . . . the emblematic . . . figure of the state of exception."[1] The essays here thus examine the biopolitics of the plantation form to explain "how particular populations are rendered vulnerable to processes of death and devaluation over and against other populations, in ways that palimpsestically register older modalities of racialized death but also exceed them" (Hong and Ferguson 2011: 1–2).

Poststructuralist theory's critique of the West's supposed rational social organization challenged conceptions of the subject. If the modern state is structured by its power over life and death rather than its composition by a polity of autonomous subjects amalgamated through collective rationality, then what of "man," its ideal citizen? The Enlightenment conception of man as a rational, conscious individual produced the subject of human rights and democratic citizenship; however, this ostensibly universal category in fact distinguished white men from those considered irrational, primitive, and ignorant of the rule of law—including women, blacks, and other nonwhite peoples. In the 1990s a burgeoning posthumanism critiqued the modern conception of the human as a historically contingent construct rather than transcendent truth (see, e.g., Jackson 2013: 671–73). This line of inquiry is usually traced to poststructuralist critiques of epistemological certainty, but anti- and postcolonial writers such as Frantz Fanon, Aimé Césaire, and later Sylvia Wynter had since the mid-twentieth century noted that the category of man is circumscribed by its foundational role in the modern Enlightenment project that gave rise to colonial slavery. This other genealogy provides a crucial corrective to posthumanism's continued investment in Western rationality and hierarchies of knowledge. We ask how a racially aware posthumanism illuminates what we mean by Black Lives Matter and why we still need to declare it.

As we reconsider the time and space of the plantation from beyond the liberal humanist idiom, we must guard against "reductive claims" of dehumanization that "obscure more nuanced argumentation" about the ways that racist ideologies construct and sustain hierarchical relationships among humans (DeLombard 2018: 805). As Jeannine Marie DeLombard explains, "Far from denying black humanity, slaveholders extracted profit from recognizing and exploiting that humanity" (800). Conversely, it was the slave's status as both human and property that made slavery abhorrent to abolitionists and unassimilable to our notions of humanness today. How to account for the compatibility of human and property status in the racial ideologies of the plantation slavery era? Bearing in mind this important caveat to distinguish between the liberal humanist subject man, which excluded people of African descent, and the species category of the human, which did not, we might ask, How did eighteenth- and nineteenth-century law and science, as mechanisms of biopower, divide the human species into hierarchically arranged racial subcategories to enable slavery and its legacies?

Taking my cue from DeLombard's study of nineteenth-century slave law in this issue, I would like to consider briefly the example of Supreme Court chief justice Roger B. Taney's opinion in *Dred Scott v. Sandford* (60 U.S. 393 [1857]), which famously held that people of African descent in the United States were considered "so far inferior that they had no rights which the white man was bound to respect" (407). Though reviled in the annals of Supreme Court history, the far-reaching decision reflected the position of the pro-slavery faction leading up to the Civil War.[2] On the issue of citizenship, Taney ruled that people of African descent, even if freed or born to free parents, cannot become citizens of the United States or find protection under the provisions of the US Constitution. They form no part of "the political body" (404) because the "degraded condition of this unhappy race" (409) proves its exclusion from "universal" (407) conceptions of civilized man and, therefore, from the founding documents' declarations of the rights of man. For though the Declaration of Independence's statement that all men are equal and endowed with unalienable rights "would seem to embrace the whole human family . . . it is too clear for dispute that the enslaved African race were not intended to be included, and formed no part of the people" (410). In other words, though this race is human, its members are not among the men referred to by the declaration. Further, the Constitution establishes "the negro race as a separate class of persons, and show[s] clearly that they were not regarded as a portion of the people or citizens of the Government then formed" (410). Taney thus codifies the exclusion of black people from liberal humanism's man to compromise their legal personhood.[3] This reading of the nation's founding documents renders people of African descent bare life. They exist in a permanent state of exception outside the political body of the sovereign state and subject to the "absolute and despotic power" (409) of the state.

Furthermore, in the hierarchy of human races, the "negro African race" (406) is different from other races not only in degree but also in kind. For "this population was altogether unlike the Indian race" (403) and "the subjects of any other foreign Government" (404) who may become naturalized US citizens.[4] Though Taney considers the "uncivilized" Indians "a free and independent people, associated together in nations or tribes and governed by their own laws" (403), he recognizes no such existence for the "negro African race" prior to or apart from slavery.[5] Slavery's mark is eternal because in colonial law black people "were never thought of or spoken of except as property" (410), and those who had been emancipated were "regarded as part of the slave population rather than the free" (411). Moreover, "no one of that race had ever migrated to the United States voluntarily; all of them had been brought here as articles of merchandise" (411). In thus canonizing the natal alienation of US slavery, Taney reserves this special unassimilable status for this "subordinate and inferior class of beings who had been subjugated by the dominant race, and, whether emancipated or not, yet remained subject to their authority" (404–5). The opinion thus works through a tautology whereby members of one race were imported as slaves due to the race's inferior status, and its inferior status is proved by the fact that its members are slaves. The tautological reasoning required to rationalize liberal humanist democracy's relegation of only one race to the status of human-as-property, such that its property status is tantamount to its human status, blurs the boundaries of humanity even as it upholds the claim that (white) man is but a subset of the species.

In sum *Scott v. Sandford* reasons that people of African descent cannot be US citizens and have no rights under the Constitution because they are part of a slave race distinct from civilized man.[6] Thus we might yet consider how the slave's "mixed character" as both human and property made for a hybrid that consternated philosophical, moral, and political categories of humanity. As Saidiya V. Hartman (1997: 5) puts it, "Although the captive's bifurcated existence as both an object of property and a person . . . has been recognized as one of the striking contradictions of chattel slavery, the constitution of this humanity remains to be considered." Yet, in reading the opinion this way, am I simply deconstructing its racializing logic along conventional lines, pointing to a node in the "historical nexus when slavery and race conjoined," as if to find "in the coupling of European colonial slavery and racial blackness a history both inevitable and determined" (Best 2012: 454)? That is not the goal or method of this revision of the plantation form and its permutations. As Stephen Best reminds us, we cannot simply map the slave past onto the present without "divesting history of movement and change" or find in slavery's dispossession the ethical glue of political affiliation without potentially sacrificing "effective political agency" (454). For these reasons, recent work in black posthumanism has sought less to restore humanity to those rendered differently human than to transform the framework of liberal humanism. For posthumous rehabilitation to humanist Man does not help us recover the modes of being of those rendered bare life by the necropolitics of colonial plantation slavery and its afterlives.

This recent work in racially aware posthumanism, new materialism, environmental criticism, and other methods marks a shift from analyzing Western processes of racialization to uncovering the response, experience, and agency of those oppressed by slavery, colonialism, and imperialism. The new critical assemblage also formulates the question of agency through a "flow of knowledge, archives, and geographic spaces" that includes the Caribbean, a region often sidelined within Latinx or American studies (Fiol-Matta and Gómez-Barris 2014: 494). This turn in transnational American studies, which in its earlier phase focused more on the discursive structures of US imperialism than on the forms of resistance and self-making devised by the colonized and enslaved, also signals a shift in postcolonialism away from the Fanonian psychoanalytic subject and preoccupation with melancholia, which arguably provide only ambivalent possibilities of representing subaltern agency. The essays here thus seek to discover what exceeds, escapes, remains outside, or is made new through, around, and in spite of slavery and later formations of white supremacy. Yet they respect the limits of the archive, avoiding fantasies of historical subjects of unfettered agency, resistance, and revolution. This search for modes of being within the plantation structure and succeeding states of exception offers one way to rewrite histories of slavery other than as dehumanization, dispossession, and determinism.

Monique Allewaert's essay in this issue, "Super Fly: François Makandal's Colonial Semiotics," does just this work of reconsidering what counts as knowledge, agency, and object of study in relation to the transnational circuits of eighteenth-century colonial plantation slavery in Saint-Domingue (now Haiti). Allewaert examines the ritual practices of the legendary hero François Makandal, whose fetish making and alleged poisoning of whites, as well as his evasion of execution by transforming into an insect, was said to inspire the Haitian Revolution. She considers the textual evidence in the French colonial archive as well as the vernacular history that circulates in Haiti even today, finding that the archival evidence on Makandal is, in fact, as fully implicated in the very practices of syncretic assemblage it ostensibly documents. That is, both the French colonial text about Makandal's fetish making that Allewaert examines and Makandal's fetishes themselves constitute material artifacts that mediate among domains of knowledge, culture, and environment. In this way, she reconsiders the archival text as something that acts on the world, like a fetish, rather than something that provides authoritative knowledge about fetish making. This approach to the artifact checks contemporary scholars' tendency to privilege colonial European knowledge about enslaved nonwhite peoples and proposes new ways of reading the archive of slavery.

Jeannine DeLombard's "Dehumanizing Slave Personhood" makes a crucial intervention in black posthumanism by clarifying that slavery recognized and exploited black humanity rather than denying it. For this reason, she argues, we can best understand slavery and its carceral afterlives by focusing on the figure of the legal person rather than the human or citizen. Examining a nineteenth-century case of slave law, *United States v. Amy* (1859), DeLombard demonstrates how the case shows the "lethal legacy of slave personhood as a debilitating mixture of civil death and criminal culpability." That is, the law recognized the slave as a legal person primarily to subject her to criminal prosecution and punishment. The result is that slave law naturalized black humanity as criminality, a legacy that persists in the mass incarceration, police misconduct, and racist profiling in US law and culture today, all of which enable the prison-industrial complex to exploit black humanity for profit. Against this criminal visibility and civil invisibility, black people have long offered a politics of counter-civility. Analyzing the dash cam video of Sandra Bland's encounter with Texas state trooper Brian Encinia in 2015, DeLombard explains how videos of police misconduct reveal in real time and space the confrontation between the criminalization of black people and African Americans' counterassertions of civil personhood.

Shifting to the early twentieth century, Jarvis C. McInnis's essay examines circuits of control, communication, and self-determination in plantation spaces of what he calls the global black south. Here the plantation takes a corporate form—in the Delta and Pine Land Company (DPL), which employed thousands of black sharecroppers, tenant farmers, and day laborers in the Mississippi delta, and in the United Fruit Company (UFCO), which operated across the Caribbean and Central America, including the site in Panama he discusses. McInnis uncovers the production and circulation of the *Cotton Farmer*, a paper published by the black tenant farmers of the DPL and circulated through the DPL's eighteen plantations in the 1920s. Learning that the *Cotton Farmer*'s editor received a subscription request from a reader in Panama, which the editor speculated was due to the paper's positive attitude toward Marcus Garvey, McInnis traces this route, as well as those of laborers who migrated throughout the US South, Caribbean, and Central America, to reveal "a dynamic, yet relatively underexplored geography of black transnational mobility and diasporic affiliation" that works within and against the modern management practices of the corporate plantation. Like Allewaert, McInnis attends to the biopolitical mechanisms of plantation control of bodies, labor, cultural practices, and knowledge, even as plantation laborers enact modes of self-determination, affiliation, and communication within their spatial-political constraints.

Like McInnis, Benjamin Child's essay, "The Plantation Counterme-lodies of Dunbar and Du Bois," proposes that black engagement with agriculture during the most repressive Jim Crow era of sharecropping and tenancy "both reflect[s] and create[s] forms of resistance" despite the structural legacies of slavery. Child argues that Paul Lawrence Dunbar's plantation poems and W. E. B. Du Bois's cotton novel, *The Quest of the Silver Fleece* (1911), provide imaginative accounts of agricultural life that transform the necropolitical legacies of the plan-tation into a politics of possibility by showing how "the subject and the nation are inscribed on the ground itself." This interembodiment of human and nonhuman nature is not just metaphorical but material and historical in, for example, Dunbar's poems of a tree used for a lynching or a Civil War battleground that absorbed the miscegena-tional blood of both black and white soldiers. Contrary to the usual accounts whereby the slave plantation's transition to Jim Crow tenancy perpetuates black political and personal dispossession, Child traces in Dunbar's and Du Bois's "agropolitical texts" a radical black embodied selfhood and political agency grounded in the rural landscape.

Julius B. Fleming Jr. picks up on this reworking of the meaning and effect of southern land and plantation ground in his study of the Free Southern Theater's staging of radical plays in the Jim Crow South dur-ing the civil rights movement. Fleming documents how the Free Southern Theater "used plantations, porches, and cotton fields" in Mississippi to stage plays such as Samuel Beckett's *Waiting for Godot* (1954) for black audiences. Fleming claims that these time-conscious performances "revise[d] the oppressive histories of time rooted in the material geographies of the US South," thereby calling audiences to action. In other words, the staging of these plays on the actual grounds of the former slave plantations called attention to the ways that slavery's necropolitics worked through insisting on or requiring black patience with oppression and suffering in order to change the audience's relationship to the time and space of the slave plantations and their afterlives.

Roberta Wolfson's essay "Race Leaders, Race Traitors, and the Necro-politics of Black Exceptionalism in Paul Beatty's Fiction" also con-siders spaces of black community and modes of political organiz-ing but in the contemporary postracial moment rather than during the civil rights era. She examines contrasting examples of black exceptionalism—a race hero and a race traitor—in two of Beatty's novels to explain "the necropolitics of black exceptionalism." That is, US society celebrates or censures exceptional black figures that are marshaled as evidence of a color-blind society only to entrench the social death and civic exclusion of black people generally. As Wolfson illuminates, Beatty places these singular black celebrities in the contemporary necropolitical sites of the basketball court and the segregated urban neighborhood, comparing these spaces to the plantation and its exploitation of black bodies for white entertainment and profit. Beatty's satirical fictions counter this exploitation with modest proposals for political agency and affiliation through mass suicide and the reintroduction of slavery and segregation, proposals that Wolfson explores in relation to the fraught question of how to organize effective black activism in the neoliberal present.

In his influential work *Habeus Viscus* (2014), Weheliye asks what agency or resistance might look like under forms of extreme subjection such as slave plantations or concentration camps (2). Noting the question embeds problems of method and epistemology because the terms *resistance* and *agency* tend "to blind us, whether through strenuous denials or exalted celebrations of their existence," he nonetheless calls for "new modes of analyzing and imagining the practices of the oppressed in the face of extreme violence" (2). This collection goes some of the way toward answering that call. What stands out here is less the brutality and persistence of the plantation and its permutations than the creative agency black people have deployed despite them. From passage into insect life, to assertions of civil presence in the face of police misconduct, to recalibrations of plantation time and space through performance, the essays here excavate the afterlives of bare life and civil death to demonstrate that "racializing assemblages of subjection . . . can never annihilate the lines of flight, freedom dreams, practices of liberation, and possibilities of other worlds" (2).

Gwen Bergner is an associate professor of English at West Virginia University. She is the author of *Taboo Subjects: Race, Sex, and Psychoanalysis* (2005) and articles on race, US imperialism, and transnational feminism in *PMLA, American Quarterly,* and *American Literary History,* among other publications. Her essay on Edwidge Danticat's *The Dew Breaker* is forthcoming in the first edited collection on Danticat.

Notes

I would like to thank my coeditor, Zita Nunes, for her comments and suggestions on a draft of this introduction. I would also like to thank Monique Allewaert for her help in conceptualizing the topic of this issue.

1 Weheliye (2014: 37) notes that Paul Gilroy also connects the plantation to the camp.
2 For a concise account of the political debates over slavery related to *Dred Scott*, see Jaffa 2008.
3 Henry Chambers (2007: 218) says that *Dred Scott* recognized and accepted "tiered citizenship" and "tiered personhood" under the Constitution, though black people were not afforded *any* citizenship and their "tier of personhood . . . was well below that of other non-citizens." In fact, Taney's opinion denies that any rights adhere to black personhood, though he purposely misreads colonial law to do so.
4 In practice, US statutes barred many groups based on race and nationality, including Native Americans, from becoming naturalized US citizens. See López 2006 for a legal history of the role of race in naturalization law.
5 I use Taney's terminology for race to convey but not to naturalize nineteenth-century conceptions.
6 Chambers (2007: 218) sums up Taney's equation of blackness with slavery thus: "Because African slaves had been treated as property when brought to the United States, the Negro race was a degraded one whose degradation was passed on to each of its members. Given that supposed history, free black people were to be treated as free slaves rather than free people with slave ancestors. Indeed, Taney suggested that free black people were regulated more like slaves than like other non-citizens."

References

Agamben, Giorgio. 1995. *Homo Sacer: Sovereign Power and Bare Life.* Translated by Daniel Heller-Roazen. Stanford, CA: Stanford Univ. Press.
Agamben, Giorgio. 2005. *State of Exception.* Translated by Kevin Attell. Chicago: Univ. of Chicago Press.
Best, Stephen. 2012. "On Failing to Make the Past Present." *Modern Language Quarterly* 73, no. 3: 453–74.
Chambers, Henry. 2007. *"Dred Scott*: Tiered Citizenship and Tiered Personhood." *Chicago-Kent Law Review* 82, no. 1: 209–32.
DeLombard, Jeannine Marie. 2018. "Debunking Dehumanization" (a review essay). *American Literary History* 30 no. 4: 799–810.
Fiol-Matta, Licia, and Macarena Gómez-Barris. 2014. "Introduction: *Las Américas Quarterly.*" *American Quarterly* 66, no. 3: 493–504.

Foucault, Michel. 2003. *Society Must Be Defended: Lectures at the Collège de France, 1975–1976.* Translated by David Macey. New York: Picador.

Hartman, Saidiya V. 1997. *Scenes of Subjection: Terror, Slavery, and Self-Making in Nineteenth-Century America.* Oxford: Oxford Univ. Press.

Hong, Grace Kyungwon, and Roderick A. Ferguson. 2011. Introduction to *Strange Affinities: The Gender and Sexual Politics of Comparative Racialization,* edited by Grace Kyungwon Hong and Roderick A. Ferguson, 1–22. Durham, NC: Duke Univ. Press.

Jackson, Zakiyyah Iman. 2013. "Animal: New Directions in the Theorization of Race and Posthumanism." *Feminist Studies* 39, no. 3: 669–85.

Jaffa, Harry V. 2008. "*Dred Scott* Revisited." *Harvard Journal of Law and Public Policy* 31, no. 1: 197–217.

López, Ian Haney. 2006. *White by Law: The Legal Construction of Race.* New York: New York Univ. Press.

Mbembe, Achille. 2003. "Necropolitics." Translated by Libby Meintjes. *Public Culture* 15, no. 1: 11–40.

Weheliye, Alexander G. 2014. *Habeus Viscus: Racializing Assemblages, Biopolitics, and Black Feminist Theories of the Human.* Durham, NC: Duke Univ. Press.

Monique Allewaert   Super Fly:
François Makandal's Colonial Semiotics

Abstract In this article I collate vernacular and elite academic stories about François Makandal, focusing particularly on his production of fetishes, which I (following his usage) call *macandal*. I show that the codes at work in macandal artifacts involve a materialism and semiotics that together constitute a critical methodology. I then use the methodology at work in macandal artifacts to read one key piece of the archive pertaining to Makandal: his judge and executioner Sébastien-Jacques Courtin's *Mémoire*.
Keywords indexical signs, colonial archive, interpretive methods

In November 2018 I visited the Musée Ogier-Fombrun in Montrouis, Haiti, with two Haitians I'd recently met in Port-au-Prince. Our guide recounted a story that incorporated the vestiges of the sugar plantation under our feet into a narrative of the entire country. His story moved from Haiti's indigenous Taíno origins to plantation slavery in French colonial Saint-Domingue to the Bois Caïman ceremony said to have launched the Haitian Revolution to the emergence of the country as the first and only black republic in the Western Hemisphere.

The slave-turned-maroon François Makandal played a key role in this story. Makandal, who was born in the colony, was cast as an avatar of the revolution to come because he had supposedly led a poisoning operation that aimed to drive whites from the colony. Although Makandal was caught and then burned at the stake in Cap-Français in 1758, the museum guide suggested that his poisoning campaign was the first act of an essentially political resistance that

American Literature, Volume 91, Number 3, September 2019
DOI 10.1215/00029831-7722092   © 2019 by Duke University Press

inspired slaves to rise up thirty-three years later in 1791. This story of Makandal circulates widely inside and outside Haiti, perhaps most famously in Alejo Carpentier's novella *The Kingdom of This World* (*El reino de esta mundo*) ([1949] 1957), which adds to the story a commonly recounted detail that Makandal passed from human form into that of "a buzzing mosquito" to escape execution by colonial courts and to continue his campaign (45).[1]

Since the 1980s, historians based in France and the United States have challenged this account. Drawing on French archives and on colonial dictionaries and sociolinguistics, Pierre Pluchon (1987), David Geggus (1991, 1992, 1994, 2002), and Christina Mobley (2015) have argued that Makandal was not really poisoning whites. Indeed, these historians suggest he was probably not really poisoning anybody, at least not in the sense that twentieth- and twenty-first-century audiences understand. Rather, he was making fetishes. That he passed into insect life is, for these historians, so clearly fabulistic that they scarcely comment on it. These scholars emphasize that Makandal was born in Africa, almost certainly in the Kongo (present-day Republic of Congo, Democratic Republic of Congo, and Angola). In the story they tell, Makandal came to the attention of white colonial authorities because he was participating in an African-derived socioreligious practice that white colonists deemed heretical. In these narratives, Makandal's production of fetishes might well have been socially important to Africans in the colony and might have contributed to the emerging syncretic practice of vodou, but they were not part of a poisoning campaign and had no revolutionary political motivations in the mid-eighteenth century.

Because I find historians' evidence for Makandal's African birth compelling, I mentioned this to the museum guide. The guide responded with silence. If the Haitian docent at the museum responded to the conclusions of professional American and French historians with silence, these professional Western historians have little to say about the stories of Makandal that still circulate everywhere in Haiti, and they treat the novelists and politicians who trade in this story as mythmakers whose narratives are apocryphal and epiphenomenal.[2]

To negotiate these silences, it is necessary to recognize that the mutual disregard of Haitian vernacular historians and professional Western historians derives from their drawing on two different archives, two different theories of the archive, and at least two different methods of interpreting the archive.[3] The story I heard from my Haitian guide was drawn from an archive of oral histories, which have passed into print culture from the nineteenth century (Hérard Dumesle, Thomas Madiou) through the twentieth and into the twenty-first (Jean Price-Mars, Guy Endore, Jean Fouchard, Alejo Carpentier, Nalo Hopkinson). The method of interpreting this archive involves the compilation of stories supplemented by a tactic of circumlocution and irony that addresses tensions in this accumulation of histories, memories, and stories.[4] The story told by professional historians is gathered from an archive of documents produced by French colonial elites, most of which are only accessible to those who travel to France and even then only to those who know how to orient themselves in these archives, including the reading of microfiche, familiarity with eighteenth-century Francophone elites' modes of expression, the capacity to decipher eighteenth-century handwriting, and the academic affiliation necessary to enter the archive at all. The method of interpretation here involves locating, consulting, and cross-referencing multiple accounts of the same event that are themselves situated within larger periodizations and other disciplinary frames pertaining to colonialism, law and punishment, and religion in ancien régime France.

In this article, I attempt a reading of Makandal that integrates these approaches by drawing on both archives and both methods of interpretation. I foreground three points that emerge in vernacular Haitian accounts of Makandal and in those of professional historians. First, whatever Makandal was doing that brought him to the attention of colonial authorities was linked to the production of artifacts that have alternatively been called *fetishes, macandal, power objects*, and *gris-gris*. The colonial court decreed his production of these artifacts "seduction, profanation, and poisoning" (Pluchon 1987: 172). Second, he predicted that he would evade final capture by white colonial authorities by passing into insect life. Third, the French colonial court's punishment—an old-fashioned punishment called the *amende honorable* that culminated in burning at the stake—did not go off as planned because Makandal leaped from the flames and into the crowd. Though he was recaptured and again thrown into the flames, the witnessing public (composed of persons of all racial positions and statuses) was evacuated when he leaped from the fire. Because of this, only a few colonial administrators witnessed his execution.

Fetishism, insect passage, and the failure of the colonial court's punishment to fulfill its office. I trace the close relationships among these three points of convergence between vernacular and professional academic stories of Makandal to offer a sustained analysis of a key document in the French colonial archive: an extraordinary handbook discussing Makandal's so-called fetishism that was produced by Sébastien-Jacques Courtin, the very same judge who presided over Makandal's trial and who sentenced him to death. This handbook focused entirely on Makandal's fetishism or *macandalism*.[5] A fetish or *macandal* is an assemblage of fragments of heterogeneous Atlantic world practices and knowledges.

Courtin's handbook is not just a document *about* macandalism but *is itself* a sort of macandal. To access the document as a macandal, it is necessary to attend not simply to this artifact's propositional content but also to the mediations it effects. At stake in this argument is a different method for approaching and interpreting the archives of slavery. Most professional academics working with written artifacts in eighteenth-century colonial archives focus primarily on the propositional content of texts—on what their words and numbers say and mean and, sometimes, what is unsaid or otherwise absent from this propositional content. But making sense of Courtin's macandal requires an interpretive method that departs from the account of language, meaning, and truth that subtends these academic analytical methods. By the codes that govern the production and interpretation of macandal, language does not primarily mean (offer a certain propositional content) but rather mediates (performs the work of holding together and allowing transfer between distinct domains). I explore how macandal mediate between human and nonhuman natures; between nonlinguistic and linguistic materialities; between French colonial organizations of land, bodies, and affect and creole variations on West and Central African organizations of the same that allowed Africans in the diaspora modicums of pleasure and liberty; and finally, between vernacular and elite stories and methods of telling and interpreting these stories.

By elaborating the methods that guide the production and use of macandal and applying these methods to Courtin's handbook, I consider the validity of a series of claims that traditional historians can only discount or treat as epiphenomenal. For one, Makandal really did effect a sort of poisoning, more aptly a metamorphic semiosis by which one thing could transform into another, as when he turned colonial documents from serving as "good" expressions of Catholicism into vehicles mediating Atlantic world contests far afield of French Catholicism. Moreover, his macandalism had a relation to insect life so close he might well have passed into insect form. By passing into the realm of insects and other minute particulars of the terrestrial world, Makandal really did evade capture by the colonial court. Finally, in evading capture, as well as in the practice of macandalism, Makandal's work had the revolutionary political significance that Haitians have long ascribed to it, even in the middle of the eighteenth century.

From the Fetish to the Macandal

My effort to move beyond the silences of professional historians to Haitian vernacular traditions and of Haitians to professional historians' information depends on an analysis of the fetish and of then passing from the term *fetish*, a term of European origin that privileges European archives, to the term *macandal*, a term of Central African origin, through which it might be possible to offer an alternative account of the archive and the codes for engaging it. What is a fetish? William Pietz (1985: 5) proposes that the etymology of *fetish*, which derived from the Portuguese-based *feitiço*, indicates that the word and the concept are not native to any particular culture but emerged from "cross-cultural spaces" on the coast of West Africa. To Pietz's geography I would add Central Africa and the West Indies, as well as South and North America, which were all key zones of cross-cultural contact. Because *fetish* is a term and a concept that derived from cross-cultural contact, Pietz emphasizes that the term does not designate West (or Central) African artifacts and practices that preceded contact with Europeans. Further, he proposes that it cannot be reduced to the sense given by Europeans traveling in and out of these contact zones, namely, a pejorative way of designating African beliefs and practices that supposedly confounded spiritual and material claims.[6]

Middlemen and -women who negotiated between the different cultures brought into sustained contact by colonial mercantilism could not help but recognize that what was valuable in one culture was not equally valuable in another. Thus, people working across cultures understood that value was not a quality inherent in objects but was, instead, socially produced and historically determined. As my overview of Pietz's argument suggests, the Atlantic fetish that emerged from these spaces of cross-cultural contact is quite different from what Karl Marx called the commodity fetish, designating capitalist economists' failure to recognize the social determination of value. After all, the Atlantic fetish arises from the need to work through the *problem* of determining value in a cross-cultural space, whereas the commodity fetish took value—namely, that of the commodity—as a given and as given in the object itself.

This difference between the Atlantic fetish and the European fetish, however, continually recedes in Pietz's analysis. For instance, noting the circulation of the term *fetish* in structuralist writing, Pietz (1985: 9–10n21) suggests that an analysis of Atlantic world fetishes might challenge structuralist linguistics that poses the fetish as a "nonverbal material signifier" (9), marking the limit of symbolic language and with it the limit of structuralism's field of inquiry. However, because Pietz focuses almost exclusively on philosophical problems in the Western canon, he offers scarcely a hint of how language might work beyond this limit or of what, if any, relation fetishes might have to language.

Examining the case of macandalism offers a corrective to Pietz's overly Western focus by situating analysis of the Atlantic fetish in a colonial contact zone. This context allows for the elaboration of the alternate materialism of the sign that Pietz alludes to but does not pursue. To be sure, many of the extant documents pertaining to this case were written by Europeans and white Creoles in eighteenth-century Saint-Domingue, and for this reason, they are also part of a European discursive field that continues to be prioritized and reified by academics. Yet the documents pertaining to this case do not simply express the positions and practices of the French colonial state. They evoke and often directly cite the voices and claims of diasporic African actors, sometimes transcribing their words as they were spoken in the emerging Haitian language and sometimes recording fragments of a range of African languages, since the enslaved and maroons in the colony had come from several African communities. Consider one of the key source documents that Sébastien-Jacques Courtin, the chief legal authority in Saint-Domingue in the late 1750s, produced in the wake of Makandal's trial and execution. Courtin calls his document *Mémoire*, which in eighteenth-century French denoted a formal summary based on firsthand observation, something akin to a natural history. Such a designation would seem to position Courtin's text in a growing body of European natural histories. Yet, his firsthand observation includes accounts of the Kreyòl speech that Brigitte, a woman Courtin identifies as Makandal's wife, used to activate the artifacts.[7] He also records a song voiced by those who use the artifacts, which he transcribes as *"Ouaïe, Ouaïe, Mayangangue (bis) zamis moir mourir, moi aller mourir, ouaie, ouaie, Mayangangue"* (*"Ouaïe, Ouaïe, Mayangangue* [refrain] my friends die, I will die, *Ouaïe, Ouaïe, Mayangangue"*). He notes that he cannot determine either the figurative or the literal meaning of the word *Ouaïe*, which, he explains, has a particular power for Brigitte and other diasporic Africans whom he interviewed.

Courtin also uses several African words, chief among them the word he transcribes as *macandal*, which he uses to designate the artifacts Makandal creates. Courtin's term *macandal* is a transformation of a Kongo-language word, perhaps either *mak(w)onda* (which designates an amulet [Geggus 1992: 29]) or the Yombe *makanda*, meaning "packets of animal, vegetable, or mineral matter wrapped in a leaf" (Mobley 2015: 218).[8] In what follows, I use *macandal* to designate the artifacts Makandal and his associates produced and used. The proximity of this word to Bantu words recognizes the relation of Makandal's practice to similar practices of Central African origin generally designated as *nkisi*. Moreover, the transcoding of this word from an African language into a European one, from the spoken word to an alphabetic script, as well as the clouding of the name's origin that follows on this transcoding, recognizes that this was no longer simply an indigenous Central African practice but one that was changing because of its movement into the cross-cultural Atlantic world, where it was in contact with Fon, Yoruba, Islamic, American Indian, and various European practices and languages.

Courtin's polyglossic text might be read as an example of what Deborah Jenson (2004) calls *oraliture*, which describes colonial writing that mediates the Kreyòl spoken language of colonial Saint-Domingue. Jenson notes that the use of Kreyòl by all classes in the colony "position[ed] . . . all speaking subjects within the parameters of the slave economy" (88). Given that Kreyòl was a language that developed because of the economic and colonial policies of the French mercantilist state but that was substantively developed by enslaved African speakers who were the majority of Kreyòl speakers, the identifications and desires that follow on speaking and writing in Kreyòl were not simply those of the French elite.

As oraliture, Courtin's text circulates in the same material and discursive field as the macandal it discusses. How, specifically, is Courtin's text inflected by this cross-cultural field? The document's full title is *Mémoire sommaire sur les prétendues pratiques magiques et empoisonnements prouvés aux procès instruits et jugés au Cap contre plusieurs Nègres et Négresses dont le chef nommé François Macandal, a été condamné au feu et executé le vingt janvier mille sept cent ciquante huit* (*Summary Report on the Supposedly Magical Practices and Proven Poisonings at the Trials Carried Out and Judged at Le Cap against Several Negroes and Negresses Whose Chief Was Named François Macandal, Condemned to the Fire and Executed the 20th of January 1758*). Courtin's main concern is macandal, which, he claims, caused the various slow-acting illnesses and deaths that affected persons of all origins and statuses in the colonies. At the close of the text, Courtin summarizes the dangers posed by macandal artifacts, focusing primarily on the fact that because the composition and use of the artifacts violated Christian theology and French laws mandating Catholicism, the production and use of the artifacts gave rise to a community of persons who operated outside of colonial law and were therefore a political and social threat to the colonial order.

The text offers a loosely organized ethnography of macandal, their production, and their personal and social uses. Courtin has a macandal in his keeping, for example, that includes a crucifix, which he finds especially repulsive for its "diabolical" perversion of Catholicism. Further, Courtin contends, the addition of pomades to completed artifacts makes them ever uglier. His main point, however, is that the diasporic African practice he documents has real effects, namely, producing malaise, illness, and death. He also describes reports from enslaved and maroon informants that might seem to contradict eighteenth-century French epistemologies: for instance, informants report that well-crafted macandal can speak words to their owners.[9] Rather than suggesting such things are improbable, impossible, or delusional, he simply indicates that he did not himself witness such speech acts. Because Courtin is a French colonial magistrate, we might expect him to simply impose a European epistemology on macandalism. And, to some extent, he does. By punishing Makandal and his accomplices via the *amende honorable*, he enfolds these artisans and their underground activity within a set of European cultural codes concerning heresy. However, his effort to witness the practice of macandalism meant that he worked in close contact with the enslaved and maroons to determine how these packets were understood to work and to what end, often reporting his interlocutors' claims and transcribing certain important terms and phrases verbatim. Despite sometimes admitting that he doesn't understand what his African interlocutors meant or why they did things, Courtin does not confine diasporic African practice to unreality. Rather, the recognition of his own incomprehension of certain parts of the ways these artifacts were used reinforces his sense of the real effects of these practices, which he casts as the real cause of colonial mortality and the colonial temperament.

At once presenting Makandal and his collaborators as producing a theopolitical underground that was absolutely familiar to European courts and as, at the same time, partaking in a practice with codes, meanings, and effects that he could not quite fully grasp or document, Courtin's text testifies to two competing epistemologies in the colony: that of the French state he represents and that of the diasporic Africans he interviews. His text attempts to hold together these two epistemologies and their attendant organizations of nature and the social field so as to dissolve the latter into the former and secure European rule. However, the effect of the text is to evince a third epistemology and, with it, a third organization of nature and the social field, one in which French and diasporic African organizations jostle against each other. This recognition of an African epistemology and the reality that follows on it, even if blunted in this colonial text, is why his *Mémoire* can argue that macandal are both unimportant, aesthetically unappealing artifacts and supremely important practices. This is how in the title of his manuscript he can suggest that Africans in the colony have no deep knowledge of what they do and simultaneously are wily interlocutors constantly outwitting him to pursue ends he cannot entirely determine. This is how he can announce that macandal are at once supposedly magical and at the same time real poison. In the cross-cultural space encoded in macandal, each of these seemingly oppositional things is true. This equivocity at the core of Courtin's text led his contemporaries to disparage him: for instance, Jean Laborde dismissed Courtin and his report as equally as superstitious as the diasporic Africans he interviewed.[10]

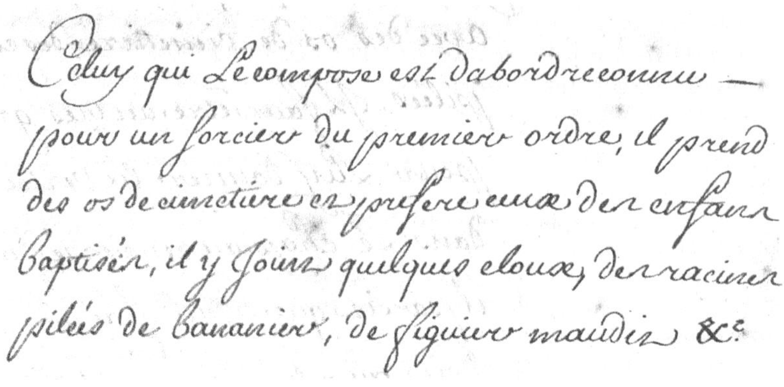
Celuy qui Le compose est d'abord reconnu — pour un sorcier du premier ordre, il prend des os de cimetière et prefere ceux des enfans baptisés, il y joint quelques cloux, des racines pilées de bananier, de figuier maudit &c.

Figure 1 Courtin lists the ingredients in one of Makandal's macandal artifacts. Courtesy of Les Archives Nationales d'Outre Mer

If Courtin's text indicates that European cultural codes and realities were becoming creolized in the cross-cultural space of the West Indies, it also offers a good deal of evidence that African cultural codes and realities were becoming creolized as well. "Here is how one makes a macandal," Courtin writes. First, one gathers a number of materials, which Courtin lists as bones (preferably of baptized children), metal nails, the crushed roots of banana trees, bits of a figuier maudit ("cursed fig tree"), and finally, "etc.," to indicate further ingredients of this category of what he classes as inconsequential things (see fig. 1). One adds to these ingredients those that Courtin groups in another class: holy water, incense, and the Catholic host.[11] These ingredients are put into a cloth with dirt and holy water, and then they are wrapped many times to form a packet that Courtin describes as "about the size of between 2 to 4 thumbs that is more or less the shape of a sausage." While binding together these ingredients, the artisan makes invocations in French, Kreyòl, and what Courtin supposes is Arabic because of the repetition of the word *Allah*.[12] The now-actuated artifact is then doused in holy water and sold: in fact, Courtin explains that it is generally commissioned. It is often used in ritual dances and is frequently reactivated by the addition of pomades, incantations, and processes of knotting.

On the one hand, this artifact is recognizable as a variation on the nkisi artifacts that are still produced in the Central Africa, which suggests it is an American restaging of an existing Kongo practice. Yet this description of macandal and their production also confirms

Pietz's argument that in the Atlantic world "fetish" artifacts spliced together different cultural codes and systems of valuation. For example, this particular artifact includes vestiges of Catholic practice and value like holy water bundled together with banana root, which is likely linked to an African practice, since bananas were prevalent in Central Africa and often used in ritual and medical practices.[13] Historians focusing on the Kongo origins of Makandal's practice have suggested that Courtin must have been wrong when he said the enslaved and maroons he interviewed used the Arabic phrase "Allah" (Mobley 2015: 288, 296). However, it is possible that the practices of Islamic slaves were also incorporated into the American production of these Kongo-derived artifacts. This macandal combines French Catholic and diverse African ingredients, practices, and terms with the roots of the West Indian figuier maudit. Its presence in the artifact indicates that Makandal and his collaborators were reckoning with the Caribbean natural world and developing a Caribbean mode of root doctoring.[14]

If eighteenth-century Saint-Domingue was a cross-cultural space of *creolité*, it was also a space of dramatic power imbalances. To read Courtin's artifact in ways that avoid replicating these power imbalances it is necessary to do more than tease out the diasporic African perspective by using African-derived names; it is also necessary to tease out the diasporic African interpretive codes at work in the production and use of macandal and then to use them to interpret Courtin's macandal. Attending to the codes of Kongo nkisi artifacts to which the macandal are related, as well as to those of Fon and Yoruba practices with which they came into contact in the Americas, offers a method of creating a less-Eurocentric critical approach.[15]

Later anthropologists of nkisi make clear that each artifact has a distinct provenance. This is probably because, like macandal, they were and are commissioned for personal reasons, thus their design and significance can be as diverse as the people who commissioned them. Still, a relatively coherent set of codes is at work in their composition and activation, whether in Central and West Africa or in the West Indies.[16] Most importantly, nkisi, *bo*, and macandal are made up of a series of partial objects.[17] For instance, Courtin notes the inclusion of crushed banana roots, bones, and bits of a cursed fig tree.[18] Sometimes entire objects were brought into a macandal, as is the case with the occasional incorporation of crucifixes. It is likely that entire objects also function as partial objects; the crucifix, for example,

functions as a useful—because highly portable—fragment in meto-
nymic relation to a whole set of Catholic rituals to which Africans
were often forcibly introduced and not as a symbol of Christianity as it
was understood by Western Europeans.[19]

These partial objects function indexically. This point is implicit in
Wyatt MacGaffey's (2000: 86) explanation that the materials gathered
into nkisi are parts that stand for larger wholes, such that a beak
might reference a bird as well as Bárbero Martinez-Ruiz's account of
the referential functions of Kongo semiosis. The terms *indice* and
indexically inform art historian Suzanne Preston Blier's (1995: 223,
224) analysis of the fragments integrated into similar bo artifacts in
Yorubaland. MacGaffey's and Blier's descriptions might be elaborated
by Charles Sanders Peirce's (1998: 5) definition of indexes as the category of signs that "show something about things, on account of being
physically connected with them."[20] Unlike icons and symbols, Peirce's other two categories of signs, indexes express continuity with circumstances to which they remain in relation. Indexes signify precisely
by virtue of their material relation to their referents.

Above all, indexes indicate a domain of language in which the materiality of the world and the materiality of the sign are coconstitutive.[21]
These macandal artifacts' collation of indexes requires that those who
interpret them contend with this special category of signs that have
been given rather short shrift in historical and literary criticism until
recently because both disciplines have generally presumed a Saussurean account of the sign. This posits as its first principle the arbitrari-
ness of the sign, which in turn suggests that the sign is a purely formal and conventional symbol (Saussure 2016: 67). This purely formal
sign implies a break between the realm of language (where conventions and formal structures allow for the production of meaning) and
that of the material world of nonhuman nature (to which language has
an only arbitrary and thus, generally speaking, nonmeaningful relation) (Saussure 2016: pt. 1, chap. 1).[22] Interpreting macandal artifacts
and their unusually dense collation of indexical signs turns new attention to signs that do not signify as symbols (conventional signs by
Peirce's definition) do, yet that circulate within symbolic language.
Attending to the indexical function of these signs also offers some
sense of the speech acts that Courtin's informants said were sometimes performed by these artifacts since these partial objects on their
own (or brought into new relation in the artifacts) recall, and speak to
and of, their material circumstances. Attending to indexicality also

links up to MacGaffey's (2000: 84) claim that the ingredients in Kongo nkisi can be punning "material metaphors" for the things or powers with which they are associated.

If macandal artifacts' partial objects are in relation to the scenes that they represent by indexing them, then on being cut from these scenes and put into a different set of relations, these indexical signs also achieve a distinction or difference from these scenes. Without being symbols in the Peircean sense since they are not conventional signs, they are partially removed from the circumstances from which they are engendered. For instance, speaking of Dahomey cosmology, anthropologist Melville J. Herskovits (1938: 2:244) offers the example of taking a fragment of a root close to a rock that partakes of the "spirit" of a historical event that occurred in this location (that is to say, the rock functions as a concretization of history, and the things in proximity to this rock are associated with that history). We might posit that, in this case, the root functions as an index of an event sedimented in that particular place. If this root signifies precisely because of its material relation to its circumstance, it is also distinct from it on becoming a partial object. After all, the historical event sedimented in place has become portable by virtue of the index. Moreover, in being separated from its circumstance, this root also changes its circumstance. First, on the index's extraction from the milieu that engenders it, this milieu is changed. Second, the index carries only a part of its circumstance and only a part of it as it existed before its separation from its circumstance. Finally, this indexical sign is put in relation to other indexical signs on the ground of the artifact. This process of gathering indexes and then mixing them would make the particular materiality of this historical event register differently for the commissioner of the artifact. This difference could be that of producing a partial liberation from a historical event that is also being materially referenced, brought into the present, and transformed by the index.[23]

To put to the test my claim that the ingredients of macandal are indexes and that attending to their indexicality broadens thinking on language beyond professional critics' mostly symbolic accounts of signs, consider the roots of the figuier maudit reported by Courtin. This particular tree—also sometimes called the figuier sauvage or the strangler fig—is indigenous to the American tropics, so it was new to both Europeans and Africans in the colonies (see fig. 2). The French naturalists who named the tree were particularly focused on

Figure 2 Engraving of the "figuier sauvage," another name for the figuier maudit in Jean Baptiste Labat's *Nouveau voyage aux isles de l'Amerique*. Courtesy of the Newberry Library's Ayer Collection, Ayer 1000.L15 1722 Special Collections

the tree's mode of reproduction, which Dominican naturalists in the West Indies described as occurring via two different modalities—*franc*, or seed-grown propagation, and what they called bastard or maroon propagation (Nicolson 1776: 232). This latter mode of propagation was cast as autonomous reproduction in which parts of trees produced new trees, sometimes within an existing tree, which led to what one eighteenth-century Dominican naturalist called "arbicide" (233) and which is dramatized in French Dominican natural historian and plantation owner Père Labat's mid-eighteenth-century drawing of the tree. Here he depicts the trailing roots of new trees born from parts of old ones hanging down from a host tree of the same species, which the new trees will eventually overwhelm. One Dominican naturalist (Jean Baptiste du Tertre) suggested that the figuier maudit propagated flies as well as figs; Père Labat suggested that only some of its fruit hosted flies and more fully developed an account of cross-species parasitism (Labat 1724: 55–57). The problem of fertility is central to such writing, whether in attention to the tree's unwanted and some-times "arbicidal" "maroon" propagation or in accounts that argued for, or against, the idea that trees can produce insect progeny. These problems linked to fertility are mitigated by the French naturalists' use of the name figuier maudit, which references a parable in the gospels of Matthew and Mark in which Christ, on seeing a fig tree that doesn't bear fruit, cursed this tree, after which it subsequently died. The evangelists indicate that the parable's moral is that the divine word is an expression of spirit that is separate from and determines material nature (Mark 11:20–26). This fable of the power of the word over nonhuman nature likely informed the French naming of this trop-ical tree with its threatening reproductive capacities, for the name announces the sovereignty of the name and the word over the thing that it references in ways that clearly echo French naturalists' hopes that their names and other representational technologies would con-trol the strange fertilities and cross-species metamorphoses of all sorts that occurred in plantation colonies.

Why did Makandal use roots of the figuier maudit in the artifact Courtin had in his possession? It is impossible to answer this question precisely since every macandal is singular. Moreover, because indexi-cal signs are in material relation to their circumstances, they are meaningful only in their contexts or when these contexts are known. Still, natural histories from the colonial period offer several clues. Père Labat and Père Nicolson (an eighteenth-century Dominican priest and natural historian) note that the wood of this tree was used by the enslaved community to craft utensils (Labat 1724: 19; Nicolson 1776: 232). For this reason, the tree may have been associated with eating and other food-related rituals. Wild fig trees were also used as antidotes to various poisons in eighteenth-century Barbados (Handler and Jacoby 1993). This suggests that substances in the tree had (or were thought to have) curative effects and were used for this reason. Third, since white creoles and Europeans also called this the maroon fig, there might have been an association between this fig tree and the communities of self-liberated slaves also called maroons.

Thomas Madiou's history of Haiti offers a tantalizing clue about the status of the figuier maudit among early nineteenth-century black peasants, which again suggests the tree's importance to the colony's black community. He recounts a political intrigue that played out in 1812 when a representative (Henri Christophe) of one political party staged an appearance of the Virgin Mary in a figuier maudit in order to mobilize the Haitian peasantry to his side (Madiou 1989: 5:111–26). His rival (Alexandre Pétion) attempted to undermine his ploy by ordering a Catholic priest to visit this same tree and declare that if it really bore any special properties, the tree would not succumb to fire, at which point he doused it in oil and put a match to it. The tree burned. The gathered peasantry was scandalized, but not simply because this second political operative had proven that the first had duped them by having a fraudulent Virgin Mary masquerade in the tree but because burning this tree was—to use Madiou's term—*sacrilegious* whether or not the Virgin Mary was in it (5:112). The point to draw from Madiou's account is that the early Haitian peasantry understood the figuier maudit as a vector for a power that exceeded that of the Catholic God and saints. Moreover, neither of these political rivals (Christophe or Pétion) was able to harness this arboreal power in the service of their political ambitions, even if that power was understood as extending into the political realm, as indicated by the struggle over how to mobilize the tree to further political ambitions.

The early nineteenth-century Haitian peasantry's expectation that the figuier maudit's power precedes and exceeds that of these rival political parties makes perceptible an aural pun in the French name still half audible in the Kreyòl appropriation of this name: *figuier "maudit"* is a close homophone for *figuier mot dit*, that is to say, "the word spoken by the fig tree."[24] This homophony vests the power of signification in the tree. In this homophony, nonhuman nature and signs are not antipodal (as they are in the parable that inspired the French naturalists' naming, which puts the power of the word over nature and that of spirit over matter) but coimplicated. The key point is that the diasporic African valuation of the figuier maudit and heavy use of indexical signs in macandal production suggests aesthetic and interpretive codes and an episteme that develop from the relay between nonhuman material forces and human creation. These codes presume that phenomena like trees, social organizations, and structures of power (like Catholicism) are coextensive and not separated onto spiritual and material planes.

Macandal do not consist only of indexical signs. Courtin makes clear that the indexes gathered into the artifact must be knotted together. These acts of tying occur via rope, potions, and spoken incantations.[25] The colors of the ropes, the styles of knotting, and the spoken incantations have conventional significance and might be thought of as the symbolic portion of the production of macandal. The entire operation of gathering partial objects, arranging them, and then knotting them is intended to catalyze a reaction. This reaction is thought to change the expression of the material circumstances relevant to the commissioner. For instance, Courtin reports that the macandal that his court investigated were sometimes produced to make a master less brutal toward the commissioning slave. Such an artifact would be tied to the master's bed, where it acted as a channel for the master's feelings and actions, thereby shielding the enslaved individual. As this example suggests, an actuated macandal was meant to mediate events, attitudes, and other material circumstances that affected its commissioner.

While macandal did include a symbolic component, this component did not close them off from their material surrounds. Rather, they remained intensely indexical artifacts that managed relations of contiguity, not only in their creation but also in their ongoing work of mediating how the material surround redounded on its bearer. In short, while West Indian macandal production did include a symbolic element, these artifacts did not so much *mean* as *mediate*. The indexes gathered into the macandal bear portions of a particular material surround into the ground and arrangement of the macandal. By virtue of the artifact's mediation, the bearer stands to gain a different relation to human-scale phenomena (the body and its pleasures and pains, the threat of specific enemies) and to inhuman-scale ones (the forces of history and the phenomenal world in and through which historical force manifests).

In the conceptual grammar at stake in Makandal's practice, the artifact acts as something like a prism that refracts the material circumstances (whether bodily, psychological, or spiritual) that accrue to the person for whom it is commissioned. The artifact's effect on material phenomena is rather like the effect of angled glass on the expression of light. Light, in passing from the medium of air to that of angled glass, slows and refracts, thereby changing its material properties. Moreover, the perception of this light by observers also changes as light becomes more palpably visible as it diffuses into a spectrum. In the same way that light is material both before and after passing through a prism, the events that pass through the macandal artifact are material before and after their passage, but this materiality is differently expressed and perceived by virtue of this passage.

On Insects and Indexes

The slight transformations at stake in the selection of indexical signs and in their collation in the macandal offer a clue to what was at stake in Makandal's prophecy that he would escape punishment by passing into insect life. Courtin's document makes clear that Makandal understood himself to be a craftsman of these artifacts and that his associates understood this as well. And he was jailed, punished, and executed for producing them. It is fitting that his prophecy about evading execution would bear a relationship to the very practice, his life's work, for which he was being executed.

The possibility that insects and insect relics were used in macandal, as well as the possibility that insect cocoons served as signs for these artifacts themselves, might offer some further insight into Makandal's prophecy. Though we do not know all the indexical components of Makandal's artifacts, later anthropologies of nkisi indicate that dead and live insects as well as insect leavings were often used in their composition. Karl Laman (1963: 2:74) writes that live insects are joined with the partial objects put into nkisi. In 1900 Nsemi Isaki (1974: 36), a Kongo informant, explained that insect cocoons were frequently included in nkisi to "stitch together" the various indexes, as though the insect's action redoubled and was a sign of the artisan's actions.[26] Discussing twentieth-century artifacts, MacGaffey (2000: 86) notes that bagworm cocoons are often attached to nkisi and explains that they "serv[e] no other function than to enhance by its remarkable character the apparent sacredness of the *nkisi*; in form [the cocoon] is itself a miniature *nkisi*." Granted, these accounts offer evidence of a Kongo, not an American, practice. Moreover, the earliest of these accounts was transcribed nearly a hundred and fifty years after Makandal's death. Still, these details open the possibility that insects may also have been used in macandal. Isaki's and MacGaffey's accounts raise a number of questions. It is possible that insects were included in Courtin's capacious "etc." and that they were used as signs for the artifact or of the artisan's binding together of indexes. If so, in predicting passing into insect life, Makandal may have aimed to suggest he would himself become a sign for the practice of macandalism as well as promise that this practice could unfold on infinitesimal scales that would remain unseen by the colonial court while at the same time remaining powerfully and ubiquitously present in the colony.

While I do not have proof that insects were used in Afro-Caribbean artifacts, we might also use the logic of indexes and indexical signs themselves to offer a reading of Makandal's prophecy. As I have shown, indexes carry with them the materiality of the circumstances or things with which they are associated: these small-scale fragments testify to and repeat (with a difference) larger bodies, forces, or historical events. Makandal certainly knew what the colonial court had in mind for him: if the court managed to hold him, they would burn his body to ashes, as the colonial arrêt mandated. Since Makandal understood that the court meant to eliminate macandalism by turning his body to ashes, his prophecy could be a recoding of this punishment from the perspective of *macandalists* who believed that fragments of bodies, things, and places retained and carried with them properties of the things from which they came. By this account, Makandal's prophecy unfolds entirely within the understanding of signs, knowledge, and aesthetics at stake in macandalism, and it concerns how the act of becoming small—in fact, incinerated—allowed him to retain a certain power as an index. Here Makandal prophesizes his becoming small, partial, and in this sense like the insect whose smallness is redoubled and emphasized by the French and English name of the class, which means that which is in sections. Makandal knew the end of the public ritual to which he was to be subjected: his prophecy foretold that being burned to ashes would amount to becoming a proliferating set of indexes. Makandal vowed that incineration would transform him into a series of fragments of the colonial scene that, instead of simply referencing or returning this scene or the formalities (the amend honorable) that the French colonial court used to organize it, passed from this scene. Cinders carried to the air as this Atlantic event turned to ashes, yet each of these cinders its own index—and one that might be used to proliferate Makandal's practice on human and nonhuman scales.

Here the colonial court's legal formalisms inadvertently produced a material residue that became a proliferating set of indexes. The pulverizing power of the colonial plantation and the French state converted Makandal's body and life into fragments, which were not only effects of imperial power but also bore traces of the body and life from which they came. The fragments—that is to say, the indexes—produced by the touch of imperial power also bear vestiges of the body, life, and power crushed by this imperial power and might be tied to other indexes to create new artifacts, new macandal. By this reading, the revolutionary nationalist mythos that pieces together indexes from this and other Atlantic events might be said to construct an artifact that, like any macandal, reorients the material plane of the user. In this case, the myth produces a mediating structure through which the user sees the past as a prelude to the nationalism she desires or is in fact achieved. By this logic, the mythographical approach to Makandal is not epiphenomenal but a continuation of this indexical artifactual practice.

Turning the Colonial Archive to a Colonial Aesthetic Theory

If the revolutionary nationalist myth is its own macandal, might not my own engagement with this archive also draw together indexes of this Atlantic event that reroute the colonial archive so that it doesn't simply offer evidence of the fetish (of Courtin's encounter with radically different epistemologies and valuations brought together in the Atlantic world) but of a macandal (of Makandal's encounter with radically different epistemologies and valuations as well as his effort to organize this difference, through Central and West African aesthetic and semantic codes and practices)? To assay this final turn, I direct us again to Courtin's *Mémoire*, which until now I have used as flatly as possible in order to avoid treating him as a transparent source that testifies to the past as it was and in so doing replicating the imperial geopolitics and temporalities sedimented in the text.

Like Makandal's artifacts, Courtin's artifact was crafted by hand. Courtin ends manuscript lines with tildes and dashes that have no grammatical or diacritical function (see fig. 3). According to paleographers, these sorts of nonsignifying marks in seventeenth- and eighteenth-century French writing, especially legal writing, served to

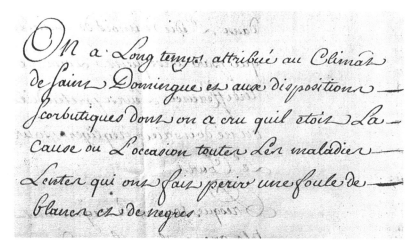

Figure 3 The tilde that Courtin uses at the end of manuscript lines. Courtesy of Les Archives Nationales d'Outre Mer

Figure 4 Seventeenth-century legal writing that demonstrates the legal convention of using a tilde to prohibit the addition of further content on the right margin of the page. Courtesy of the Hathi Trust

fill in blank space so as to make it impossible for others to add to manuscript texts (see fig. 4).[27] Sometimes Courtin did add marginalia to his manuscript: it was added on the left margin, indicated with a star, and he placed a star in the manuscript where this text should be inserted. If tildes on the right margins guarded against additions by

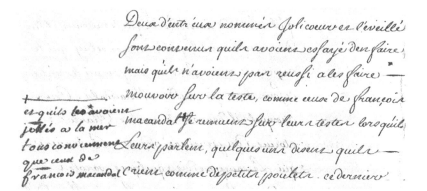

Figure 5 This demonstrates Courtin's practice of adding content to the left margin with a star in the margin and in the text indicating where the added material should be inserted. Courtesy of Les Archives Nationales d'Outre Mer

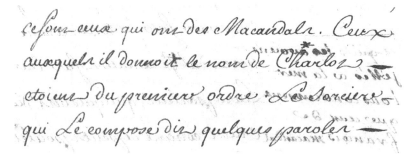

Figure 6 This demonstrates the migration of the ink marking additions in the left margin onto the right margins of succeeding pages. Courtesy of Les Archives Nationales d'Outre Mer

other hands and stars on the left margin indicated additions, and if each sign is allotted to the left or right side of the page, the ink Courtin put to the page exceeded this organizational principle. It seeped into paper and pressed onto verso and contiguous pages, carrying these marks from the left to the right margin and back again, as we see in figures 5 and 6, where an insertion on the left margin of one page seeps into its verso, where it verges on the right margin that was to bear no further additions.

The press of these foreclosing tildes and additive stars backward and forward onto recto and verso and then to contiguous pages are surely indexes that might be given significance by we latter-day readers of macandal. After all, if I call attention to Courtin's stars and his tildes and to their accidental superimposition on each other, they signify precisely because of their connection to material circumstances in the scene of the document's production. Most obviously, these stars and tildes point to Courtin's intention to organize the page, the space of writing itself, so that it would align with French legal and cultural codes.

Yet the migration of these marks such that the space that was to foreclose addition bears additions into the text also points to a failure to maintain French cultural codes in the colonies, a failure that comes from the circumstance of writing in the colonies in which material circumstances that shaped this scene of writing subverted Courtin's intentions. It is possible that Courtin was writing with ink imported from Paris.[28] Conservation specialists expect that ink that would be relatively stable in Paris (and well maintained when in metropolitan archives) might bleed from one page to the next if used in documents stored in tropical locales (see Rouchon et al. 2009).[29] Thus if Courtin used Parisian ink to write the *Mémoire*, then the plantation colony's high humidity might have caused the ink to migrate through and across pages, especially if the document was stored in the colony for any length of time. The fact that it was read by a number of other colonial figures suggests it probably was. It is also possible that Courtin used locally produced ink.[30] Galls, which result from insect parasitism of trees and plants, were the predominant ingredient of nearly all writing inks in the eighteenth century. If Courtin's ink was indeed produced in the colonies, with colonial materials, and likely by slave labor, the galls used to make that ink might well have resulted from the action of colonial insects on colonial trees, which in turn passed into and redirected Courtin's organization of the page. Père Nicoloson's (1776: 232) natural history notes that the fruit of the figuier maudit looks exactly like "gall nuts," which opens the tantalizing possibility that this fruit (which, like most figs, also depends on insect parasitism) may sometimes have been used in the production of colonial ink. In this case, the reorientation of the space of the page would have followed on the actions of the colonial insects through which Makandal promised to continue his artisanal practices. Here, insects would literally be the agents through which the indexes signifying French codes passed outside of these codes.

Whether Courtin's ink was Parisian ink or whether it was of colonial manufacture, the seeping of ink through the page makes clear
that the *Mémoire* transmits the material conditions of its place of
inscription. In fact, like the indexes gathered into macandal, this ink
transmits into the artifact a vestige of these material conditions—at
once its place of production, the juridical event that motivated its production, the diasporic African practices that motivated the juridical
event, and the epistemologies and valuations at stake for all the actors
gathered on this scene. Finally, as is the case with the macandal's
indexes, here the world that is referenced passes into the sign such
that world and sign are coimplicated, and we might remediate this
colonial scene by virtue of the materiality of the artifact. In this sense,
Courtin's text is not only a fetish but also a macandal. Because of this,
Courtin's manuscript doesn't only bear traces of what Michel Foucault
called the lives of infamous men caught in imperial and national
archives at the moment they were crushed by power. The inadvertent
signs that seep across Courtin's *Mémoire* indicate that the crush of
colonial power leaves a residue of material circumstances that bear
traces of epistemologies and an aesthetics that, far from being eradicated by Courtin's court and far from being eradicated by Courtin's
vade mecum on fetishism, passes into it and reorients it if we know
how to see and interpret it.

Reading Courtin's *Mémoire* as a fetish-turned-macandal demonstrates that the archives of slavery need not simply replicate the temporalities, geopolitics, and epistemological conditions of the past.
To be sure, the lives, experiences, and subjectivities cut short and
occluded by slavery and racism cannot be returned. Moreover, the
repercussions and aftereffects of these losses continue to shape not
only archives, the knowledges gained from them, and the methods
used to access them but also experiences of the present that are still
determined by the world-making and -destroying impulses of colonial-
isms.[31] Indeed, the silences of Haitian vernacular historians to elite
professional historians and of professional historians to Haitian
vernacular tradition are themselves aftereffects and indexical signs
of colonialism's continuing force.

Still, prioritizing diasporic African productions, perspectives, meanings, and analytical methods makes visible in this archive of slavery the residue of an episteme and semiotics seemingly pulverized,

indicating the possibility of redirecting the interpretation of the archive in order to trace the world-shaping power of stories that otherwise recede into the haze of "mere" mythology. Macandal and other artifacts on the frontiers of Western canons demand that professional critics work with vernacular critics and storytellers to develop interpretive methods to think anew about historiographic method and aesthetic experience while also attending to the circulation of nonhuman materialities in the semiotic fold. This attention to nonhuman materialities requires attention not only to trees and insects that are increasingly the focus of new materialisms and ecocriticism but also to history and its expressions of power that have long been at stake in materialisms. Attending to the shaping force of history on archives and on other institutional structures of our present is the only way to affect the mediating processes necessary to spin stories, syntheses, analyses, and conversations that pass beyond its impasses and silences.

Monique Allewaert is an associate professor of English at the University of Wisconsin, Madison.

Notes

Thanks to several scholars and audiences whose feedback helped me to develop this article. First, thanks to Gwen Bergner who invited me to participate in an MLA panel where I presented the earliest incarnation of this work and who then shepherded the piece through the editorial process. Thanks, too, to Mel Chen and the audience at the UC Berkeley Department of Gender and Women's Studies, to Amanda Goldstein and Antoine Traisnel and the audience at the University of Michigan English Department, to the audience at the Northwestern English Department, to the audience at the Newberry Library, to Marty Rojas and Jennifer Jones and the audience at the University of Rhode Island English Department, to Vesna Kuiken and the audience at SUNY Albany English, to Branka Arsić and the audience at Columbia English, to Anne Cheng and Rob Nixon and the audience at the Princeton Humanities Institute and the Princeton Environmental Humanities Institute, and to the audience at UW-Madison's Center for Culture, History, and Environment. Thanks, too, to several colleagues whose criticisms and engagements helped sharpen my thinking, especially Jill Casid, Lesley Curtis of Sagely, Joe Fitzpatrick, Terry Kelly, and Frédéric Neyrat. Thanks, especially, to Sophie Sapp Moore, who introduced me to Jhemson Pompilus and to Jhemson and Toni (Berthony) Saint Gardien for bringing me to Montrouis.

1   This story of Makandal has been told since the early postcolonial period, when the Haitian writer Hérard Dumesle (1824) invoked his name as an avatar of the revolutionary spirit he associated with the August 1791 Bois Caïman ceremony. François Duvalier appropriated for his own pseudo-populist ends Haitian folk mythologies, including that of Makandal, whom his government featured on the gourde.

2   If these professional historians are silent about what Haitians and consumers of popular cultural artifacts might say about Makandal, Geggus's (2010) biting review of Karol K. Weaver's discussion of Makandal in *Medical Revolutionaries* (2006) makes clear that from some of these historians' perspective any person with proper training must give up "jejune" and "novelette-like" popular accounts.

3   Here I reference and draw on Michel-Rolph Trouillot's (2015) well-known discussion of the silencing of Haitian history and on critics like Sibylle Fischer (2005) and Sophie Sapp Moore (2018), who provide accounts of the effects of silencing and disavowing certain parts of Haitian history. Marlene L. Daut's (2015) *Tropics of Haiti* also offers an important addition to Trouillot's work.

4   It might seem that this is a credulous and simply additive method—or an idealization of simple belief in the interests of populist political and cultural ends—but Haitians quite savvily understand the ambivalences and uncertainties of oral stories.

5   I will primarily use this term because it is what Courtin and Makandal used and because it emphasizes the perspectives and names of Africans in the Atlantic world.

6   As Pietz makes clear, this European sense of *fetish* was used to justify slavery, as the bugbear and ground for eighteenth-century Enlightenment philosophy and then in Marxist, sociological, and psychoanalytic discourses that built their own claims from this Enlightenment philosophy.

7   Courtin's approximately thirty-page manuscript is available at the Archives Nationales Outre Mer (ANOM) F3/88 in the collection Moreau de Saint-Méry. A microfiche version is available at the Archives Nationales Paris. For a transcription of the manuscript, see Pluchon 1987: 208–19. Although subsequent critics have sometimes quibbled with Pluchon's transcription and translation, his is the best version of the manuscript for those without access to French archives. I have shared copies of my archival materials with Elizabeth Maddock Dillon, who will be making them available in the Early Caribbean Digital Archive.

8   Also see Burnard and Garrigus 2016, which retreads Geggus's (1992) argument.

9   Courtin recounts an episode in which two of Makandal's imprisoned associates, Joliecoeur and L'Éveillé, are supposedly stunned when the court

proves Makandal's capture by presenting him to his jailed associates. Courtin imagines that the jailhouse reunion should prove to these men that Makandal cannot avoid capture by colonial authorities and is astonished by the fact that these men, one of whom he singles out for his intelligence, are delighted to be reunited with Makandal and are not angry with him or chagrined by their own credulity.

10 Laborde complained that Courtin was superstitious and his pamphlet on fetishism corrupted good sense and reason. See Pluchon 1987: 219n48.

11 Courtin's separation of the profane and the sacred ingredients of the macandal attempts to reintroduce order and idealism to a practice whose materialism demands the leveling of the two.

12 A number of scholars, particularly those interested in the Kongo origins of Makandal's practice like Geggus and Mobley, have called into question Courtin's claim that Makandal spoke or uttered words in Arabic.

13 Willem Bosman (1967: 407), for instance, writes of the Slave Coast that "their Banana is besides what they eat with it, the Staff of their Life." The French word for *banana*, *banan*, is close to the current-day Kikongo word for powerless people, *banaana*, which raises the possibility that the banana root was intended as an intercultural pun.

14 Gwendolyn Midlo Hall (1992) suggests that the figuier maudit was of West African provenance. I do not see evidence for this. In *Tout-Monde* (1993), Édouard Glissant associates the figuier maudit with the West Indies and uses it to suggest a *creolité* that navigates between discourses of rootedness of rhizomatic proliferation. On this point see Bongie 1997.

15 To be sure, nkisi, *bo*, and other power objects are not the same, and the differences among these are important.

16 It is important to note differences between African languages and origins as well as West Indian cultures, and I strive to do so even if I here produce an analytic that draws on a range of African and West Indian anthropologies. The production of this analytic draws on MacGaffey's (2002) analysis of the migration of Bantu concepts into Haiti.

17 These partial objects are selected for the power they take in from the objects or situations to which they belong. See Blier 1995: 217, 277; and Hurston 2009: 238, 239–40.

18 That "fetish" artifacts are composed of partial objects is confirmed by virtually every account of these artifacts in the Atlantic world and repeatedly puzzles British and French observers as well as creoles. See Earle 2005; Grainger 2000; Moseley 1799; and Moreau 1958, to note just a few. For later anthropological accounts of partial objects in similar Kongo nkisi see Laman 1963: 3:67–80. See also MacGaffey 2000, esp. 78–96; and MacGaffey 1988.

19 Courtin's interviewees express a range of positions on Catholicism. Makandal seems entirely pragmatic about Catholicism and its rituals

(he uses a crucifix in a macandal only by request). Brigitte expresses derision toward Christianity and claims the rituals in which Africans engage are pastiches of Catholic practice. Mercure claims to be a devout Catholic, but Courtin doubts this. At this relatively early moment, Catholicism is not totally integrated into the syncretic practices and religions that emerged in the Caribbean. A number of scholars have argued that people in the eighteenth-century Kongo already had significant contact with Christianity. See Thornton 2002; see also Thornton 2003.

20 Peirce's examples of indexes range from photographs to the vocative case to weathervanes. While we might be tempted to think of indexes as signs that point back to an extradiegetic context, it might be more apt to conceive indexes as signs that bear a residuum of their referents into a semiotic field.

21 Attending to indexical signs ultimately complicates Paul de Man's (1970: 6) account of language and the literary, which depends on the difference, and then comparison, of "human language . . . to a natural thing"; see also de Man 1973. For a discussion of Peircean semiotics in the upper Amazon, see Kohn 2013. For an account of diasporic Kongo semiotics, see Martinez-Ruiz 2012. I have no room to discuss this problem further in this article.

22 This generally received account of the Saussurean sign does not consider Saussure's short engagement with the potentially big problem of onomatopoeia or idiosyncrasies in Saussure's oeuvre, like his never-published theory of anagrams. On this point see Wunderli 2004.

23 This sort of a sign that exists in material relation to its circumstance yet also achieves distance from it can help to explain the so-called magical thinking of Afro-American and African practices in which signs (whether fragments or spoken or written words) are conceived as having power over material circumstances. The process I have just described is one in which a circumstance that exceeds human agency is managed—but not eliminated—via the interface of the indexical sign. This might be called magic. It could also be called one function of art, which can serve as a mediation between human and inhuman forces.

24 The primary term for *word* in Kreyol is *pawòl*, so the homophony is not obviously evident in spoken Kreyòl. However the term *mot* can also signify *word*, and as in the French, it remains a latent meaning and, according to Jhemson Pompilus, offers a sense of "sa ou di," "sa li di," or "sa yo di" ("what you say," "what it say," "what they say") (personal correspondence, March 2019). Thanks to Sophie Sapp Moore and Jhemson Pompilus for their help with the Kreyòl.

25 Knotting and tying are central to both the Congo nkisi tradition and Yorubaland bo objects. See MacGaffey 2000: 78–96; and Blier 1995: 239–70.

26 Isaki's description of nkisi is in Janzen and MacGaffey 1974; see Isaki 1974: 35–36 for reference to cocoons and their function.

27 My thanks to Jill Gage and Lia Markey at the Newberry for their information on this point.
28 Advertisements in *Les Affiches américaines* indicate that in the 1780s imported Parisian and Spanish inks were available in Port-au-Prince and probably throughout the colony.
29 On the effect of tropical conditions on ink, see Rouchon et al. 2009: 236.
30 Hans Sloane (1707) and Père Labat (1724: 452) both note that colonial acajou could be used as a substitute for gum arabic. Logwood, or *campêche*, was also used in inks in Saint-Domingue and could be a component of this ink. Campêche ink, which was almost certainly locally produced since Saint-Domingue was one of the main exporters of this product, was forbidden in public documents thirty years later. This suggests it was a common ingredient of earlier inks. See McClellan 2010: 219.
31 Here I am thinking of Saidiya Hartman's work: 2008.

References

Blier, Suzanne Preston. 1995. *African Vodun: Art, Psychology, and Power*. Chicago: Univ. of Chicago Press.
Bongie, Chris. 1997. "Resisting Memories: The Creole Identities of Lafcadio Hearn and Edouard Glissant." *SubStance* 26, no. 3: 153–78.
Bosman, Willem. (1704) 1967. *A New and Accurate Description of the Coast of Guinea: Divided into the Gold, the Slave, and the Ivory Coasts*. London: Frank Cass.
Burnard, Trevor, and John Garrigus. 2016. *The Plantation Machine: Atlantic Capitalism in French Saint-Domingue and British Jamaica*. Philadelphia: Univ. of Pennsylvania Press.
Carpentier, Alejo. (1949) 1957. *The Kingdom of This World*. Translated by Harriet de Onís. New York: Knopf.
Courtin, Sébastian-Jacques. 1758. *Mémoire sommaire sur les prétendues pratiques magiques et empoisonnements prouvés aux procès instruits et jugés au Cap contre plusieurs Nègres et Négresses dont le chef nomme François Macandal, a été condamné au feu et executé le vingt janvier mille sept cent ciquante huit*. Archives Nationales Colonies, Paris: AN F3 88.
Daut, Marlene L. 2015. *Tropics of Haiti: Race and the Literary History of the Haitian Revolution in the Atlantic World, 1789–1865*. Liverpool: Univ. of Liverpool Press.
de Man, Paul. 1970. "Intentional Structure of the Romantic Image." In *Romanticism and Consciousness*, edited by Harold Bloom, 65–77. New York: Norton.
de Man, Paul. 1973. "Semiology and Rhetoric." *Diacritics* 3, no. 3: 27–33.
Dumesle, Hérard. 1824. *Voyage dans le nord d'Hayti, ou, Révélations des lieux et des monuments historiques*. Port au Prince: Imprimerie du Gouvernement.

Earle, William. 2005. *Obi, or, The History of Three-Fingered Jack.* Edited by Srinivas Aravamudan. Toronto: Broadview.

Fischer, Sibylle. 2005. *Modernity Disavowed: Haiti and the Cultures of Slavery in the Age of Revolution.* Durham, NC: Duke Univ. Press.

Fouchard, Jean. 1981. *The Haitian Maroons: Liberty or Death.* New York: E. W. Blyden Press.

Geggus, David. 1991. "The Bois Caïman Ceremony." *Journal of Caribbean History* 25, no. 1: 41–57.

Geggus, David. 1992. "Marronage, Voodoo, and the Saint Domingue Slave Revolt of 1791." *Proceedings of the Meeting of the French Colonial Historical Society* 15: 22–35.

Geggus, David. 1994. "The Haitian Revolution: New Approaches and Old." *Proceedings of the Nineteenth Meeting of the French Colonial Historical Society* 19: 141–55.

Geggus, David Patrick. 2002. *Haitian Revolutionary Studies.* Bloomington: Indiana Univ. Press.

Geggus, David. 2010. Book review. *Medical History* 54, no. 3: 408–9.

Glissant, Édouard. 1993. *Tout-Monde.* Paris: Gallimard.

Grainger, James. 2000. *The Sugar Cane.* In *The Poetics of Empire: A Study of James Grainger's "The Sugar Cane"*, edited by John Gilmore. London: Athlone.

Hall, Gwendolyn Midlo. 1992. *Africans in Colonial Louisiana: The Development of Afro-Creole Culture in the Eighteenth Century.* Baton Rouge: Louisiana State Univ. Press.

Handler, Jerome S., and JoAnn Jacoby. 1993. "Slave Medicine and Plant Use in Barbados." *Journal of the Barbados Museum and Historical Society* 41: 74–98.

Hartman, Saidiya. 2008. "Venus in Two Acts." *Small Axe* 12, no. 2: 1–14.

Herskovits, Melville J. 1938. *Dahomey: An Ancient West African Kingdom.* New York: J. J. Augustin.

Hurston, Zora Neale. (1938) 2009. *Tell My Horse: Voodoo and Life in Haiti and Jamaica.* New York: Harper.

Isaki, Nsemi. (1900) 1974. "Sacred Medicines (Min'kisi)." In Janzen and MacGaffey 1974: 34–38.

Janzen, John M., and Wyatt MacGaffey. 1974. *An Anthology of Kongo Religion: Primary Texts from Lower Zaïre.* Lawrence: Univ. Press of Kansas.

Jenson, Deborah. 2004. "Mimetic Mastery and Colonial Mimicry in the First Franco-Antillean Creole Anthology." *Yale Journal of Criticism* 17, no. 1: 83–106.

Kohn, Eduardo. 2013. *How Forests Think: Toward an Anthropology beyond the Human.* Berkeley: Univ. of California Press.

Labat, Jean Baptiste. 1724. *Nouveau Voyages aux Isles de l'Amérique.* Vol. 2. La Haye: Husson, Johnson, Gosse, van Duren, Alberts, and le Vier.

Laman, Karl. 1963. *The Kongo.* 3 vols. Lund: Häkan Ohlssons Boktryckeri.

Les Affiches américaines. 1784. "Supplément aux *Affiches américaines.*" January 3. Available from University of Florida Digital Collections, http://ufdc.ufl.edu /AA00000449/00027/2x.

MacGaffey, Wyatt. 1988. "Complexity, Astonishment, and Power: The Visual Vocabulary of Kongo Minkisi." *Journal of Southern Bantu Studies* 14, no. 2: 188–203.

MacGaffey, Wyatt. 2000. *Kongo Political Culture: The Conceptual Challenge of the Particular.* Bloomington: Indiana Univ. Press.

MacGaffey, Wyatt. 2002. "Twins, Simbi Spirits, and Lwas in Kongo and Haiti." In *Central Africans and Cultural Transformations in the American Diaspora,* edited by Linda M. Heywood, 211–26. Cambridge: Cambridge Univ. Press.

Madiou, Thomas. 1989. *Histoire d'Haiti.* 8 vols. Port au Prince: Editions Henri Deschamps.

Martinez-Ruiz, Barbaro. 2012. *Kongo Graphic Writing and Other Narratives of the Sign.* Philadelphia: Temple Univ. Press.

McClellan, James E., III. 2010. *Colonialism and Science: Saint Domingue in the Old Regime.* Chicago: Univ. of Chicago Press.

Mobley, Christina Frances. 2015. "The Kongolese Atlantic: Central African Slavery and Culture from Mayombe to Haiti." PhD diss., Duke Univ.

Moore, Sophie. 2018. "Futures Otherwise: Radical Life on Haiti's High Central Plateau." PhD diss., Univ. of California, Davis.

Moreau, Médéric de St. Mery. 1958. *Description topographic, physique, civile, politique et historique de la partie français de l'isle Saint-Domingue.* Paris: Société de l'Histoire des Colonies Françaises.

Moseley, Benjamin. 1799. *A Treatise on Sugar.* London: G. G. and J. Robinson.

Nicolson, Jean. 1776. *Essai sur l'histoire naturelle de l'isle de Saint-Domingue: avec des figures en taille-douce.* Paris: Gobreau Libraire Quai des Augustins.

Peirce, Charles Sanders. (1894) 1998. "What Is a Sign?" In *The Essential Peirce: Selected Philosophical Writings (1893–1913),* vol. 2, edited by Nathan Houser and Christian Kloesel, 4–10. Bloomington: Indiana Univ. Press.

Pietz, William. 1985. "The Problem of the Fetish, I." *RES: Anthropology and Aesthetics,* no. 9: 5–17.

Pluchon, Pierre. 1987. *Vaudou sorciers empoisonneurs: De Saint-Domingue à Haiti.* Paris: Karthala.

Rouchon, Véronique, Blandine Durocher, Eleanora Pellizzi, and Julie Stordiau-Pallot. 2009. "The Water Sensitivity of Iron Gall Ink and Its Risk Assessment." *Studies in Conservation* 54, no. 4: 236–54.

Saussure, Ferdinand de. (1916) 2016. *Course in General Linguistics.* Translated by Roy Harris. London: Bloomsbury.

Sloane, Hans. 1707. *A Voyage to the Islands of Madera, Barbados, . . . and Jamaica with the Natural History of the Herbs and Trees [. . .].* London: Printed by B. M. for the author.

Thornton, John K. 2002. "Religious and Ceremonial Life in the Kongo and Mbundu Areas, 1500–1700." In *Central Africans and Cultural Transformations in the American Diaspora*, edited by Linda M. Heywood, 71–90. Cambridge: Cambridge Univ. Press.

Thornton, John K. 2003. "Cannibals, Witches, and Slave Traders in the Atlantic World." *William and Mary Quarterly* 60, no. 2: 273–94.

Trouillot, Michel-Rolph. 1995. *Silencing the Past: Power and the Production of History*. Boston: Beacon.

Wunderli, Peter. 2004. "Saussure's Anagrams and the Analysis of Literary Texts." In *A Cambridge Companion to Saussure*, edited by Carol Sanders, 174–85. Cambridge: Cambridge Univ. Press.

Jeannine Marie DeLombard   Dehumanizing Slave Personhood

Abstract Afrohumanism is crucial to the forward-looking "project of thinking humanity from perspectives beyond the liberal humanist subject, Man" (Weheliye 2014: 8). It is another question, however, whether such a humanist approach provides the best historical analytic for understanding slavery and its carceral afterlives. This question becomes particularly pressing when we consider that today's prison-industrial complex, like the American slaveholder of the past, extracts profits by strategically exploiting—rather than denying—the lucrative humanity of its captive black and brown subjects. To illustrate these claims, this article examines a seldom-discussed slave case, *United States v. Amy* (1859), which was tried before Supreme Court chief justice Roger B. Taney two years after his infamous decision in *Dred Scott v. Sandford* (1857). Centering on the figure of the legal person rather than the human or the citizen, *United States v. Amy* alerts us to the lethal legacy of slave personhood as a debilitating mixture of civil death and criminal culpability. Nowhere, perhaps, is that legacy more evident than in viral videos of police misconduct. And nowhere do we see a more vivid assertion of black counter-civility than in the dash cam video of the late Sandra Bland's principled, outraged response to her pretextual traffic stop by Trooper Brian Encinia. The essay closes by considering Bland's arrest and subsequent death in custody in the context of her own and other African Americans' efforts to achieve and maintain a civil presence in an American law and culture where black personhood remains legible primarily as criminality.

Keywords humanism, US law and culture, incarceration, police brutality, viral videos

Today, the carceral afterlives of slavery make themselves manifest in racist profiling, police misconduct, and mass incarceration.[1] Activists, public intellectuals, and scholars often protest this state of affairs with humanitarian appeals. "Hundreds of years ago, our nation put those considered less than human in shackles; . . . today we put them in cages," observes Michelle Alexander (2012: 141) in

American Literature, Volume 91, Number 3, September 2019
DOI 10.1215/00029831-7722104   © 2019 by Duke University Press

her indispensable *The New Jim Crow: Mass Incarceration in the Age of Colorblindness*. "This is the dehumanization of African-American people," sociologist and minister Michael Eric Dyson (in Goodman 2014) insisted of the St. Louis County grand jury's failure to indict white Ferguson, Missouri, police officer Darren Wilson in the shooting death of African American teenager Michael Brown. The Black Lives Matter movement emerged as a "space for the celebration and humanization of Black lives" (Garza 2014) in response to the un-redressed killings of Brown, Eric Garner, Trayvon Martin, and the increasingly visible number of African Americans caught in the crosshairs of racism and police power. Ava DuVernay's powerful 2016 documentary on race and criminalization after slavery, *13th*, closes with CNN political commentator Van Jones intoning, "the opposite of criminalization is humanization," and activist critic Malkia Cyril insisting, "it's about rehumanizing us as a people."

This commentary appears against the backdrop of a resurgent Afrohumanism in the academy. Building on the work of Hortense Spillers and Sylvia Wynter, Alexander G. Weheliye (2014: 19) speaks of the necessity of making "the human . . . a central object of knowledge in black studies." To this end, he suggests, "If racialization is understood not as a biological or cultural descriptor but as a conglomerate of sociopolitical relations that discipline humanity into full humans, not-quite-humans, and nonhumans, then blackness designates a changing system of unequal power structures that apportion and delimit which humans can lay claim to full human status and which cannot" (3). Such a critical prioritizing of the human is consistent with Wynter's (2003: 260) insight that "our present ethnoclass (i.e., Western bourgeois) conception of the human, Man, which overrepresents itself as if it were the human itself," threatens "the full cognitive and behavioral autonomy of the human species itself/ourselves." This endeavor thus mounts an important challenge to poststructuralist-cum-posthumanist discourses whose efforts to dispense with the human often serve to entrench further its overrepresentation as Western, bourgeois "Man," on the one hand, while identifying a more diverse humanity with nonhuman animals, on the other (Weheliye 2014: 9–10).

Clearly, Afrohumanism is crucial to the forward-looking "project of thinking humanity from perspectives beyond the liberal humanist subject, Man" (8). It is another question, however, whether such an approach provides the best historical analytic for understanding slavery and its afterlives in American culture.[2] More than twenty years ago, Saidiya V. Hartman (1997: 5) demonstrated that "the recognition of humanity and individuality acted to tether, bind, and oppress" the black subject both during and after slavery. Whether we think of the slave girl Phillis's forced, unpaid secretarial work for the Wheatley family in colonial Boston or the practice of leaving traveling slaves' children behind as hostages during sojourns in free jurisdictions, it is clear that enslaved African Americans were valued for and controlled through the cognitive capacity and affective qualities that distinguished them as fellow human beings (see Wong 2009: 77–182). Unquestionably, slaveholders maintained social control over and extracted profits from enslaved people through myriad dehumanizing practices. That brutal treatment did not, however, mean that whites thought slaves and other people of African descent were not human.[3] Quite the contrary, as Christopher Freeburg (2017: 89) contends, "white subjects need to strip blacks of their personhood because of their humanity and not in spite of it" (see also Cassuto 1997: xiii). Accordingly, historian Walter Johnson (2016) concludes, the liberal rhetoric of dehumanization is "misleading, harmful, and worth resisting." An inhuman practice, slavery actively exploited a recognized black humanity. *Moby-Dick*'s Ishmael acknowledges as much when he alludes to "that common decency of human recognition which is the meanest slave's right" (Melville 2002: 202).

Unlike Ishmael, we are heirs to an abolitionist discourse that influentially, albeit problematically, constructed slavery as a process of dehumanization and animalization. One of the most effective, influential, and underappreciated rhetorical tactics of the transatlantic anti-slavery movement was to transform enslavers' conscious economic exploitation of the human capacities of those targeted for enslavement into an unchristian *denial* of black humanity. British pottery manufacturer and reformer Josiah Wedgwood's medallion of a nearly naked kneeling slave mutely imploring, "Am I Not a Man and a Brother?" (1787), became a durable abolitionist meme. Featured on everything from stationery to handkerchiefs, the icon solicited assent to the widely accepted fact that slaves were human beings by calling that very fact into question. This problematic tactic achieved the laudable goal of inserting a "metaphysical opposition" into the ancient concept of human property (Mussawir and Parsley 2017: 49). The product of a broader nineteenth-century evangelical reform movement, this sentimental abolitionist rhetoric shaped the humanitarian discourse that surfaced in the wake of World War II (Hunt 2007: 116). Combined with the contemporaneous rise of the human sciences, this discursive background ensured that, as Weheliye (2014: 21) observes, the emergent "interdiscipline" of black studies "made humanity an avowed ideological and ontological battleground." To impose this presentist humanist perspective on slavery retrospectively, however, risks dangerously misunderstanding the legal-cultural logics of racism.

Focusing on imputations of black criminality, this article contends that the through-line connecting slavery to mass incarceration is not the denial but the exploitative recognition of black humanity. Today's prison-industrial complex, like the American slaveholder of the past, extracts profits by strategically commodifying the humanity of its captive black and brown subjects. To speak of the carceral afterlives of slavery in this way is to succumb, Stephen Best (2012: 453) would caution, to the critical fallacy "that the slave past provides a ready prism for apprehending the black political present"—and thus to fail to appreciate the "radical alterity of the past" (455). The figure is a suggestive one. Consider the simultaneously clarifying and distorting effects of a prism on a beam of light. Rather than dispensing with the slave past as a lens through which to view the political present, we might better attend to its refracting effect. Viewed through the prism of the slave past, the seemingly linear history of racist dehumanization bends sharply to follow an oblique trajectory. The line is still there, of course, but it takes us in a radically divergent discursive direction—that of legal personhood.

As Best's own work illuminates (2004), one of the most alien aspects of the slave past is a concept of humanness that did not exclude property status. If, then, we share Weheliye's understanding of "racialization" as "a conglomerate of sociopolitical relations" and "blackness" as designating "a changing system of unequal power structures," then the "status" to which we need to direct our attention is not that of the human but of the person. Like nineteenth-century Americans, we tend to use these words interchangeably in everyday speech; indeed, they are often confused in the relevant scholarship (see, for example, Hunt 2007: 21). As John Bouvier explains in the nation's first legal lexicon, *A Law Dictionary Adapted to the Constitution and Laws of the United States of America*, "in law, man and person are not exactly synonymous terms."[4] Whereas "any human being is a man, whether he be a member of society or not, whatever may be the rank he holds, or whatever may be his age, sex, &c.," Bouvier elaborates, legally, "a person is a man considered according to the rank he holds in society, with all the rights to which the place he holds entitles him, and the duties which it imposes." A human being is a particular bundle of fluids and tissues; legal persons, by contrast, are varying bundles of rights and duties, powers and obligations. Perversely, it is the very naturalization—the humanization and thus racialization—of the artificial slave person that leads us, obliquely, to the carceral present.

To illustrate these claims, this article examines a seldom-discussed slave case, *United States v. Amy* (1859). The case was tried in Richmond, Virginia, before a circuit-riding Supreme Court chief justice Roger B. Taney two years after his infamous decision in *Dred Scott v. Sandford* (60 U.S. 393 [1857]). *United States v. Amy* demonstrates that in the antebellum period it was not only insightful black and brown critics of American racism who took "the humanness of African Americans as a given" (Pratt 2016: 2). Rather, the case reminds us, slavery was *premised* on that assumption. Centering on the figure of the legal person rather than the human or the citizen, *United States v. Amy* alerts us to the lethal legacy of slave personhood as a debilitating mixture of civil death and criminal culpability.

Nowhere, perhaps, is that legacy more evident than in viral videos of police misconduct. And nowhere, I suggest, do we see a more vivid counterassertion of black civility than in the dash cam video of the late Sandra Bland's principled, outraged response to her pretextual traffic stop and subsequent arrest by State Trooper Brian Encinia in Waller County, Texas. The article closes, then, by considering Bland's arrest and death in custody in the context of her own and other African Americans' efforts to achieve and maintain a civil presence in an American law and culture where black personhood remains legible primarily as criminality. For too many African Americans, this Ellisonian dilemma of being caught between a "hypervisible" criminal culpability and an invisible civil capacity is, poet Claudia Rankine (2014: 49) suggests in her "American lyric," what it means to be a *Citizen*.

■ ■ ■

Amy was enslaved by Samuel W. Hairston, of Patrick County, Virginia (*Quarterly Law Journal* 1859: 163). She was indicted under a federal statute against mail theft for stealing "letters" (apparently "with . . .

money in them") from that county's post office (202). Beyond this brief, mysterious, and almost certainly misleading glimpse, the case tells us nothing about Amy or her experiences. It does, however, provide a great deal of insight into the intertwined cultural and legal logics of slavery at the moment of its fullest doctrinal development in the United States. Specifically, the case illustrates that slaveholders recognized and consciously exploited the humanity of the enslaved, even as it suggests how criminality, the attribute that enabled law to recognize the enslaved person as a responsible legal agent, became attributed to the African American collective, free and enslaved, before and long after the Civil War.

United States v. Amy provides the rare opportunity to observe a group of white male southern legal professionals, all of whom represent slaveholding interests, as they debate not only the contours of slave personhood but, remarkably, the relationship of that legal artifice to humanness. John Howard, speaking "for the owner of the defendant," sought to protect Hairston's property interest in Amy by mounting the defense that "a slave is not a 'person' amenable to the act" (*Quarterly Law Journal* 1859: 164). (The case report paraphrased the March 3, 1825, federal statute thus: if "any person shall steal a letter from the mail, the offender shall, upon conviction, be imprisoned no less than two nor more than ten years"; quoted at 163). In other words, Howard argued that Amy's enslaved status should shield her from criminal prosecution as a responsible legal person. James D. Halyburton, the presiding judge, convicted Amy of the theft but purposely overruled this point of law so as to enable review by Chief Justice Taney. Taney, of course, had provoked national controversy with his gratuitous observation in *Dred Scott* that by the time of the nation's founding, Americans of African descent had "been regarded as . . . so far inferior, that they had no rights which the white man was bound to respect" (*Dred Scott v. Sandford* 60 U.S. 393 [1857], at 407). Taney's obiter dictum ignored, but by no means ended, what a growing cohort of legal historians have shown to be pervasive everyday legal activity by both enslaved and free African Americans throughout the United States (Welch 2018; Jones 2018). Indeed, Amy's very appearance at the Fourth Circuit Court in Richmond spoke to the juridical "respect" occasionally accorded to the procedural "rights" of enslaved defendants. Taney upheld Amy's conviction, ruling that, in keeping with the language of the US Constitution, the federal statute's use of the word *"person* . . . may be construed as including slaves" (*Quarterly Law Journal* 1859: 163). As Taney noted, the case hinged on "the two-fold character which belongs to the slave" as *"person* and also *property"* (199). What was not in dispute was Amy's humanness, which each of the participants not only took for granted but expressly affirmed over the course of the proceedings.

In taking up the question of slave personhood, Richmond's Fourth Circuit addressed itself to one of the foundational categories of Western law. Under Roman law, slave and other forms of personhood were not "metaphysical" but "purely technical and functional" categories (Mussawir and Parsley 2017: 48). Thus, although "slaves" constituted one of the two main divisions of the law of persons in Gaius's *Institutes* (c. 161 CE), slaves could also be treated as "things" (1.9–12, 2.1, 2.13). *Persona* was literally a term of art, purportedly deriving from the ancient Greek *prosōpon*, the mask an actor used to indicate a particular character or role. Personhood, Alain Pottage (2002: 275) and other legal theorists insist, remains the product of "legal rhetoric as *techne*; that is, as an art, technique, craft, or strategy." For Edward Mussawir and Connal Parsley (2017: 46), this origin story "expresses a fundamental element crucial to an emergent legal science: the difference that is necessary in law in order to separate the identity of a real living subject from that of a purely artificial, fabricated role that is reserved and instituted at the level of juridical existence." Prior to the medieval insertion of the person into a "transcendent, theological, metaphysical, or meta-juridical frame" (47) they note, "the Roman law did not mould its persons on a pre-existing biological human substrate" (49).[5]

At the current moment, when it is the *artifice* of legal personhood that provokes outrage—typically, in the form of the corporation—it feels counterintuitive to suggest, as Mussawir and Parsley do, that "calls for an outdated law to 'better reflect life'" may "have limitations both as jurisprudence and as political action" (57). Analysis of *United States v. Amy* addresses this seeming contradiction by examining the legal, political, and cultural effects of naturalizing the particular form of legal personhood assigned to the slave. As we shall see, the definitive African descent of the slave person in American law and culture encouraged the ongoing identification of African Americans with a civilly incapacitated legal agency primarily legible as criminality.

Like other antebellum legal thinkers, Timothy Walker, author of the first US legal textbook, saw the growing abstraction of legal personhood as directly proportionate to the increasing democratization of American law. Unlike in England, Walker noted in his *Introduction to American Law: Designed as a First Book for Students* (1846: 205), the American law of persons had achieved an exemplary democratic simplicity "in consequence of our entire abolition of privileged orders." The American "doctrine of equality" assumes that "in theory at least, all men start equally; they are born with equal rights; and their distinctions in after life, are mainly made by themselves" (205). The exceptions that he would go on to enumerate—wives, slaves, Indians—confirm legal historian Susanna L. Blumenthal's (2016: 55) observation that, in fact, the nineteenth-century American "legal model never entirely displaced the traditional English law of persons. American jurists continued to speak in terms of status relations." The difference was that instead of artificial distinctions, status now derived from "what were regarded as natural differences in people's mental and physical attributes" (7). In this way Americans' "gradual dismantlement of a 'law of persons' with roots in feudal society" enabled their creation of a "default legal person" (7). Abstracted as it was, this model of a "free and independent man" was presumed to be male, white, able-bodied, and of sound mind (7). This default legal person stood in contrast to his variously incapacitated and subordinated counterparts such as the wife, the slave, and the child—each of which, of course, represented a form of legal personhood.

Under Roman law, natural attributes such as age and sex could determine slave status for the purpose of manumission or under the doctrine of *partus sequitur ventrem* (the condition of the child follows that of the mother). But, as Thomas Jefferson claims in *Notes on the State of Virginia* (1788), Roman slaves were distinguished from the master class only by "condition," not "nature" (152). Whereas Roman slavery was, for Jefferson and others of like mind, merely a matter of formal status, American slavery grounded that status in natural difference. "Among the Romans, . . . [t]he slave, when made free, might mix with, without staining the blood of his master," explains the likely father of Sally Hemings's children (154). "But with us," Jefferson continues, the emancipated slave, ideally, "is to be removed beyond the reach of mixture" (154). As the legal artifice of slave personhood became naturalized, it became increasingly identified with "the blacks on the continent of America," whether enslaved or free (151).

We can observe this naturalization-cum-racialization in the best-known summary of the doctrine Taney alludes to in *United States v. Amy* as "two-fold character." In number 54 of the *Federalist Papers* (1788), Virginian James Madison, in the persona of "Publius," addresses the US Constitution's already controversial three-fifths clause, which counted a state's slave population at that fraction of the free population in the apportionment of taxation and representation. Publius rejects the assumption that "slaves are considered merely as property, and in no respect whatever as persons" (Madison, Hamilton, and Jay 1988: 332). Because "they partake of both these qualities," he maintains, the "federal Constitution" correctly follows state and local law in viewing slaves "in the mixed character of persons and of property" (332). He goes on to explain, "in being compelled to labor, not for himself, but for a master; in being vendible by one master to another master; and in being subject at all times to be restrained in his liberty and chastised in his body, by the capricious will of another—the slave *may appear* to be degraded from the human rank, and classed with those irrational animals which fall under the legal denomination of property" (332; emphasis added).

Criminality resuscitated slave personhood from this civil death. As Publius goes on to clarify, "in being protected . . . against the violence of all others, even the master of his labor and his liberty; and in being punishable himself for all violence committed against others—the slave is no less evidently regarded by the law as a member of the society, not as a part of the irrational creation; as a moral person, not as a mere article of property" (332). In practice, the formal protection of slaves against violence spoke more to their value as property than their status as persons (Wahl 1998: 126–320). In any case, slaves' potential to become perpetrators of unlawful violence necessitated punitive recognition of their responsibility to the rule of law. Reanimated as a criminally responsible defendant, the civilly dead slave is no longer to be seen "as a part of the irrational creation" or "a mere article of property" but "as a member of the society" and "as a moral [i.e., social] person." Because legal personhood comprises duties as well as rights, the officially administered punishment of enslaved offenders amounted to punitive recognition of their accountability to the political community of which they, in the breach, were retroactively acknowledged to be members (DeLombard 2012).

Publius appears to adopt Roman law's "purely technical and functional" approach to legal personhood, slave personhood in particular. Thus far, the account of the slave's "mixed character" resists naturalizing what appears to be a gender- and even race-neutral category of legal personhood (Madison, Hamilton, and Jay 1988: 332). In fact, in the United States as in the colonies, slave personhood was born from coupling legal classifications of sex and race. The doctrine of *partus sequitur ventrem*, combined with the restriction of bound servitude to those of African descent, naturalized a matrilineal racial blackness as at once the purported cause and a very real effect of slave personhood (see Spillers 1987). In *Federalist* 54, however, Publius only once identifies "Negroes" with the "slaves" alluded to but not named by the Constitution. Publius insists that it is with "great propriety" that the Constitution "views" slaves in "the mixed character of persons and property," because that is "the character bestowed on them by the laws under which they live"—the same state and local "laws [that] have transformed the Negroes into subjects of property" in the first place (332). Conversely, Publius reminds his readers, "if the laws were to restore the rights which have been taken away, the Negroes could no longer be refused an equal share of representation with the other inhabitants" (332). Publius's references to, alternatively, commodified or rights-bearing "Negroes" confirms the law as "*techne*; . . . as an art, technique, craft, or strategy" (Pottage 2002: 275) that produces different kinds of artificial legal persons. To identify "Negroes" with the "mixed character" of slave personhood was, then, to associate African Americans not only with civil incapacity but with criminality.

■ ■ ■

Amy, Chief Justice Taney's ruling confirmed, was just such a civilly dead, criminally culpable person. What makes the case so revealing is the opposing attorneys' unexpected and unorthodox inquiry into the relevance of the slave's humanity to her legal personhood. John M. Gregory, district attorney for the United States, had an easy task. The federal prosecutor had only to remind the court of the well-established legal doctrine that "slaves are property; but it is equally true that they are recognized in all modern communities where slavery exists as persons also," noting that "they are recognized as persons in every State in the Union, and punishable as persons for the commission of offences in violation of the penal laws" (*Quarterly Law*

Journal 1859: 169). Gregory enlivened his otherwise self-evident doctrinal argument, however, by abruptly departing from professional convention. "I deem it would be a rather useless waste of time to refer more particularly to authorities," he asserted, adding, "I cannot prove more plainly that the prisoner is a person, a natural person at least, than to ask your honors to look at her! There she is. She is beyond doubt a human being, and it is not pretended she is not of sound mind" (170). With this impassioned appeal to vernacular common sense — that a person is a human — the US district attorney exposed the artifice of legal reasoning, the fiction of slave personhood in particular. He did so, we should recall, not to assert Amy's inherent rights and equality as a fellow human being but to win a ruling that would merely (and temporarily) change the terms of her captivity, from private enslavement to federal custody.

John Howard, the defense attorney, was quick to point out "the great mistake into which . . . the learned counsel for the United States has fallen" in making "profert of Amy in open court" "as if in triumphant and conclusive proof that a slave is a person, a natural person, at least, a human being" (170). As Howard pointed out, the prosecution's unorthodox resort to Amy's embodied humanness in place of the relevant legal authorities "entirely overlooks a broad, radical, and most important distinction, which is the basis of all our civil and criminal jurisprudence in respect to slaves": this is the distinction between "the legal character and attributes of the African slaves in the United States, who are purely *chattel slaves* — with their character and attributes as *natural persons*" (170). As we have seen, this crucial distinction was that between slaves' obvious humanness and their status as a particular kind of legal person. Howard's argument — that Amy was not indictable as a "person" under the terms of the statute — would lead him to fudge the terms of this distinction.

The challenge facing the defense attorney was well-nigh insurmountable: to persuade the court to make what was, in effect, an exception to the doctrine of culpable slave personhood so as to ensure that Hairston would retain his property right to Amy and her labor. Briefly, Howard sought to prove that Amy was not a legal person under the statute by arguing that not only does "the utter civil non-entity of the slave" deprive her of any rights under the law but it also removes her from any legal obligations or duties (177). This formulation flew in the face of the doctrinal logic of the slave's mixed character. Howard therefore sought to limit jurisdiction over the latter to *state* law. States' punitive recognition of criminous slaves, Howard argued, formed "part of their municipal polity and police . . . , upon the idea that by tying the self-interest of the master the more closely to the commonweal, greater diligence would be encouraged on his part, alike by coercion and kind treatment[,] to keep his slaves in due subordination and goodly courses" (193). Basically, Howard sought formal authorization for what was commonly referred to as "plantation justice." He envisioned private, extralegal disciplinary control over slaves that would be minimally under the purview of state governments, while being protected from oversight by the federal government—whose own twofold character as a union of slave and free states was, by 1859, perceived as a dangerous threat to slaveholders' property. Nowhere did such a brief require any consideration of Amy's humanness; at its most persuasive, Howard's argument addressed how punitive recognition of Amy's legal obligations as a criminally culpable person would have impinged on Hairston's right to her as his property.

Howard's awareness of the irrelevance of Amy's humanness to the legal question of her personhood did not, however, prevent him from emphasizing her humanity so as to entrench her property status. The prosecution's unorthodox, off-topic introduction of humanness into the legal dispute over slave personhood prompted the defense attorney to a revealing admission. "It is true," Howard acknowledged, "that the negro did not cease to be a *natural person*, a human being, by becoming a slave" (172). Indeed, he maintained, "the very idea of a *slave* is a human being in bondage. A slave is, and must, of necessity, continue to be a natural person, although he may be a legal *chattel*" (172). Later, Howard offered the following remarkable concession: "If it be said that although a *chattel*, he [the slave] cannot be divested of his characteristics as a natural person, a human being,—a human body inspired with intellect, feeling, volition—that is conceded—(it is that which makes him so valuable a chattel)" (176). Howard's own tangential observations on the slave's humanness merely articulate what slaveholding practice had long made clear: race slavery involved the profitable exploitation of recognized black humanity.

Howard's resort to the animal kingdom to elaborate his point would appear to complicate this reading. After he had acknowledged that the slave's value lies in his or her distinctly human "intellect, feeling, and volition," Howard argued that "the natural character of the *chattel* must determine the manner and kind of treatment it receives from its owner or others. Thus a horse, or a dog, a slave, or a pet lamb, would not be treated as a bale of goods" (176). Disturbing as Howard's bland analogy of enslaved human beings to nonhuman pets and livestock is, it alerts us to the need for analytical precision. Howard's white supremacist ideology, in keeping with that of the slaveholding class he literally represented, was far more insidious than abolitionists and many modern critics would have it. Howard and his slaveholding client Hairston did not justify their inhuman treatment of the enslaved Amy by refusing to recognize her as a fellow human being—as "a Woman and a Sister," in the words of the abolitionist motto. Instead, as Howard frankly acknowledged, slaveholders consciously exploited the slave's humanity as "that which makes him so valuable a chattel." Not unlike today's prison-industrial complex, antebellum slaveholders cannily extracted profits from the humanity of their black and brown captives while treating them like nonhuman animals.

Repeated assertions to the effect that "New World slavery . . . positioned black subjects as nonhumans" take the humanitarian high ground at the risk of ignoring the conceptual bedrock of American racism (Weheliye 2014: 144n18). *United States v. Amy* was argued and decided well after the rise of a new scientific racism that sought empirically to establish racial inferiority. Crucially, however, even the most notorious proponents of scientific racism—Samuel George Morton, Josiah Nott, Louis Agassiz, and others associated with the American school of ethnology—argued for racial inferiority *within* humankind. A polygeneticist like Agassiz (1850: 141–42) understood his task as "to settle the relative rank among these races," that is, to establish a hierarchy *among* the "different races of men." As in Bouvier's account of legal personhood, scientific discourse in slaveholding America tended to focus its discriminatory, white supremacist energies on ascribing a "status" hierarchy among differently racialized groups of humans rather than on excluding groups from *human* status. The critical challenge, in Wynter's (2003: 261–62) terms, is to understand the specific scientific, legal, economic, political, and social forms of stratification that result in the "Black population group" being "still made to occupy the nadir . . . rung of being human."[6]

Today, Howard's analogy of the defendant's chattel status to that of nonhuman animals would seem to include *United States v. Amy* in the "archives of dehumanization" (Pratt 2016: 118). In fact, the argument for the defense illustrates how a narrow critical focus on the category of the human can occlude other, more relevant forms of racist subjectification. Consider another instance where Howard appears to slight, if not outright deny, slave humanity in his effort to reject Amy's culpability as a responsible "person" under the federal statute against mail theft. Howard alludes to "laws against cruelty to animals," as well as "laws prescribing death or punishment for certain animals in case of dangerous or troublesome insubordination, roving, or ferocity," to argue that "these laws" do not "recognize any legal or civil rights in the brute creation—[in] the animals protected, or punished" (*Quarterly Law Journal* 1859: 177). "And so," he analogizes, "with the laws punishing offences committed upon, or committed by slaves. *The slave is still but a chattel, in which no legal or civil personal right inheres.* The fact that he is protected by the law, or is punished by the law, is no concession to him of legal rights or responsibilities, any more than in the case of other chattels, the accidents of whose natural characteristics are animate existence, and some sort of intelligence, volition, and feeling" (177). The glaring flaw in his analogy is that it was precisely the criminous slave's "legal . . . responsibilities" under the doctrine of mixed character that distinguished her from the victimized, insubordinate, roving, or ferocious animals whom the law might well protect, confine, forfeit, or exterminate but could not punish.[7] As noted, Howard's professional commitment to defending the property interests of Amy's master (rather than Amy herself) and thus ensuring her continuing enslavement does not prohibit him from acknowledging her humanity. Indeed, he emphasizes that her humanness is the source of her comparatively high value among other chattels. The irony here is that Howard's enthusiastic recognition of captive black humanity seeks to realize a vision of near-absolute private control that would reduce enslaved existence to something very like the "bare life" described by philosopher Giorgio Agamben (1998), with the emphatically human slave stripped of legal personhood as its *homo sacer.*

Howard's frank acknowledgment of Amy's humanity while denying her legal personhood brings to mind Hannah Arendt's concerns regarding the human rights movement that was emerging in the wake of World War II. Of those rendered stateless in early twentieth-century Europe, Arendt (1994: 295) notes in *The Origins of Totalitarianism,* "innocence, in the sense of complete lack of responsibility, was the mark of their rightlessness as it was the seal of their loss of political status." If, as she maintains, "the first essential step on the road to total domination is to kill the juridical person in man" (447), the "best criterion by which to decide whether someone has been forced outside the pale of the law is to ask whether he would benefit by committing a crime" (286). Arendt, whose brilliant critique of racist oppression was compromised by her own racism toward people of African descent (Gines 2014), nevertheless offers a helpful clarification of the difference between inhuman treatment and subhuman status. To characterize hereditary slavery as a "crime against humanity," as she did, was not to say that slaves had been denied *their* humanity (Arendt 1994: 297). "Slaves still belonged to some sort of human community; their labor was needed, used, and exploited, and this kept them within the pale of humanity," Arendt argues: "To be a slave was after all to have a distinctive character, a place in human society—more than the abstract nakedness of being human and nothing but human" (297). Just such a reductive acknowledgment of black humanity, she goes on to argue, impeded contemporary African Americans' civic inclusion as free members of the polity. In modern nation-states built on the indispensable artifice of political equality (the origin story that "all men are created equal"), Arendt suggests, racism manifests itself in an inability to see those perceived as ethnically "alien" as fellow citizens, regarding them instead as mere humans (302). Her case in point is "the Negro in a white community" (302). Excluded from "that tremendous equalizing of differences which comes from being citizens of some commonwealth . . . no longer to partake in the human artifice," the racial other is reduced to "some specimen of an animal species, called man" (302). This, of course, is exactly what Howard's catalog of animate, volitional, affective chattels accomplishes in its equivalency of "a horse, or a dog, a slave, or a pet lamb." In this way *humanization* becomes a tool of, rather than a shield against, degradation.

More to the point, Howard anticipates slavery's carceral afterlives when he seeks to "kill the juridical person" in the enslaved by coupling their "complete lack of responsibility" not with the dangerous "innocence" of the stateless but with an innate criminality. Remarkably, in this trial over a slave's alleged mail theft, it is the attorney for the *defense*, not the prosecution, whom we find pointedly referring to "the peculiar peccadilloes of theft for which" the "negro slave . . . would seem to be endowed with an inborn genius and proclivity" (*Quarterly*

Law Journal 1859: 180). Howard offers these observations about a racial propensity for crime as he seeks to extend "the utter legal incapacity and impersonality of the slave" beyond civil death, to include criminal liability as well (175). His redundant reference to "inborn genius" seeks to transmute the criminal culpability that constitutes artificial slave personhood into a natural "negro" attribute, regardless of condition. Having done so, he can then speak authoritatively of "the broad and complete contrast between the social, civil, and political condition of the dominant and the slave race" (181). The slave is no longer a particular kind of artificial legal person but the representative of a larger "race." With this understanding, Howard can insist that "so absolute and wide-pervading is the ethnological, civil, social and political difference between the dominant and the subject races—the white *American sovereign* and the black *African slave*—that they are not, and cannot be, governed by the same system of penal laws" (179). Howard's call to limit prosecution to the terms of the relevant slave codes blurs into a call for a separate criminal justice system for "the dominant and the subject races" based on innate "ethnological" differences rather than formal differences in "civil, social," or "political" standing. Such a bifurcated legal system, of course, need not end with abolition and emancipation.

Regardless of whether Taney shared Howard's view of an innate black criminality, the chief justice clearly understood that to exempt the enslaved from criminal accountability would pose a threat to legal order. Taney's brief decision repeatedly emphasizes the dangers that would ensue "if a slave is not within the law" (199). "It is true that a slave is the property of the master," Taney affirmed. "And it is equally true that he is not a citizen, and would not be embraced in a law operating on that class of persons. Yet, he is a person, and is always spoken of and described as such in the State papers and public Acts of the United States" (198). Even if we share the commitment to identifying, animating, and cultivating "alternative forms of life that elude law's violent embrace," *United States v. Amy* should alert us to how the coconstitutive legal and cultural processes of racialization operate by differentiating how various groups of humans are held "within the law" as persons, rather than biopolitically "disciplin[ing] humanity into full humans, not-quite-humans, and nonhumans" (Weheliye 2014: 127). The slave partook of the human artifice not as citizen but as a uniquely disempowered, obligated juridical (or legal) person. Taney's ruling affirms, then as now, the disciplinary necessity of maintaining a racist legal order by the ascription of a racialized personhood in which criminal culpability is the counterpart to civil death.

As one of the nation's most infamous expounders of racist legal thought, Taney joined other white, southern legal professionals in taking slaves' humanity for granted, understanding that it was the contours of slave personhood that mattered most for the preservation not only of slavery but of the white supremacist nation built on it. Despite its unorthodox deviation into the realm of the human, *United States v. Amy* makes it clear that from both a cultural and a legal perspective the humanity of enslaved African Americans was key to "the very idea" of slavery, as well as to the enhanced value of that particular form of property. Far from liberating, the recognition of enslaved black humanity was enlisted on both sides in efforts to intensify the slave's captivity, either as federal prisoner or as private *homo sacer*. Revealing as the tangential discussion of slave humanity is in *United States v. Amy*, the case suggests that slavery, like its carceral analogue, rested on the peculiar fractional, and fracturing, logic of a personhood that combined civil death with criminal culpability.

If *United States v. Amy* is the prism through which we look at the political present, it is in the argument for the defense that we see the artifice of slave personhood bending in the direction of the human. Howard may have lost the case, but the defense attorney's effort to eliminate even the punitive legal agency of the artificial slave person while redefining criminality as an inborn racial trait was a prescient one. Today, the same logic threatens to place African Americans practically, if not formally, "outside the pale of the law," consigned by the police power to the "rightlessness" that Arendt identifies with "loss of political status."

■ ■ ■

It has become commonplace to attribute the racialization of crime and the criminalization of race in the United States to the postemancipation transfer of a captive African American population "from plantation to prison" in the aftermath of the Civil War (Oshinsky 1996; Green 2008; DuVernay 2016). After all, the Thirteenth Amendment provides that "neither slavery nor involuntary servitude, except as a punishment for crime whereof the party shall have been duly convicted, shall exist within the United States" (U.S. Const. amend XIII,

§1). In fact, the story begins nearly a century earlier, when, soon after the nation's founding, the new states of the Northeast began gradually to abolish slavery (DeLombard 2012: 51–163). This "first" Reconstruction coincided with the equally gradual rise of the penitentiary as an alternative to public corporal punishment. Not coincidentally, by the time the Pennsylvania State Penitentiary for the Eastern District opened its doors in 1829, "Prisoner Number One" in the world's best-known penal experiment was an eighteen-year-old African American man, Charles Williams (Eastern State Penitentiary n.d.). A literate black farmer from Harrisburg, Williams was sentenced to "two years confinement with labor" for the theft of "one twenty-dollar watch, one three-dollar gold seal," and "a gold key" (ibid.). When the prison admitted its first female prisoners two years later, all four were African American (Patrick 2000: 363). While it is unquestionably true that "the presumptive identity of Black men [and women] as 'slaves' evolved into the presumptive identity of 'criminal,' and we have yet to fully recover from this historical frame" (Stevenson 2016: 12), we need to realize that this process commenced not with the Thirteenth Amendment (1866) but at the end of the *previous* century, with the nation's founding, the legal doctrine of the slave's mixed character, and the first Reconstruction.

The opposing lawyers' digressive affirmations of slave humanity in *United States v. Amy* throw into sharper relief the increasingly naturalized slave personhood that not only stood at the heart of this nearly forgotten case but that continues to inform African Americans' status in US law and culture today. Obscure though the case may be, *United States v. Amy* nevertheless suggests that the continuum connecting slavery to today's mass incarceration, police misconduct, and racist profiling is the continuing refusal to see African Americans as persons "within the law" in civil rather than criminal terms (see Hartman 1997: 125). For too many Americans, what we might after Tavia Nyong'o and Kyla Wazana Tompkins (2018) call black "counter-civility" remains the inscrutable obverse of a personhood that in US law and culture has historically been legible only as criminality.

Since the early colonial period, African Americans plaintiffs have persistently countered such legal-cultural ascription by exacting both official and community recognition of their standing in a steady stream of everyday civil proceedings. From recording title deeds to suing common carriers, African American civil litigants forcefully countered the legal and cultural identification of black personhood with civil incapacity and criminal culpability (see Welke 2001; Welch 2018; and Jones 2018). Black counter-civility insists on African Americans' standing as empowered legal (rather than natural) persons bearing the civil rights that are traditionally distinguished from the duties or obligations associated with criminal law. As such, this concept carries the "various significations" that Bouvier reminded readers of his *Law Dictionary* emanated from the word *civil*. When "used in contradistinction to *barbarous* or *savage*," it does not refer to mannerly decorum but, rather, to "a state of society reduced to order and regular government; thus we speak of civil life, civil society, civil government, and civil liberty." Bouvier goes on to explain that "it is sometimes used in contradistinction to *criminal*, to indicate the private rights and remedies of men, as members of the community, and in contrast to those, which are public and relate to the government; thus we speak of civil process and criminal process, civil jurisdiction and criminal jurisdiction."[8]

Black counter-civility should not, therefore, be confused with the "politics of respectability" theorized by historian Evelyn Brooks Higginbotham (1993). Citing the admonitions of Bill Cosby and Barack Obama, Dyson dismissively glosses this "brand of moralizing activism" as "the belief that good behavior and stern chiding will cure black ills and uplift black people and convince white people that we're human and worthy of respect" (Dyson 2016: 199; see also Alexander 2012: 212–17, 225–28). Rather than targeting the self-fashioning and conduct of African Americans, black counter-civility directs scrutiny toward the actions of others, often whites, whom it seeks to hold accountable under the rule of law.

We see a stark dramatization of how this black counter-civility differs from a politics of respectability in the dash cam video of motorist Sandra Bland's encounter with State Trooper Brian Encinia in Waller County, Texas. On July 10, 2015, Encinia pulled Bland over for an alleged failure to signal. When Bland questioned the trooper's authority to order her first to put out her cigarette, then to step out of her car, Encinia threatened her with a Taser, maneuvered her off-frame, violently rendered her supine, handcuffed her, and jailed her at $5,000 bail. Three days later she was found hanged in her cell.

The circumstances that brought Bland back to Texas represent a determined effort to assert and maintain a civil personality free from slavery's legacy of criminalized blackness. It was widely reported that Bland had returned to Texas from Chicago to take a job at her alma mater, Prairie View A&M University. Less well known is that she had driven more than one thousand miles to accept a temporary position at $13.80 per hour, having accumulated "$7,579.00 in court fines resulting from five traffic stops in various Chicago suburbs (including a DUI)" (Smyser 2015). Bland had seen firsthand how so-called prison profiteers benefit from the mass incarceration of people of color in the United States (Herivel and Wright 2007). In 2010, an insolvent Bland elected to "sit out" her traffic fines with a thirty-day stint in Houston's Harris County Jail (Smyser 2015). This was during the period when, under scrutiny from the US Department of Justice for civil rights violations, the perpetually overcrowded public facility routinely transferred overflow prisoners to private prisons run by LaSalle Corrections and Emerald Enterprises (Tilove 2012). Strategically opting for incarceration as an alternative to payment, Bland nevertheless helped to generate profit for corporate investors by contributing to the overcrowding that authorized outsourcing to private facilities. Like so many people of color targeted by the police, Bland found her options increasingly limited as a result of the growing trend for cost shifting as a form of economic sanction against defendants—guilty or not.[9] Bland's misdemeanors made it hard for her to find steady work. When Encinia pulled Bland over, however, her most recent period of unemployment was the result of conscience, not presumed criminality. Newly politicized by Black Lives Matter, Bland had made the principled decision in April 2015 to quit her secure, if low-paying, administrative assistant job at Cook's Correctional ("Innovative Food Service Products for Corrections"), on the basis of what we might call racial conflict-of-interest (Nathan 2016).

The legal and media inquiries into the three days leading up to Bland's death inadvertently reveal the extent to which her experience at Waller County Jail was structured by her potential profitability as a carceral subject. A video distributed by the Waller County sheriff shows the indigent Bland using the jail's staff telephone "as a courtesy" to make six or seven free calls to friends and family in an effort to raise the $515 bond for her $5,000 bail ("Motion," *Reed-Veal v. Encinia* S.D. Tex. [2015], 9). Her mobile phone confiscated, Bland was likely not in a position to use the somewhat more private phone in her cell, which operated through a "pin account (charged to the detainee)" or a

$14.99 per-call collect charge (*Reed-Veal v. Encinia* S.D. Tex. [2015], 2; see also Nathan 2016). Just one of the many revenue streams that make even public prisons and jails profitable for corporate investment, such extortionate telecommunications services had by 2015 provoked sufficient public outrage to prompt the Federal Communications Commission to "comprehensive reforms of Inmate Calling Services, . . . to ensure just[,] reasonable[,] and fair rates" (Office of the Federal Register 2015). The long-awaited FCC rule was published on December 18, 2015—five months after Bland's death. Bland's last documented contact with staff occurred when she used the cell's emergency intercom to inquire about using the phone in the cell; told to use her PIN, she did not make a phone call and was found dead roughly an hour later (Nathan 2016). Bland's experiences with the criminal justice system reveal the carceral afterlives of slavery. Misapprehended on this and likely other occasions as a criminal rather than a civil subject, Bland was a rich source of potential profits in her very human need for shelter, clothing, bedding, food, medical care, and contact with family and friends.

But it is in the disturbing dash cam video of her arrest that Bland engages in the centuries-long tradition of black counter-civility. In the following excerpts from the fifty-minute video released by the Texas Department of Public Safety, Bland makes it clear that she perceives the pretextual stop as profiling:

> **Encinia:** You mind putting out your cigarette, please? If you don't mind?
> **Bland:** I'm in my car, why do I have to put out my cigarette.
> **Encinia:** Well, you can step on out now. . . .
> **Bland:** Why am I . . .
> **Encinia:** Step out of the car!
> **Bland:** No, you don't have the right. No, you don't have the right.
> **Encinia:** Step out of the car.
> **Bland:** You do not have the right. You do not have the right to do this.
> **Encinia:** I do have the right, now step out or I will remove you.
> **Bland:** I refuse to talk to you other than to identify myself. [crosstalk] I am getting removed for a failure to signal? (Grim 2015)

Bland challenges Encinia's arbitrary demand that she put out her cigarette by asserting her rights as a property owner. Encinia rejects her
claim when he replaces the possessive pronoun (Bland's "step out of
my car") with the definite article ("step out of *the* car"). In response to
her continued questioning of his authority, Encinia threatens to use
force:

> **Encinia:** Step out or I will remove you. I'm giving you a lawful
> order. Get out of the car now or I'm going to remove you.
> **Bland:** And I'm calling my lawyer.
> **Encinia:** I'm going to yank you out of here. (Reaches inside the
> car.) . . .
> **Encinia:** I will light you up! Get out! Now! (Draws stun gun and
> points it at Bland.)
> **Bland:** Wow. Wow. (Bland exits car.) (Grim 2015)

By reluctantly complying with Encinia's order-cum-threat, Bland does
not engage in a politics of respectability. Far from it. Rather, Bland's
vehement, expletive-laced exchange with Officer Encinia offers a model
of counter-civility:

> **Bland:** For a failure to signal? You're doing all of this for a failure
> to signal?
> **Encinia:** Get over there.
> **Bland:** Right. yeah, lets [*sic*] take this to court, let's do this.
> **Encinia:** Go ahead.
> **Bland:** For a failure to signal? Yup, for a failure to signal!
> **Encinia:** Get off the phone!
> **Bland:** (crosstalk)
> **Encinia:** Get off the phone! Put your phone down!
> **Bland:** I'm not on the phone. I have a right to record. This is my
> property. Sir?
> **Encinia:** Put your phone down right now. Put your phone
> down! . . .
> **Bland:** Oh I can't wait 'til we go to court. Ooh I can't wait. I can-
> not wait 'til we go to court. I can't wait. Oh I can't wait! (Grim 2015)

As with her repeated assertion of her procedural rights, Bland's insistence on defining her phone, her car, and even her cigarette in terms
of "property" relations represents a determined effort to retain her status as a civil rather than a criminal person.

Bland did not get the day in court she so ardently anticipated. Like too many other people of color, she did not survive her encounter with law enforcement to answer formally whatever criminal charges could be produced against her, nor was the officer subject to criminal prosecution.[10] Bland's death was ruled a suicide; Encinia was fired and indicted for perjury for lying in his police report; Bland's family settled their wrongful death suit for $1.9 million; following the settlement, the charges against Encinia were dismissed. In place of the public justice offered by criminal proceedings, the only redress available to Bland's family—again, like so many others—was through damages in a civil suit (Fisher, Higham, and Hawkins 2015).[11] In these circumstances, the slave's mixed character survives as a chiasmus in which the sole alternative to the civil death of the criminal is a countercivility that is only posthumously recognizable, through a civil suit for wrongful death.

As the searing example of Bland's arrest reminds us, black countercivility has for centuries been misconstrued, willfully or otherwise, as criminality. In 1797 condemned formerly enslaved activist Abraham Johnstone broke with convention in his published gallows "confessions" by refusing to confess his guilt for the murder of his neighbor, "Guinea Negro" Thomas Read. Instead, he implied, he had been framed by two white men who had previously instigated a civil suit between the two black farmers. In his *Address . . . to the People of Colour* (1797) Johnstone makes it clear that the slave's mixed character followed him from his Delaware bondage into freedom in New Jersey. Soon after settling onto his leased Gloucester County farm, Johnstone recalled, "I was improving the place fast and doing well for myself, which made me an object of envy and hatred" in the local community— as indicated by the persistent rumors that he'd stolen carpets from a boarding-house keeper and meat from local smokehouses and slaughterhouses (39). He was convicted on circumstantial evidence and hanged on July 8, 1797, for a murder in which a body was never produced. A little more than a century later, slavery reparations activist and organizer Callie House was convicted by an exclusively white male jury on trumped-up charges of mail fraud; House spent November 1917 to August 1, 1918, imprisoned in the Missouri State Penitentiary in Jefferson City before her early release for good behavior (Berry 2005: 188–211). Johnstone and House are just two among legions of African Americans who, since the founding, have had their civil—and often civic—actions literally misapprehended as criminality.

Long after the abolition of slavery and the formal end to de jure segregation, many Americans remain unable (or unwilling) to perceive African Americans as persons with civil standing. For too many of their fellow citizens, African Americans' peaceful occupation of both public and private spaces too often remains legible only as criminality. This failure to identify black civil personality is what prevented onlookers and police officers alike from seeing Tamir Rice as a boy playing in a public park, Dajerria Becton and her friends as teenagers enjoying a pool party, or Philando Castile as a citizen with the right to bear arms.

African American detainees, prisoners, and parolees find that, like their enslaved forebears, their profitability lies in the exploitation, rather than the denial, of their humanity. The various commercial enterprises that have become known as the prison-industrial complex extract their profits from inmates' distinctly human need for a range of lucrative services, ranging from Cook's Correctional's custom-made tableware to exorbitant telecommunications systems that at once provide and restrict access to support networks of friends and family (Haverty 2016). Privatized carceral services such as health care reap gains through rigid cost-benefit accounting of inmates' all-too-human vulnerabilities (Jacobs 2007; Hylton 2007; Zielbauer 2007). It is cruelly apt, then, that the American Correctional Association should, in the current revision of its original, Reconstruction-era "Declaration of Principles" (1870), give pride of place on its website to "humanity" (ACA n.d.). The ACA's canny (not to say cynical) participation in humanitarian rhetoric suggests the danger of ignoring the fact that, far from denying black humanity, today's prison-industrial complex, like historical race slavery, is a financial enterprise purpose-built to extract profits from the conscious, explicit exploitation of that humanity.

■ ■ ■

Unquestionably, one of the most important critical contributions of Afrohumanism, or black posthumanism, is "the transformation of the human into a heuristic model and not an ontological fait accompli" (Weheliye 2014: 8). But that very principle requires that we be clear about when the subject of critical inquiry is the human—and when it is *not*. To understand US slavery and its carceral afterlives, we must attend to the legal person, especially in its avatar as slave person, bearing what *Federalist* 54 identifies as the mixed character of civilly dead property and criminally responsible person. For it is their fellow Americans' failure (or refusal) to recognize African Americans in their civil capacity that, repeatedly, horrifically, creates all those deadly situations characterized by the excessive use of force by law enforcement.

I adopt the term *situations* from the video series by poet Claudia Rankine and her husband, documentary photographer John Lucas (2016). Their *Situations* capture those moments when African American citizens are subject to the hyperscrutiny and misapprehension that leads to black and brown body parts being "criminalized already [into] weapons," which in turn leads to the traumatic repetition of the situation—"flashes, a siren, a stretched-out roar"—in which "you are not the guy and still you fit the description because there is only one guy who is always the guy who is always fitting the description" (Lucas and Rankine 2016; Rankine 2014: 101, 105).[12] "Criminalized already": that is not the description of a dehumanized animal—animals are not currently subject to prosecution—but to a particular form of personhood, one with its roots in a slavery that, like today's prison-industrial complex, exploited human beings *as* human beings for profit while rendering them, in Howard's words, "utter civil nonentit[ies]." Nor is it only "the guy" under the flashing light of the police car. It is, Rankine (2014: 34) reminds us, Serena Williams having to ask interviewer Piers Morgan, after winning the 2012 Olympic gold medal for the United States in women's singles tennis, "if she looks like a gangster to him"—and being told, "Yes." (This, after Williams was reviled for Crip-walking in her impromptu victory dance.)

In her "American Lyric," Rankine enfolds these moments of criminalized hypervisibility within the countless everyday occasions when black men and women are utterly invisible *as civil persons* to their fellow Americans. Rankine deftly limns this failure to recognize black civil presence in a scene of a fellow customer's inadvertent—if not exactly innocent—line jumping at the pharmacy: "Oh my God, I didn't see you . . . no, I really didn't see you" (77). It is in such instances of Ellisonian invisibility, as much as in the misapprehension of black counter-civility for criminality, that we glimpse the thriving, albeit deadly, afterlives of slavery.

Jeannine Marie DeLombard is associate professor of English at the University of California, Santa Barbara. The author of *Slavery on Trial: Law, Print, and Abolitionism* (2007) and *In the Shadow of the Gallows: Race, Crime, and American Civic Identity* (2012), she is currently at work on a third book project, "Bound to Respect: Democratic Dignity and the Indignities of Slavery."

Notes

1 "Within the text of the law there is an afterlife of slavery" (Best 2004: 13). (But see Best 2012, discussed below. This article was in press upon the publication of Best 2018; I was therefore unable to frame my account of counter-civility as a response to Best's very persuasive criticism of scholarship on civil death as one of the afterlives of slavery.) Rather than focusing on embodied persons in the context of property relations (Hartman 1997; Best 2004; Allewaert 2013; Luck 2014), my larger project builds on the scholarship of the "mixed-character" doctrine (Gross 2000; Dayan 2002; Dayan 2011: 39–70, 140–76) to explore how the naturalization of slave personhood has at once enabled and limited the democratization of status—civil standing, in particular—in American law and culture.

2 Of course, the concept of the human is itself constantly shifting. See Arendt 1994: 298; and Boggs 2013: 24, 27. Cristin Ellis (2018: 4) questions the critical stress on "recognition," making the excellent point that "racism functioned, in the antebellum context . . . to justify *indifference* to the fact of Black humanity. For under its empirical redescription, (biological) humanness strictly vouches for a basically *physiological* commonality across the human species that makes no definite claim about the moral equality of all members." My project focuses on the *terms* of recognition—that is, of the status of persons rather than biopolitical membership in the (always shifting) category of the human.

3 Thus, in his inquiry into this very question, David Brion Davis (2015: 17) is careful to define *dehumanization* in terms of status as much as of biopolitical inclusion: "[It is] the eradication not of human *identity* but of those elements of humanity that evoke respect and empathy and convey a sense of dignity. Dehumanization means the debasement of a human, often the reduction to the status of an 'animalized human,' a person who exemplifies the so-called animal traits and who lacks the moral and rational capacities that humans esteem."

4 John Bouvier, *A Law Dictionary* [. . .], rev. 4th ed. (1852), s.v. "person."

5 My approach diverges from that of Monique Allewaert (2014: 13), who, without contending with this longer legal history, emphasizes this biological substrate to theorize the "parahuman body of the slave person" and does not address the specific combination of rights and duties that constitute the legal artifice of slave personhood.

6 Although here Wynter (2003: 261) characterizes "the Black population group" as occupying the lowest rung of the human ladder, elsewhere she speaks of racial exclusion to sub-/nonhuman status. This ambiguity is captured by her designation "Human Other" (266), which in some places seems to suggest inclusion within the category of the human and elsewhere its definitive opposite. Although Wynter's magisterial survey brilliantly

summarizes and integrates a range of historical periods and ideologies, the frequent shifts between a "barely human" (309) status and "not-quite-humanness" (301) does not seem to correspond to the particular epochs Wynter considers.

7   On slave personhood in the context of the English common law of deodands, see DeLombard 2012: 58, 331n44.

8   John Bouvier, *A Law Dictionary* [. . .], 2nd ed. (1843), s.v. "civil."

9   Recently revived, cost shifting dates back to the birth of the prison, where it disproportionately affected—and exploited—women, especially women of color. See Levinston 2007; and Manion 2015: 37–38.

10   Bland was charged with assaulting a public servant on the basis of Encinia's (false) claim that she kicked him (Montgomery 2015). For the transcript of Encinia's discussion with his sergeant of how to charge Bland, see Hager 2015.

11   In addition to the settlement, in 2017 Bland's family achieved passage of the Sandra Bland Act in the Texas legislature, which "mandates county jails divert people with mental health and substance abuse issues toward treatment, makes it easier for defendants to receive a personal bond if they have a mental illness or intellectual disability, and requires that independent law enforcement agencies investigate jail deaths" (Silver 2017).

12   Rankine's line echoes the trenchant critique offered by Tyquan Brehon, who estimates being "unjustifiably stopped by the police more than 60 times" before he turned eighteen: "They never say, 'This is why I'm stopping you.' When you're young and you're black, no matter how you look, you fit the description" (quoted in Dressner and Martinez 2012).

References

Agamben, Giorgio. 1998. *Homo Sacer: Sovereign Power and Bare Life*. Translated by Daniel Heller-Roazen. Stanford, CA: Stanford Univ. Press.

A[gassiz], L[ouis]. 1850. "The Diversity of Origin of the Human Races." *Christian Examiner and Religious Miscellany* 49, no. 1: 110–45.

Alexander, Michelle. 2012. *The New Jim Crow: Mass Incarceration in the Age of Colorblindness*. Rev. ed. New York: New Press.

Allewaert, Monique. 2014. *Ariel's Ecology: Plantations, Personhood, and Colonialism in the American Tropics*. Minneapolis: Univ. of Minnesota Press.

American Correctional Association. n.d. "Declaration of Principles: Humanity." www.aca.org/ACA_Prod_IMIS/ACA_Member/AboutUs/Dec.aspx ?WebsiteKey=113f6b09-e150-4c56-9c66-284b92f21e51&hkey=a975cbd5 -9788-4705-9b39-fcb6ddc048e0&Principles=2#Principles (accessed August 29, 2016).

Arendt, Hannah. (1951) 1994. *The Origins of Totalitarianism*. New York: Houghton Mifflin Harcourt.

Berry, Mary Frances. 2005. *My Face Is Black Is True: Callie House and the Struggle for Ex-Slave Reparations.* New York: Knopf.

Best, Stephen. 2004. *The Fugitive's Properties: Law and the Poetics of Possession.* Chicago: Univ. of Chicago Press.

Best, Stephen. 2012. "On Failing to Make the Past Present." *Modern Language Quarterly* 73, no. 3: 453–74.

Best, Stephen. 2018. *None Like Us: Blackness, Belonging, Aesthetic Life.* Durham, NC: Duke Univ. Press.

Blumenthal, Susanna L. 2016. *Law and the Modern Mind: Consciousness and Responsibility in American Legal Culture.* Cambridge, MA: Harvard Univ. Press.

Boggs, Colleen Glenney. 2013. *Animalia Americana: Animal Representations and Biopolitical Subjectivity.* New York: Columbia Univ. Press.

Cassuto, Leonard. 1997. *The Inhuman Race: The Racial Grotesque in American Literature and Culture.* New York: Columbia Univ. Press.

Davis, David Brion. 2015. *The Problem of Slavery in the Age of Emancipation.* New York: Vintage.

Dayan, Joan. 2002. "Legal Slaves and Civil Bodies." In *Materializing Democracy: Toward a Revitalized Cultural Politics*, edited by Russ Castronovo and Dana D. Nelson, 53–94. Durham, NC: Duke Univ. Press.

Dayan, Joan [Colin]. 2011. *The Law Is a White Dog: How Legal Rituals Make and Unmake Persons.* Princeton, NJ: Princeton Univ. Press.

DeLombard, Jeannine Marie. 2012. *In the Shadow of the Gallows: Race, Crime, and American Civic Identity.* Philadelphia: Univ. of Pennsylvania Press.

Dressner, Julie, and Edwin Martinez. 2012. "The Scars of Stop-and-Frisk." *New York Times*, June 12. www.nytimes.com/2012/06/12/opinion/the-scars-of-stop-and-frisk.html?_r=1&ref=nyregion.

DuVernay, Ava, dir. 2016. *13th.* Los Angeles: Kandoo Films.

Dyson, Michael Eric. 2016. *The Black Presidency: Barack Obama and the Politics of Race in America.* Boston: Houghton Mifflin Harcourt.

Eastern State Penitentiary. n.d. "Timeline: 1829 October 25." www.easternstate.org/research/history-eastern-state/timeline (accessed June 6, 2019).

Ellis, Cristin. 2018. *Antebellum Posthuman: Race and Materiality in the Mid-Nineteenth Century.* New York: Fordham Univ. Press.

Fisher, Marc, Scott Higham, and Derek Hawkins. 2015. "Uneven Justice." *Washington Post*, November 3. www.washingtonpost.com/sf/investigative/2015/11/03/uneven-justice/.

Freeburg, Christopher. 2017. *Black Aesthetics and the Interior Life.* Charlottesville: Univ. of Virginia Press.

Garza, Alicia. 2014. "A Herstory of the #BlackLivesMatter Movement." *Feminist Wire*, October 7. www.thefeministwire.com/2014/10/blacklivesmatter-2/.

Gines, Kathryn T. 2014. *Hannah Arendt and the Negro Question.* Bloomington: Indiana Univ. Press.

Goodman, Amy. 2014. "Dehumanizing the Black Lives of America: Michael Eric Dyson on Ferguson, Police Brutality, and Race." *Democracy Now!*, December 1. www.democracynow.org/2014/12/1/dehumanizing_the_ black_lives_of_america.

Green, Tara T., ed. 2008. *From the Plantation to the Prison: African-American Confinement Literature.* Macon, GA: Mercer Univ. Press.

Grim, Ryan. 2015. "The Transcript of Sandra Bland's Arrest Is as Revealing as the Video." *Huffington Post*, July 22. www.huffingtonpost.com/entry /sandra-bland-arrest-transcript_us_55b03a88e4b0a9b94853b1f1.

Gross, Ariela J. 2000. *Double Character: Slavery and Mastery in the Antebellum Southern Courtroom.* Princeton, NJ: Princeton Univ. Press.

Hager, Eli. 2015. "What You May Have Missed in the Sandra Bland Video." *The Marshall Project*, July 22. www.themarshallproject.org/2015/07/22 /what-you-may-have-missed-in-the-sandra-bland-video#.DP1QNYl1F.

Hartman, Saidiya V. 1997. *Scenes of Subjection: Terror, Slavery, and Self-Making in Nineteenth-Century America.* New York: Oxford Univ. Press.

Haverty, Natasha. 2016. "Video Calls Replace In-Person Visits in Some Jails." *All Things Considered*, December 5. National Public Radio. www.npr.org /2016/12/05/504458311/video-calls-replace-in-person-visits-in-some-jails.

Herivel, Tara, and Paul Wright, eds. 2007. *Prison Profiteers: Who Makes Money from Mass Incarceration.* New York: New Press.

Higginbotham, Evelyn Brooks. 1993. *Righteous Discontent: The Women's Movement in the Black Baptist Church, 1880–1920.* Cambridge, MA: Harvard Univ. Press.

Hunt, Lynn. 2007. *Inventing Human Rights: A History.* New York: W. W. Norton.

Hylton, Wil S. 2007. "Sick on the Inside: Correctional HMOs and the Coming Prison Plague." In Herivel and Wright 2007: 179–203.

Jacobs, Steven J. 2007. "Mapping the Prison Telephone Industry." In Herivel and Wright 2007: 235–49.

Jefferson, Thomas. 1788. *Notes on the State of Virginia.* Philadelphia: Prichard and Hall. Documenting the American South, https://docsouth.unc.edu /southlit/jefferson/jefferson.html.

Johnson, Walter. 2016. "To Remake the World: Slavery, Racial Capitalism, and Justice." *Boston Review*, October 26. http://bostonreview.net/race/walter -johnson-slavery-human-rights-racial-capitalism.

Johnstone, Abraham. 1797. *Address of Abraham Johnstone, a Black Man [. . .].* Philadelphia.

Jones, Martha S. 2018. *Birthright Citizens: A History of Race and Rights in Antebellum America.* Cambridge: Cambridge Univ. Press.

Levinston, Kristen D. 2007. "Making the 'Bad Guy' Pay: Growing Use of Cost Shifting as an Economic Sanction." In Herivel and Wright 2007: 52–79.

Lucas, John, and Claudia Rankine. 2016. *Situations.* claudiarankine.com/.

Luck, Chad. 2014. *Body of Property: Antebellum American Fiction and the Phenomenology of Possession.* New York: Fordham Univ. Press.

Madison, James, Alexander Hamilton, and John Jay. (1788) 1988. *The Federalist Papers*. New York: Penguin.

Manion, Jen. 2015. *Liberty's Prisoners: Carceral Culture in Early America*. Philadelphia: Univ. of Pennsylvania Press.

Melville, Herman. (1851) 2002. *Moby-Dick: An Authoritative Text*. Edited by Hershel Parker and Harrison Hayford. 2nd ed. New York: Norton.

Montgomery, David. 2015. "New Details Released in Sandra Bland's Death in Texas Jail." *New York Times*, July 20. www.nytimes.com/2015/07/21/us /new-details-released-in-sandra-blands-death-in-texas-jail.html?_r=0.

Mussawir, Edward, and Connal Parsley. 2017. "The Law of Persons Today: At the Margins of Jurisprudence." *Law and Humanities* 11, no. 1: 44–83.

Nathan, Debbie. 2016. "What Happened to Sandra Bland?" *Nation*, April 21. www.thenation.com/article/what-happened-to-sandra-bland/.

Nyong'o, Tavia, and Kyla Wazana Tompkins. 2018. "Eleven Theses on Civility." *Social Text*, July 11. https://socialtextjournal.org/eleven-theses-on -civility/.

Office of the Federal Register. 2015. "Rates for Interstate Inmate Calling Services." *Federal Register: The Daily Journal of the United States Government*. www.federalregister.gov/articles/2015/12/18/2015-31252/rates -for-interstate-inmate-calling-services.

Oshinsky, David M. 1996. *"Worse Than Slavery": Parchman Farm and the Ordeal of Jim Crow Justice*. New York: Free Press.

Patrick, Leslie. 2000. "Ann Hinson: A Little Known Woman in the Country's Premier Prison, Eastern State Penitentiary, 1831." *Pennsylvania History* 67, no. 3: 361–75.

Pottage, Alain. 2002. *"Unitas Personae*: On Legal and Biological Self-Narration." *Law and Literature* 14, no. 2: 275–308.

Pratt, Lloyd. 2016. *The Stranger's Book: The Human of African American Literature*. Philadelphia: Univ. of Pennsylvania Press.

Quarterly Law Journal. 1859. "Mail Robbery by Slave. *United States v. Amy*." 4, no. 3: 163–202.

Rankine, Claudia. 2014. *Citizen: An American Lyric*. Minneapolis: Graywolf Press.

Silver, Johnathan. 2017. "Texas Gov. Abbott Signs 'Sandra Bland Act' into Law.'" *Texas Tribune*, June 15. www.texastribune.org/2017/06/15/texas -gov-greg-abbott-signs-sandra-bland-act-law/.

Smyser, Katy. 2015. "Suburban Woman Found Dead in Jail Had Previous Encounters with Police." *Chicago NBC5 News*, July 16. www.nbcchicago .com/investigations/Suburban-Woman-Found-Dead-in-Jail-Had-Previous -Encounters-With-Police-316025661.html.

Spillers, Hortense J. 1987. "Mama's Baby, Papa's Maybe: An American Grammar Book." *Diacritics* 17, no. 2: 64–68.

Stevenson, Bryan. 2016. "A Presumption of Guilt: The Legacy of America's History of Racial Injustice." In *Policing the Black Man: Arrest, Prosecution, and Imprisonment,* edited by Angela J. Davis, 3–30. New York: Pantheon.

Tilove, Jonathan. 2012. "Houston Stops Helping Louisiana Fill Beds in Its For-Profit Prisons." *Times-Picayune,* May 20. www.nola.com/crime/index.ssf /2012/05/houston_stops_helping_louisian.html.

Wahl, Jenny Bourne. 1998. *The Bondsman's Burden: An Economic Analysis of the Common Law of Southern Slavery.* Cambridge: Cambridge Univ. Press.

Walker, Timothy. 1846. *Introduction to American Law, Designed as a First Book for Students.* 2nd ed. Cincinnati: Derby, Bradley, and Co.

Weheliye, Alexander G. 2014. *Habeas Viscus: Racializing Assemblages, Biopolitics, and Black Feminist Theories of the Human.* Durham, NC: Duke Univ. Press.

Welch, Kimberly M. 2018. *Black Litigants in the Antebellum American South.* Chapel Hill: Univ. of North Carolina Press.

Welke, Barbara Young. 2001. *Recasting American Liberty: Gender, Race, Law, and the Railroad Revolution, 1865–1920.* Cambridge: Cambridge Univ. Press.

Wong, Edlie L. 2009. *Neither Fugitive nor Free: Atlantic Slavery, Freedom Suits, and the Legal Culture of Travel.* New York: New York Univ. Press.

Wynter, Sylvia. 2003. "Unsettling the Coloniality of Being/Power/Truth/ Freedom: Towards the Human, after Man, Its Overrepresentation—An Argument." *CR: The New Centennial Review* 3, no. 3: 257–337.

Zielbauer, Paul von. 2007. "Private Health Care in Jails Can Be a Death Sentence." In Herivel and Wright 2007: 204–27.

Jarvis C.
McInnis

A Corporate Plantation Reading Public:
Labor, Literacy, and Diaspora
in the Global Black South

Abstract This essay reconstructs the history of the *Cotton Farmer*, a rare African American newspaper edited and published by black tenant farmers employed by the Delta and Pine Land Company, once the world's largest corporate cotton plantation located in the Mississippi delta. The
Cotton Farmer ran from 1919 to circa 1927 and was mainly confined to the company's properties.
However, in 1926, three copies of the paper circulated to Bocas del Toro, Panama, to a Garveyite
and West Indian migrant laborer employed on the infamous United Fruit Company's vast banana
and fruit plantations. Tracing the *Cotton Farmer*'s hemispheric circulation from the Mississippi
delta to Panama, this essay explores the intersections of labor, literacy, and diaspora in the global
black south. What do we make of a reading public among black tenant farmers on a corporate cotton plantation in the Mississippi delta at the height of Jim Crow? How did the entanglements of
labor and literacy at once challenge and correspond with conventional accounts of sharecropping
in the Jim Crow South? Further, in light of the *Cotton Farmer*'s circulation from Mississippi's cotton fields to Panama's banana fields, this essay establishes the corporate plantation as a heuristic
for exploring the imperial logics and practices tying the US South to the larger project of colonial
domination in the Caribbean and Latin America, and ultimately reexamines black transnationalism
and diaspora from the position of corporate plantation laborers as they negotiated ever-evolving
modes of domination and social control on corporate plantations in the global black south. In so
doing, it establishes black agricultural and corporate plantation laborers as architects of black
geographic thought and diasporic practice alongside their urban, cosmopolitan contemporaries.
Keywords transnationalism, black geographies, global south, Garveyism, print culture

Once touted as the world's largest cotton planta-
tion, the Delta and Pine Land Company (DPL) was a constellation of
eighteen plantations located in the rich alluvial lands of Washington
and Bolivar Counties in the Mississippi delta. With approximately
thirty-five thousand acres of land under cultivation, the company

American Literature, Volume 91, Number 3, September 2019
DOI 10.1215/00029831-7722116 © 2019 by Duke University Press

required a considerable labor force, consisting of several thousand black sharecroppers, tenant farmers, and day laborers.[1] In 1919, at the request of Reverend Addison "Ad" Wimbs, a black tenant farmer, DPL agreed to finance the *Cotton Farmer*, a plantation newspaper written, edited, and published by a committee of black tenant farmers from each plantation. The *Cotton Farmer* ran from 1919 to circa 1927 and had a paid circulation of more than thirteen hundred subscribers per year, mainly confined to DPL's properties. While the Mississippi delta had once been a thriving enclave of New Negro enterprise in the late nineteenth century, by the 1910s, widespread black land ownership had eroded into new modes of racial capitalist dispossession and dependency, such as sharecropping and tenant farming on corporate plantations. Though black sharecroppers and tenant farmers were routinely coerced into perennial cycles of debt stemming, in part, from their inability to read and comprehend labor contracts, DPL—a corporate plantation governed by modern scientific management techniques—promoted a reading and writing public as a strategy to recruit and retain (yet ultimately placate and surveil) a newly mobile black labor force. By delineating how DPL's labor policies both corresponded with and challenged predominant accounts of sharecropping and tenant farming, I argue that the history of the *Cotton Farmer* elucidates a more nuanced portrait of the entanglements of race, labor, and literacy in the rural Jim Crow South.

Despite its mostly local circulation, brief existence, and thus relative obscurity, the *Cotton Farmer*'s material and archival history also situates delta sharecroppers and tenant farmers within the hemisphere's transnational circuits of labor, trade, print culture, and political activism. Most copies of the *Cotton Farmer* were likely destroyed by the angry waters of the muddy Mississippi River, when, in 1927, the region experienced the worst river flood in US history, leaving DPL's plantations under three to fifteen feet of water from March to July and nearly wiping out the entire cotton crop for that year. The single extant issue, dated February 5, 1927, was discovered in the Marcus Garvey files at the National Archives, indicating not only the paper's unique role in cultivating a black corporate plantation reading public in the delta, already an anomaly, but also revealing a dynamic, yet relatively underexplored geography of black transnational mobility and diasporic affiliation among sharecroppers, tenant farmers, and migrant laborers during the interwar years.[2] Specifically, the issue provides evidence of the paper's circulation to an Afro-Caribbean migrant laborer in Panama and a photograph of a former DPL employee who migrated to the delta from Jamaica. This Afro-Caribbean presence at DPL situates the delta as a node within the black hemispheric literary and (labor) migration circuit that I call the *global black south*, a term I flesh out more fully below.

On the front page of the issue, Wimbs published correspondence from John J. Smith, a reader in Shepard Island, Bocas del Toro, Panama, requesting a subscription to the *Cotton Farmer*. Though surprised that the paper had traveled such a vast distance, Wimbs speculated that it "had reached Panama . . . on account of its [sympathetic] attitude towards Marcus Garvey" (Wimbs 1927). With seventeen Universal Negro Improvement Association (UNIA) divisions in Bolivar County, Mississippi, alone, the most of any county in the United States, the Garvey movement had a stronghold in the delta (Rolinson 2007: 109). It also had a significant following in Bocas del Toro and throughout Central America, due to Afro-Caribbean labor migration to the Panama Canal Zone and the infamous United Fruit Company's (UFCO) vast banana and fruit plantations. As Panama's largest banana-producing region, Bocas del Toro mirrored the Mississippi delta as a public organized around the corporate plantation (Bourgois 1989). Indeed, the two regions came into formation simultaneously and under similar conditions of foreign capital investment and black labor. Thus, Garveyism and the corporate plantation helped to facilitate the *Cotton Farmer*'s hemispheric circulation.

If Smith's subscription request indicates how corporate plantation laborers participated in a transnational periodical network, then the issue's photographic feature of a migrant laborer from "Jamaica Island" situates the delta within a hemispheric labor migration circuit as well. In the column adjacent to Smith's letter, Wimbs announced the return of Reverend A. B. Brown, a former sharecropper on DPL's Dixon Plantation, who, as Wimbs notes, was "better known on the Scott Syndicate as 'Jamaica.'" The photograph of Brown depicts him standing in front of a wood fence, dressed in a dark suit coat and dress slacks, posing with his head down, and reading what appears to be an open Bible in his right hand (*Cotton Farmer* 1927a). According to Wimbs, Brown had "cropped on Dixon Plantation for several years and each year paid his account and cleared money." How a Jamaican migrant laborer found his way to a corporate cotton plantation in the

Mississippi delta remains a mystery, but I propose that his trajectory illuminates the region's significance as a locus of black transnational activity alongside more notable port cities such as New Orleans and Mobile (Alabama), Colón (Panama), and Limón (Costa Rica).

Through the *Cotton Farmer*'s hemispheric circulation to Panama and Reverend Brown's migration from Jamaica to the delta, this essay interrogates the intersections of labor, literacy, and diaspora on the corporate plantation in the global black south. As an institution that at once extended and refined the racial and managerial logics of the antebellum plantation, the corporate plantation represents what I call an *afterlife of the plantation*. A distinct "afterlife of slavery," the afterlife of the plantation describes the institutions, logics, and practices that evolved in the wake of emancipation, yet were specifically tied to the physical spaces and biopolitical functions of the plantation as a mode of labor organization and large-scale commodity production for global markets.[3] Beginning in the late nineteenth century, corporate plantations spread throughout much of what scholars now refer to as the "global south." This essay, however, focuses on the *global black south* as a subregion of the global south that stretches from the US South to the Caribbean and the Caribbean coast of Latin America. While scholars have referred to this hemispheric cartography as the "Plantation Americas" and "the circum-Caribbean," I insist on the designation *global black south* to foreground the cultural and political contributions of southern African Americans within black transnational and diaspora studies.[4] In the field of black geographies, Katherine McKittrick and Clyde Woods (2007: 6) call for "unraveling the ostensible mysteries that take place when subaltern geographies are theorized, lived, creatively expressed, and socially produced." "In the humanities," they continue, "spatial metaphors abound through analyses of black creative texts, yet they are often theorized as detached from concrete three-dimensional geographies" (7). By resituating the *Cotton Farmer*, the corporate plantation, and the Mississippi delta within a hemispheric framework, I propose the global black south as one such "subaltern" and "three-dimensional geography" that takes seriously "the geographic knowledges that black subjects impart[ed]" as they navigated the treacherous afterlives of the plantation (6).

The essay's structure mirrors the *Cotton Farmer*'s trajectory from Mississippi's cotton plantations to Panama's banana fields. First, the essay mines disparate and rare archival sources to examine DPL and the *Cotton Farmer* as vistas into the afterlife of the plantation in the delta. Instead of perpetuating racial violence and coercion, as was typical of the neoplantation regime, DPL enacted welfare capitalism and paternalism to "manage" black workers, hence financing a corporate plantation reading public. As a record of black social life, the *Cotton Farmer* indicates how black delta residents strategically negotiated the foreclosed futures of economic independence that had initially attracted their foreparents to the region after emancipation. DPL's anomalous support for the paper and various other black domestic, social, and educational institutions enabled workers to pursue tenant farming as a seemingly viable employment option, mostly absent racial violence; yet, the company's insistence on social control and paternalism, I argue, ultimately evinces racial capitalism's insidious and protean capacity to coopt the very scripts of liberal subjecthood—that is, literacy as a marker of humanity and modality of freedom—to reinscribe and prolong plantation logics and practices.

Tracing the *Cotton Farmer*'s transnational circulation to Panama, I then reconstruct the afterlife of the plantation in the global black south as a dynamic hemispheric geography from above and below. Whereas colonialism and imperialism in the Caribbean and Latin America and Jim Crow in the United States are rightly viewed as divergent afterlives of the plantation, a comparative analysis of DPL and UFCO elucidates the corporate plantation as a biopolitical regime that produced similar conditions of black life throughout the hemisphere. As such, this essay contributes to the growing body of scholarship that repositions the US South in relation to the broader global south (Woodruff 2012; Darden 2009; Smith and Cohn 2004). At the same time, as McKittrick and Woods (2007: 5) observe, "Within and against the grain of dominant modes of power, knowledge, and space, black geographic narratives and lived experiences need to be taken seriously because they reconfigure classificatory spatial practices." Thus, rather than simply being bound to the land through violence, coercion, and debt, I show how black laborers appropriated hegemonic structures such as corporate plantation shipping and migration networks to circulate newspapers and spread ideas about labor activism and racial solidarity. Generally, scholarship in black transnational and diaspora studies in the interwar years focuses on artists and intellectuals traveling between urban cosmopolitan centers in the global north (Edwards 2003; Stephens 2005; Putnam 2013). The *Cotton Farmer*, however, broadens this cartography by illuminating the Mississippi delta and Bocas del Toro as rural New Negro enclaves, where black agricultural workers crafted geopolitical knowledges and enacted their own sharecropper and tenant farmer transnationalism from below that undermined corporate plantation disciplinary aims. Ultimately, by reconstructing the history of this rare corporate plantation newspaper, this essay makes a theoretical and methodological intervention in black transnational and diaspora studies: centering the literary, cultural and political activities of black workers in the rural plantation regions of the Americas, I maintain, elucidates *the afterlife of the plantation in the global black south* as a dynamic, yet often neglected and undertheorized region of "black geographic thought" and diasporic connectivity (McKittrick and Woods 2007: 6).

Race and Labor on a Corporate Plantation: Paternalism, Welfare Capitalism, and Social Control

Following the Civil War, the Mississippi delta was essentially a new frontier, as 90 percent of the region was covered in swamps and dense wilderness. African Americans from older parts of the South, foreign-born immigrants, southern planters, and northern businessmen poured into the area in pursuit of better economic opportunities through cotton farming on its rich alluvial soils. Though it would eventually become one of the most impoverished and racially oppressive regions in the United States, the delta was initially an enclave of New Negro enterprise, where black southerners laid claim to the new possibilities of free labor and citizenship.[5] These agrarian New Negroes agreed to cultivate the delta wilderness for white landowners in hopes of raising the down payment to purchase property of their own. Initially, their efforts were successful, as black people made up three-fourths of delta farm owners by 1900 and, in Bolivar County, established Mound Bayou as one of the earliest and most successful all-black towns in the country. By the 1910s, however, Jim Crow—the nation's newest iteration of racial capitalist subjugation, replete with disfranchisement, lynching, and land dispossession—turned this hopeful generation of freed women and men from self-determined farmers into a largely dependent proletariat, sharecropping and tenant farming on the region's corporate plantations (Willis 2000; Woodruff 2012).

Much like their colonial and antebellum antecedents, business or corporate plantations were technologies of settler colonialism combined with the efficiency of industrial factories. Their emergence throughout the US South was coterminous with "the growth of big business in the [US] North" (Woodman 2001: 809–10). In some instances, corporate plantations were established on former antebellum plantations, but many were new enterprises altogether. They "were the most modern, well-organized, closely supervised agricultural operations in the cotton South" (801). As Progressive Era enterprises, they prioritized "scientific management, which required the close supervision of a routinized and disciplined labor force" (Woodruff 2012: 2). To ensure worker efficiency and productivity, plantation managers employed practices of surveillance and social control "from plowing to sales" over their already racialized distribution of labor (Woodman 1982: 225). A prototypical corporate plantation, DPL was established in the 1910s by the Fine Cotton Spinners and Doublers' Association, a British company that invested in the Mississippi delta to produce cotton for its textile mills in Manchester, England. Combining corporate management techniques with the racial hierarchy of antebellum slavery and Jim Crow, each of its eighteen sites primarily employed black tenants supervised by a white plantation manager and a black foreman (*Manufacturer's Record* 1923: 105).

As the world's largest cotton plantation, DPL required a considerable labor force, especially since the Great Migration and World War I presented black southerners with seemingly viable alternatives to agricultural work through urban and industrial occupations. The company regularly engaged in labor expeditions to the backwoods of Mississippi, Louisiana, Arkansas, and Alabama to recruit tenants (Quinn Papers, folder 8). In plantation managers' meetings, L. K. Salsbury, DPL's executive manager from 1912 to 1927, expressed constant urgency and anxiety over recruiting and retaining enough laborers to work the plantations and stressed that surveillance of the company's workforce was imperative:

> The great difficulty we have before us now is our labor problem—not only getting labor, but keeping it. You are going to have [to do] everything you can do to maintain your present quota. . . . We must keep up with each and every tenant all the time; know what they are thinking about and what they are going to do. . . . We have got

to be firm with these negroes and see that they carry out their contracts. (DPL Company Records, box 13, folder 1923, managers' meeting minutes, June 11, 1923, 4)

For Salsbury, black laborers were an unmanageable, mercurial lot, a constant flight risk liable to break their contracts by escaping to the US North or seeking employment on neighboring plantations. He also frequently conflated "labor," a practice or service performed, with "laborers"—sentient, agential beings—indicating his low estimation of DPL's workforce and how the corporate plantation essentially reinscribed racial capitalism by reducing black ontology to black labor power. In a 1921 annual report, managers complained: "Labor conditions were unsatisfactory the entire year. Labor was high and difficult to handle, and doing as little work as possible, and we were doubtful at all times whether we received one hundred cents worth of work for each dollar paid out" (DPL Company Records, box 1, folder 1, annual report, 1921). To rectify this problem, the company demanded strict oversight and surveillance, evincing its flagrant white paternalism: "Our tenants are the best in the world," Salsbury noted at a managers' meeting, "although they are like children and need watching. Our tenants, as a rule, would have all their profits spent before they make a crop unless you hold them [their commissary accounts] down and give them only what is necessary" (DPL Company Records, box 13, folder 1923, managers' meeting minutes, March 15, 1923, 2–3).

Unlike most accounts of sharecropping and tenant farming in the Jim Crow South, DPL does not appear to have ensnared or immobilized workers by fabricating debts or through acts of physical violence, deception, or coercion. According to Merle C. Prunty Jr. (1962: 159), prior to World War II, "Contract renewals ranged from 87 to 92 per cent annually," which were "reportedly . . . unusually high rates" and thus suggested that "the Negro sharecropper considered his lot at Deltapine superior to that available to him elsewhere."[6] Frank David Quinn, DPL's stenographer who surveilled the *Cotton Farmer*'s content, recalls only a single instance of "extreme violence" against black workers. The general manager, Professor Jesse William Fox, suspected a tenant of stealing cotton and, "without giving him [the tenant] a chance to explain," started "cursing, kicking and actually stomping him [the tenant] until he ran out of the office, begging for mercy" (Quinn Papers, folder 7). They soon discovered that a plantation manager had made an accounting error, and the tenant was in fact innocent. Reflecting on the incident, Quinn recalled, "I am happy to say that this was an extreme and isolated case because that was not in any way our policy of treating tenants." Rather, as a modern corporate plantation that "wore the face of science and progressivism" (Woodruff 2012: 1), DPL sought to control laborers through welfare programs and the seemingly innocuous violence of surveillance and white paternalism. Reading against the archival grain, however, I would conjecture that if this single account of physical violence made its way into the archive, then Quinn's claim that it was an "extreme and isolated case" is highly dubious at best.

Nevertheless, by most accounts, DPL seems to have been convinced that a contented tenantry was far more productive than a fearful one and, as such, offered numerous incentives to placate employees. Salsbury stressed that "to hold the labor on the plantations of the South better living conditions must be furnished" (Smith 1923: 71). To that end, DPL reportedly provided tenants with modern, sanitary housing and medical care. As one observer noted of black domestic life at DPL:

> The old-fashioned log cabin has been entirely disappeared, replaced by comfortable sealed houses with good floors and roofs. The slab-door window is no more, but all of the company houses have ample glass windows, insuring abundant sunlight and ventilation. Wells drilled to uncontaminated water strata are supplied to each house, and welfare workers encourage the planting of vegetable gardens and flowers and the adoption of sanitary conditions, wholesome preparation of foods and other home economics. As fall approaches and the crops are laid by, the tenants are furnished with teams and wagons, and huge piles of wood are prepared for winter fuel. (Smith 1923: 71)

Contrary to this quite generous (and likely exaggerated) account of tenant housing, Lawrence J. Nelson (1999: 105) contends, "Actually, the off-ground cypress structures were crowded, their architecture usually of the 'shot-gun' variety—two rooms in a row with a door at each end, or four-room type for larger families." Whatever the specific state of tenant housing, DPL did in fact hold that improving the material conditions of black domestic life through welfare capitalism was a key strategy in keeping this newly mobile (and often fugitive) labor force rooted on its vast cotton plantations. Salsbury also offered pecuniary incentives, including bonuses and prizes for cotton picked before Christmas and even clearing tenants' debts to keep them from running off when their accounts rose too high in particularly bad crop years. Though counterintuitive, he apparently viewed tenant debt as more of a liability than an asset to the ultimate goal of maintaining labor stability.

Tenants' health care was of primary concern as well. At a cost of $20,000, DPL constructed the first and only plantation hospital in the region (Owens 1922). It was staffed by two doctors, nurses, assistants, a diet cook, and orderlies, and it was serviced by a plantation ambulance adapted from an old Ford truck (Smith 1923: 71). The hospital reported considerable success in reducing malaria, pellagra, and other diseases that incapacitated the workforce, though management policed tenants' hospital access by insisting that "doctors should always require an order from the manager . . . before examining or treating any negro" (DPL Company Records, box 13, folder 1921, managers' meeting minutes, August 5, 1921, 22). With its seeming aversion to violence and coercion and its paternalistic investment in improving black domestic life and health care, DPL was touted by one contemporaneous writer as "an almost Utopian dream being brought into an actual, practical reality" that "enabled thousands of the negro race to grow cotton under conditions which mean comfort, success and happiness for them, as well as for the company" (*Manufacturer's Record* 1923: 103). This welfare capitalism, however seemingly benevolent, was in fact self-interested and rooted in a racial capitalist logic of producing docile, immobile bodies. Ideologically, then, the corporate plantation was only marginally distinguishable from its antebellum predecessor. Nevertheless, black tenants exploited this aperture to build a range of fraternal, religious, and educational institutions that enabled their social, political, and economic advancement.

A Corporate Plantation Reading Public: Ad Wimbs, the *Cotton Farmer*, and Black Agrarian Futures

Establishing the *Cotton Farmer* was an integral part of DPL's welfare program. When Wimbs approached Quinn about establishing a plantation newspaper, Quinn "recommended to the executives that we give it a try" (Quinn Papers, folder 7). Salsbury and Fox, DPL's executive and general managers, respectively, agreed to support the endeavor, Quinn recalls, "provided that I would quitely [*sic*] supervise the news content and editorials" (Quinn Papers, folder 7). Though a "somewhat time consuming" endeavor, Quinn found that overseeing the paper's content "was most interesting because Ad Wimbs was a good common sense writer" (Quinn Papers, folder 7). In his monthly plantation managers' meetings, Salsbury routinely promoted the paper as "a valuable instrument" to the company (DPL Company Records, box 13, folder 1921, managers' meeting minutes, December 2, 1921; box 1, folder 1, annual report, 1921, 8–9). Though the paper consistently operated at a financial loss, he implored managers to ensure that it was delivered to every tenant regularly, because "we believe it has been one of the most valuable assets in *handling the labor situation* that we have ever had" (DPL Company Records, box 1, folders 1 and 2, annual report, 1919; emphasis added). Though seemingly contrary to the company's profit-driven imperative, DPL viewed this financial loss as a minor liability, an investment that would surely pay future dividends by keeping black tenants working. The *Cotton Farmer* was thus regarded as an extension of DPL's strategy of surveillance and social control over its putatively unmanageable and fugitive black labor force. It therefore represents racial capitalism's rapacious and even cannibalistic insistence on reproducing itself at all costs, exploiting and undermining one of the very tenets of liberal humanism—literacy as an emblem of freedom and subjecthood—to maintain the racial order of things.

Despite management's insidious intentions, however, the *Cotton Farmer* provides a rare glimpse at black tenant farmers in the Jim Crow South engaged in a reading and writing public. As Detweiler (1922: 13–14) observed in his study of the black press in the United States, the newspaper was generally "an adjunct of city life," because "in the city one must be able to read constantly." The *Cotton Farmer*, however, disrupts this rural/urban dichotomy by enabling a black reading and writing economy that foregrounded the unique concerns of black agricultural workers and their rural milieu. Staffed by a committee of tenant-reporters from each plantation, it was distributed every Saturday, and tenants paid an annual subscription fee of about $5 (Smith 1923; Quinn Papers, folder 7). The paper's masthead depicts a drawing of a farmer pushing a plow hitched to a mule, framed by ears of corn on the left and bales of cotton on the right. The motto, "Labor overcomes all things—everybody work," is printed just below

Figure 1 Masthead of the sole extant issue of the *Cotton Farmer*, February 5, 1927

the heading, perhaps a nod to the "dignity of labor" mantra espoused by Booker T. Washington and the Tuskegee school of racial uplift or the company's constant anxiety over recruiting and retaining laborers (see fig. 1). The content primarily covered local news from DPL's plantations, including letters from tenants about deaths and burials, the credit system, and the vagaries of agrarian life.

It also included global news and sermons; announcements about local baseball competitions, Saturday night parties, and baptisms; and classified ads publicizing the activities of the plantations' approximately thirty-one churches and numerous fraternal organizations and mutual aid societies. The paper "used many pictures," Quinn recalls, and tenants happily paid "$2 for a cut" to get their "picture in the paper" (Quinn Papers, folder 7). The sole extant issue includes an ad for Dr. Fred Palmer's skin-lightening cream, photographs of the plantation hospital and ambulance, and the portrait of Reverend Brown, or "Jamaica," cited above. Like the blues, then, the *Cotton Farmer* was a record of black social life in the "new" cotton South.

Though financially supported and surveilled by the company, the *Cotton Farmer* was still a medium in which tenants could express their grievances and disagreements with management. In a letter to the editor, a tenant addressed the managers' complaints about the problem of tenants fleeing the plantation and defaulting on their accounts. "When from sheer want a man gets up and moves away," he writes, "he should not be called a debt dodger. The weak ones that the General Manager spoke of will fall out, but many strong ones are being forced out" (*Cotton Farmer* 1927b). Reverend Brown, for instance, is reported to have left in search of a more favorable labor arrangement and autonomy over his cotton crop. "He worked on the halves but he wanted to work the same land on the fourths," Wimbs writes, "and for that cause he left as he considered himself financially able to change his method of cropping" (*Cotton Farmer* 1927a).[7] Read alongside Salsbury's anxiety over recruiting and retaining laborers and preventing them from fleeing and defaulting on their accounts, this tenant's letter and Brown's departure suggest that conditions at DPL were (obviously) not as utopian as they were made out to be and that tenants retained at least some agency over their labor and mobility despite DPL's attempts at constant supervision and control.

Wimbs possessed a rather paradoxical political philosophy that straddled the proverbial and often overdetermined accommodation-resistance binary. Hailing from Greensboro, Alabama, he was a successful businessman, minister, and politician. An active member of the Alabama Republican Party, he was an advocate for black suffrage and even ran for governor (1902) and lieutenant governor (1906) of Alabama (the first black man to do so, in fact) before moving to the delta in the late 1910s. An associate of Booker T. Washington, he took a conciliatory stance on race relations and vehemently discouraged urban and northern migration. He insisted "our people" are "cotton and corn raisers and ill adapted to the axacting [*sic*] life of the steel mills, coal mines, blast furnaces . . . and the strenuous life incident to the grind of the large cities" (quoted in *New Journal and Guide* 1923). Therefore, "the average man that remains on the cotton farms in the long run will be better off." Wimbs further warned, "Our people especially had better get it out of our heads that we can earn a living by idlesome doings and sharp practices." Rather, with its "reasonable credit prices" (quoted in *Manufacturer's Record* 1923: 105), he maintained, DPL provided a viable alternative to northern migration; thus, he cautioned black farmers that they had "better look well before you leap" (quoted in *New Journal and Guide* 1923).

Despite the widespread abuses of sharecropping and tenant farming, Wimbs was not anomalous in promoting an agrarian future based on cotton farming. In the early twentieth century, 36 percent of

African Americans still worked as farmers (Rolinson 2007: 71), and there remained considerable debate in the black public sphere about the wisdom of migrating to the US North for industrial jobs. As late as 1935, Kelly Miller (1935: 21), a Howard University sociology professor and contributor to *The New Negro* (1925), the ur-text of the Harlem Renaissance, observed, "Nowhere has the Negro thriven in numbers outside of the cotton growing states and parts of states," suggesting that most African Americans were better off in the rural, agrarian South. Thus, Wimbs's regional bias would have been consistent with popular strains of black thought that insisted on the US South's viability for self-determination and racial uplift.

Though the *Cotton Farmer* was, like the blues, a record of black social life, its ideological stance departs significantly from Woods's (2017: 16, 25) conceptualization of "the blues epistemology" as a mode of resistance to the plantation regime. Rather, it promoted a more accommodating racial philosophy. Detweiler (1922: 193) describes the *Cotton Farmer* as a "unique publication" invested in racial reconciliation and "lessening the race conflict." "The syndicate [DPL] under which the tenants work is praised," he observes. "White people are mentioned with gratitude." Quoting directly from the paper, Detweiler further notes: "Someone writes, 'The Syndicate certainly looks out for the welfare of each and every tenant regardless of circumstances. It is a real father and mother to the tenantry'" (193). In "Welfare Work on America's Largest Cotton Plantation," a 1923 photo-essay devoted to DPL's black tenants, Wimbs is quoted making a similar nod of approval toward the company's paternalism: "Under the persuasive influence of the white people, peace among my people has been so improved that now serious disagreements are but few" (quoted in *Manufacturer's Record* 1923: 106). He also supplied a letter for the essay describing the conditions of black life at DPL and a host of photographs featuring children, a kindergarten and home economics teacher, ministers, foremen, churches, the plantation hospital, and tenants enjoying an annual plantation dinner. A caption accompanying the children's photographs reads: "The reader will note the alert expression on the faces of the children and their general air of happiness and contentment" (103). The emphasis on children mirrors contemporaneous efforts by the NAACP's *Crisis* magazine, which published an annual children's issue to demonstrate racial vitality and to refute eugenicist claims about diseased black bodies and impending racial extinction.

The author(s) of the photo-essay assure readers, "The legends under all of these pictures are exactly as we found them on the photograph," and were likely written by Wimbs himself (106). Through these images and their captions, Wimbs and the author(s) sought to construct a visual narrative of black southerners thriving on the corporate plantation: "A close observation of these photographs," the author(s) believed, "will clearly reveal the look of happiness, contentment and satisfaction that appears on the faces of every one of the tenants" (105). What these images actually reveal, of course, is the performance of accommodating corporate plantation management and discipline.

It is unclear if Wimbs was in earnest in his seeming enthusiasm for white paternalism or if he simply viewed DPL as a lesser and necessary evil during a period of intensifying racial violence and socio-economic dispossession. Whatever the case, he was well aware of the challenges black southerners faced and worked diligently for their political and institutional advancement. In particular, he believed black newspapers were "one of the most powerful agencies" in the struggle for racial uplift, because the "history of the progress of the race" was often omitted from mainstream white newspapers. It was the duty of "Negro newspapers," then, "to tell of Negroes buying land, building good homes, erecting nice churches and schools, educating their children, living clean and sober lives, and doing many other helpful and encouraging things" (*Cotton Farmer* 1923).[8] To this end, he used his leadership and influence at the *Cotton Farmer* to urge DPL to erect the hospital and a host of "other educational and social facilities[,] . . . which had not been thought of until he sponsored them through his sheet" (Taylor 1935).

Unlike the antebellum plantation, where unfreedom was contingent on illiteracy, DPL promoted basic education as integral to cultivating a productive labor force. Partnering with local public school systems, they established an elementary school on each plantation, a night school, and in 1922 reportedly committed $20,000 toward building a vocational school with courses in agricultural science, elementary mechanics, domestic science, woodwork, and "a library for the negro [*sic*] tenants" (Owens 1922). Oscar Johnston, who succeeded Salsbury as executive manager following the flood, noted his preference for "deal[ing] with a tenant who can read and write and keep his own accounts; for, if intelligent, it is easier to get along and no suspicion arises as to whether he is being cheated" (Walton 1929). However,

Johnston was also flagrantly paternalistic toward tenants, proudly describing his management style as "*in loco parentis*" (Nelson 1984: 233–34). While giving black people access to literacy and education was no longer incompatible with the logics of white supremacy, Johnston intimated, it did not translate to social equality.

Alongside formal schooling, the *Cotton Farmer* itself would have certainly been a laboratory for cultivating tenant literacy. Detweiler (1922: 12) speculated that "the drop in the percentage of illiteracy [among African Americans] from 30.4 in 1910 to 22.9 in 1920 is due to the spread of newspaper circulation"; thus, the black press played "an important part in the process of educating a race" (51). The question of literacy is relative and contingent, however. "Some may be readers of the paper and yet be very slightly blessed with education," Detweiler observed. "Letters come into the newspaper offices so poorly spelled and written that they are hard to interpret" (8). Given the limited educational opportunities in the delta, the *Cotton Farmer* was undoubtedly a space of uneven literacies, where black sharecroppers and tenant farmers experimented with reading and writing, their grammatical errors and misspellings the tangible evidence of the hard-won transition from slavery to freedom and the forging of a modern black reading public in the afterlife of the plantation. Ultimately, DPL's investment in black social and educational enterprises, however modest and self-interested, seems to have buttressed Wimbs's belief that it provided a viable agrarian future for black southerners, hence his opposition to northern migration. "Where one can get a good cropper's credit, good houses to live in, good land to work, opportunities to give his or her children the chance to learn to read, write and figure, and become an expert cotton producer, and the protection of life," Wimbs reasoned, "it would be well to avail themselves of the opportunity, before that door of opportunity is closed" (quoted in *Manufacturer's Record* 1922).

The strange case of DPL and the *Cotton Farmer* presents a paradox for the history of race, labor, and literacy in the Jim Crow South. Through welfare capitalism, DPL seemingly took a comparatively less exploitative approach to managing tenants, providing improved living conditions, health care, and education, while limiting physical violence and coercion. However, it still operated under the racial capitalist logics of Jim Crow segregation, white paternalism, surveillance, and social control, thus counteracting any simplistic assessment of the company as a radical departure from the exploitative labor practices typically associated with sharecropping and tenant farming. The *Cotton Farmer* epitomizes this paradox. On the one hand, it represents a rare instance of black institution building, whereby Wimbs and his team of tenant-editors produced a vibrant reading and writing public under a biopolitical regime that derived from plantation slavery. Yet, it also demonstrates racial capitalism's wily and protean capacity to adapt itself and persist under new socioeconomic conditions. On the corporate plantation, even literacy and education—constitutive to the projects of freedom and liberal subjecthood—could be coopted to prolong colonial and antebellum plantation logics.

In 1926 three copies of the *Cotton Farmer* reached an UFCO banana plantation worker and Garveyite in Bocas del Toro, Panama, adding a transnational dimension to this already anomalous and largely local black reading public. Like the delta, Bocas del Toro was a New Negro enclave organized by the corporate plantation and populated by migrants in search of better economic opportunities. While scholars have tended to study these regions and the companies that colonized them independently, the *Cotton Farmer* serves as a literal and figural link between DPL and UFCO as similar biopolitical institutions and afterlives of the plantation in the hemisphere. Most importantly, it reveals the global black south as a dynamic black geography, wherein sharecroppers, tenant farmers, and migrant laborers forged diasporic ties and articulated geopolitical knowledges within and against corporate plantation hegemony.

The Corporate Plantation in the Global Black South: Producing Docile Bodies

In "The Biggest Cotton Plantation in the World: Another Romance of Achievement," a feature article in the *Durham (NC) Morning Herald*, Clarence J. Owens touted DPL as "a principality or empire in itself." Spanning Bolivar and Washington Counties, DPL was a monument to the eponymous heroes who "liberated" the hemisphere from European control. Bolivar County, Owens (1922) writes, "named for the heroic leader who is referred to as 'The Washington of South America,' is immediately adjacent to the county which bears the name of 'The Father of Our Country.' Thus [George] Washington and [Simón] Bolivar, at the point of whose swords the independence of a hemisphere was won, have enduring monuments to perpetuate their memory, in these counties that stand through the providence of God as high examples of economic independence." Owens's hagiographic evocation of Washington and Bolivar interpolates the Mississippi delta into a hemispheric cartography and a Pan-American mythology of republican leaders courageously wresting independence from European powers. This alleged liberation, of course, depended on the continuation of unfreedom and dispossession for black and indigenous peoples, ultimately reproducing the very inequities it claimed to abolish and thus undermining the larger project of freedom. Lauding DPL as "a principality or empire in itself," Owens (1922) unwittingly captured this ironic inextricability of freedom and empire and, more specifically, located the corporate plantation squarely within the history of settler colonialism and imperialism in the hemisphere.

Indeed, the rise of the corporate plantation in the postbellum US South was coterminous with European and US imperial efforts throughout the global south. Industrial capitalists' colonization of the delta's alluvial empire in the late nineteenth century (such as DPL) "mirrored the expansion of western capital into the colonial world at this time, as the imperial powers launched the wealth gained from the industrial revolution into their colonies in Africa, Asia, and Latin America, creating export economies based on extractive industrial and agricultural products—and employing various forms of coerced labor to produce the crops and to work in the mines and the mills" (Woodruff 2012: 9). A similar practice was afoot in the Caribbean and Latin America, whereby private enterprises such as UFCO practiced what Jason M. Colby (2006: 599) calls "corporate colonialism," that is, forging an agricultural empire by assuming "direct foreign control over production and labor in a host society." The expansionist logics and extractive practices undergirding the rise of the corporate plantation in the Mississippi delta were thus inextricably linked to US imperial and European colonial efforts in the Caribbean and Latin America.

Like the delta's cotton economy, Bocas del Toro's banana industry came into formation through foreign capital investment and black (and indigenous) labor. Once a vast expanse "of poorly drained insect- and snake-ridden tropical rain forest," UFCO "converted [the region] into one of the most productive banana farms in Latin America" (Bourgois 1989: 3). Beginning in the late nineteenth century, Afro-Caribbean workers initially migrated to the area to construct the Panama railroad and the Panama Canal, forming a New Negro enclave that, as Jennifer

Brittan (2013) observes, represented a black culture capital in Central America alongside more recognizable cities such as Harlem and Paris. Afro-Caribbean migrants were pushed by debilitating hunger and poverty after the collapse of the sugar industry in the British West Indies and pulled by the promise of better economic conditions, able to make in one hour on an UFCO labor contract what they made in one day back home. Like their counterparts in the Mississippi delta, Afro-Caribbean laborers endured debilitating health conditions clearing Panama's jungles and, as Philippe Bourgois (1989: 51) notes, "exceptionally rigid plantation labor discipline."

In this way, according to Gary Helm Darden (2009: 8), the "era of codified racial supremacy in the American South tied the region in many important ways to the theory and global practice of colonial imperialism." This was especially apparent in DPL's and UFCO's managerial techniques, whereby both companies deployed Jim Crow (or some derivation of it) to govern their nonwhite employees. Jim Crow had already been exported to Central America during the construction of the Panama Canal and to the Caribbean through the US occupation of Haiti, the Dominican Republic, and Cuba. As a US company already fluent in Jim Crow grammars and logics, then, UFCO simply extended US imperial practices to its banana enclaves through racially segregated facilities (schools, hospitals, etc.) and exploitative labor techniques. Whereas colonialism and imperialism in the Caribbean and Latin America and Jim Crow in the United States are rightly viewed as divergent afterlives of slavery and the plantation, the similarities between DPL's and UFCO's management practices and disciplinary techniques suggest that the corporate plantation was a subject-making institution that produced similar conditions of black life throughout the hemisphere.

For instance, UFCO management promoted a "strategy of keeping workers in debt in order to keep them working" (Harpelle 2003: 57). The company "extended credit to workers in order to 'hold the man on the job,'" which left "the majority of farm labourers . . . 'continuously slightly' indebted to United Fruit. Moreover, the company combined the credit system with the 'ever present threat of blacklisting' to 'stabilize' the labour force and to 'prevent promiscuous migration from farm to farm'" (57), just as DPL worked to restrict black mobility in the delta. Like cotton, "banana production required a reliable workforce and United Fruit was not opposed to using coercive means to achieve its goals" (57). Furthermore, laborers in both parts of the hemisphere faced harrowing health conditions as they cleared wildernesses, drained swamps, and cultivated plantations (Nelson 1999; Bourgois 1989). Though DPL reputedly took a less malicious approach to managing its workforce than UFCO, both firms deployed techniques of surveillance and social control to maximize production. On these corporate plantations, then, Jim Crow functioned as a technology of colonialism and imperialism—what some scholars have termed "Jim Crow colonialism"—that sought to discipline and immobilize employees (Colby 2006; Darden 2009). To be sure, there were important distinctions between DPL and UFCO, including company size and scale, commodities produced, labor processes, and degree of company influence and control over local governments; still, their shared managerial techniques aimed to produce similar kinds of docile bodies and thus demonstrate how the corporate plantation functioned as a racial capitalist and biopolitical regime across the Americas.

Sharecropper and Tenant Farmer Transnationalism: Garveyism, Print Culture, and Labor Migration

While the corporate plantation provides one way of mapping the contours of the global black south from above—linking the Mississippi delta and Bocas del Toro through similar and coterminous histories of colonization and labor management—black laborers often worked within and against these paternal, neocolonial, and imperial structures to articulate their own geopolitical knowledges and diasporic practices. The *Cotton Farmer*'s transnational circulation exemplifies how black agricultural workers appropriated hegemonic commercial and political networks to forge a black hemispheric geography from below. Furthermore, as Christopher Taylor (2012: 86) observes in his comparative analysis of sharecropper resistance in Tobago and the Missouri Bootheel, sharecropping existed as an "economic form" across the "postemancipation Americas" that "generated a form of political knowledge that can be set to work an ocean away" (92). Beyond Jim Crow and the corporate plantation, then, I propose the global black south as a circuit for the production and transmission of such political knowledge—what might be called a "sharecropper and tenant farmer transnationalism"—through print culture, labor migration, and political organizing.

On January 15, 1927, Wimbs received correspondence from John J. Smith of Shepard Island, Bocas del Toro, requesting a subscription to the *Cotton Farmer*:

Sirs: As a matter of courtesy, I have to acknowledge your very appreciative paper the "COTTON FARMER," viz: issues 16th Oct. and 30th, Oct., and 7th Nov. I presume you solicit my patronage as a subscriber. In reply beg to say, I have no objection to be a subscriber. You may continue the supply regularly. It is not financially convenient (right now) to send you the advance subscription, but will do so at a very early future, about next month.

I notice your columns are very replete with good information and instruction. Should you take job printing, you may send me your list of rates, etc. (*Cotton Farmer* 1927a)

Surprised that his local plantation newspaper had reached an international audience, Wimbs rightly speculated that it had traveled to Panama "on account of its attitude towards Marcus Garvey" (*Cotton Farmer* 1927a). Smith was indeed an active and devoted Garveyite. Before relocating to Bocas del Toro, he served as general secretary of a UNIA chapter on Farm 5, an UFCO plantation in Base Line, Panama, and he contributed at least three poems to the *Negro World* and an essay on why he became a Garveyite. A movement originally conceived in opposition to the exploitative labor practices Garvey witnessed on UFCO's Central American fruit plantations, Garveyism was an important mechanism for producing and transmitting black geopolitical knowledges throughout the hemisphere and the broader diaspora. Like the corporate plantation, the Garvey movement had a stronghold in both Central America's Afro-Caribbean enclaves and the Mississippi delta. In the 1920s there were seventeen UNIA divisions in Bolivar County, Mississippi, the most of any county in the United States, and forty-seven UNIA branches in Panama, many of which were in the Bocas del Toro region (Rolinson 2007: 109; Harpelle 2000: 6). Thus Garveyism's widespread popularity in the delta and Panama suggests that black agricultural workers in the two regions would have likely shared similar political and ideological commitments.

Wimbs's editorial activities offer further evidence of how Garveyism may have facilitated the *Cotton Farmer*'s transnational reach and its appeal to readers in Bocas del Toro and other Garveyite enclaves.

By maintaining a regular exchange with other newspaper offices, Wimbs's editorials were republished in several contemporaneous periodicals, including the *Negro World* (Smith 1923: 72). While Wimbs disagreed with the back-to-Africa component of Garvey's political philosophy, he remained sympathetic to Garvey's cause and frequently celebrated him as a superior organizer in the paper. And though DPL's management supervised the *Cotton Farmer*'s content, black delta residents were often avid readers of northern black newspapers, such as the *Chicago Defender*, the *Pittsburgh Courier*, and the *Negro World*; therefore, efforts to suppress Wimbs's engagement with Garvey's political views would have been futile. Most importantly, T. Thomas Fortune, Wimbs's friend and colleague who served as editor of the *Negro World* from 1923 until his death in 1928, often republished Wimbs's pro-Garvey editorials. In a 1924 article in the *Cotton Farmer* (subsequently republished in the *Negro World* [1924]), Wimbs compared Garvey's persecution to that of Booker T. Washington's: "We know one thing, and that is, the same element pursuing Garvey to his persecution and desired death is the same element that pursued Booker Washington to the brink of his grave, and even now throws black ink on his monument." Wimbs would continue to advocate for Garvey in the *Cotton Farmer* throughout the early to mid-1920s, including penning a fiery article casting doubt on the weight of the mail fraud charges brought against Garvey for the Black Star Line debacle and imploring President Calvin Coolidge to pardon him (*Negro World* 1925). In turn, Fortune periodically quoted Wimbs in the *Negro World* and even published an article recruiting readers to seek employment on DPL's plantations (which may account for Reverend Brown's employment there).

In contrast to his more sycophantic and pro-paternalistic positions limned above, Wimbs's defenses of Garvey unequivocally promoted black self-determination. "One thing about Garvey and his gang, they are not fussing with white folks in an effort to associate with them," Wimbs writes. "They are not with hat in hand begging the white folks for money for them to have a 'talking meeting' to save the race, and they are not fussing with the white folks about the white man's ships, but were trying to have a ship of their own even if he failed" (*Negro World* 1925). Wimbs further maintained, "If Marcus [Garvey] believe [*sic*] his plan is all right to solve what is popularly called the Negro problem in the United States and for that matter in the world, why not let him have a free rein?" (Wimbs 1927). Such a sympathetic attitude toward Garvey's right to self-determination seems to contrast significantly with Wimbs's position that DPL's black tenant farmers benefited from being "under the persuasive influence of the white people" (*Manufacturer's Record* 1923: 106). And yet, there is no evidence that he ever joined one of Bolivar County's numerous UNIA divisions; rather, he maintained that Garvey "was and is mistaken in the remedy for the ills . . . with which our race is afflicted" (*Negro World* 1925) and reminded readers, "We believe we have here 18 plantations of fine opportunities for our people and that there is no need of going to Africa" (*Cotton Farmer* 1927a). Ultimately, Wimbs seems to have taken a contradictory stance on black political futures, lingering between embracing accommodation and white paternalism on the corporate plantation, on one hand, and supporting Garvey's efforts at black self-determination, on the other, at least in principle. Notably, Garvey, too, had a checkered history of accommodating white supremacy, infamously meeting with the grand wizard of the Ku Klux Klan in 1922 and receiving regular contributions from UFCO administrators for the UNIA, despite the company's consistent mistreatment of its Afro-Caribbean employees (Harold 2007; Rolinson 2007; Harpelle 2000: 10). Such contradictory positions suggest that the global black south encompassed a range of often-competing ideological commitments and political strategies as laborers and organizers navigated the murky waters of global capitalism and white supremacy in the plantation's precarious afterlife.

Just as Garveyism would have undergirded Smith's political and ideological affiliation with the *Cotton Farmer*, it is also the most likely conduit for the paper's hemispheric circulation. An avid reader of and contributor to the *Negro World*, John J. Smith may have encountered Wimbs's editorials as early as 1923, when Fortune began republishing his pro-Garvey writings. However, in his letter to Wimbs, Smith acknowledged that he received three hard copies of the *Cotton Farmer*, indicating its physical migration from the delta to Panama. Despite the *Cotton Farmer*'s modest paid circulation, early twentieth-century black newspapers often "passed from hand to hand, especially in the South" (Detweiler 1922: 7), and each paper sold reportedly had an "average of five readers" (11). This informal practice of periodical circulation would have surely increased the *Cotton Farmer*'s readership beyond DPL's eighteen plantations and likely accounts for how it reached Panama, much like the *Negro World*. According to Colin Grant (2008: 148), "The traffic between Harlem and the Caribbean and the West Indian enclaves of Costa Rica and Panama was non-stop," so "Garvey relied on the willingness of merchant seamen to act as informal agents for the *Negro World*, carrying bundles of the paper from port to port" and "successfully distribut[ing]" them throughout the region. Traveling alongside the *Negro World*, then, the *Cotton Farmer* circulated within the transnational network of periodical exchange that Lara Putnam (2013: 124) calls the "circum-Caribbean/ transatlantic black press." This counterpublic, which extended across the Americas, was central to early twentieth-century black diasporic political organizing. In Central America, Afro-Caribbean migrants, many of whom hailed from the British West Indies, established and circulated newspapers such as the *Central American Express* and the *Workman* that, much like the *Cotton Farmer*, served as a record of black social life in the bowels of global capitalism. Unlike black southerners in the delta, however, British West Indian migrants had some of the highest literacy rates among "colonial subjects anywhere in the interwar world . . . approach[ing] those of Boston, New York, and other metropoles of the Anglophone world" (128). They often subscribed to African American newspapers as well, including the *Chicago Defender*, *Pittsburgh Courier*, *Crisis*, and *Opportunity*; thus, even if the *Cotton Farmer*'s circulation to Bocas del Toro was singular, Afro-Caribbean migrants were reading many of the same periodicals as their counterparts in the delta. Despite residing in different parts of the hemisphere and being differently literate, then, Afro-Caribbean and African American corporate plantation laborers were a part of the same transnational reading public. Savvily appropriating commercial shipping and trade networks to transport newspapers, they forged their own transnational geographies to keep abreast of the changing sociopolitical landscape of the diaspora as they became increasingly aware of their shared conditions under colonialism, imperialism, and Jim Crow (Putnam 2013).

This hemispheric periodical circulation, as Grant observes, was coterminous with transnational labor traffic. Scholarship on Afro-Caribbean labor migration in the interwar period tends to focus on movement to Central America and New York or intra-Caribbean migrations (Putnam 2013; Stephens 2005; Brittan 2013; Puri 2003). However, the *Cotton Farmer* suggests that the US South was a part of this labor circuit as well, hence Reverend Brown's migration from Jamaica to Mississippi. This movement and meeting up of workers from different parts of the hemisphere enabled not only the spread of newspapers but also the cultivation of a political consciousness around labor rights. Extant correspondence between UFCO administrators reveals that workers traveling between Mobile and Bocas del Toro, for instance, were often engaged in labor activism. One such memo requests that an administrator "quit signing on negro crew at Bocas and bringing them to Mobile, or permitting crews from his ship to be signed off at Bocas. They are carrying on regular labor traffic," he complains, "and causing unrest among our laborers at Bocas, by reason of injecting labor unionism into their heads."[9] By transporting and disseminating political knowledge between the US South and Central America, these corporate plantation laborers produced a subaltern geography that reconfigured the capitalist and biopolitical aims of corporate plantation cartographies. Whereas UFCO's primary concern was the effective transportation of plantation commodities and tourism—as evinced by the countless maps they produced to visualize their shipping and tourist routes (see fig. 2)—black laborers, many of them Garveyites, coopted these networks to spread ideas about racial uplift and self-determination and to agitate for better working conditions. Through Garveyism, print culture, and labor migration, the global black south comes into focus as a dynamic black geography wherein laborers enacted a sharecropper and tenant farmer transnationalism that contradicted corporate plantation logics. Thus, the *Cotton Farmer* broadens the cartography of early twentieth-century black diasporic practice by centering the literary, cultural, and political activities of black workers in the rural plantation regions of the Americas.

Cotton Geopolitics and Black Hemispheric Imaginaries

Though Wimbs qualified his support for Garvey's African repatriation scheme by reasserting his commitment to DPL's local, corporate plantation infrastructure, his editorials on the geopolitical economy of the cotton industry suggest that he, too, was a transnational thinker. Coincidentally, they also articulate a hemispheric imaginary that, quite presciently, maps the *Cotton Farmer*'s potential trajectory from

Passenger and Freight Routes of the
GREAT WHITE FLEET

Figure 2   A 1937 map of UFCO's tourist and shipping routes in the global black south, depicting direct routes from Panama to ports in New Orleans, Mobile, and Galveston, Texas, and thus illuminating how the *Cotton Farmer* may have circulated from the Mississippi delta to Bocas del Toro

Passenger and Freight Routes of the United Fruit Company and its subsidiaries between the Americas. Several sailings a week are available from New York and New Orleans and regularly from other ports indicated. Cruises range from 10 to 21 days according to itinerary selected. All passenger service on the Great White Fleet is first class:

EVERY PASSENGER A GUEST

the delta to Panama. Instead of shipping the region's cotton to Europe, Wimbs proposed building mills in the delta and establishing direct trade relations with other countries in the hemisphere. "Why should our cotton be shipped to Europe for distribution over the world?" he inquires in a 1921 editorial:

Let us ship from Galveston, New Orleans and Mobile direct to the spinners; and then instead of our cotton going to Germany for manufacturer [*sic*] and shipped to South America, let us spin it here in the South and ship it to the South American markets. . . . We have a product the whole world needs and must have. It would be an amazing pity to allow plutocrat financial cornerers [*sic*] to so manipulate the government agencies as to confiscate our crop. (*Cotton Farmer* 1921a)

Wimbs's hemispheric imaginary reroutes the geopolitical economy of the southern cotton industry from Europe to the circuits of the global black south. Proposing to link southern port cities—such as New Orleans and Mobile, which, incidentally, were also major banana ports and Garveyite enclaves—to South America via trade, Wimbs sought to transform the Mississippi delta into an international hub not only for cotton production but for manufacturing and shipping as well. Though obviously pro-capitalist, it was no more so than Garvey's numerous schemes for black commercial development. In fact, Wimbs's hemispheric imaginary would have certainly appealed to southern Garveyites, most of whom worked in agriculture. At the 1924 UNIA convention, for instance, Isaac Chambers, president of the New Orleans division, proposed organizing "cooperatives to empower black sharecroppers in the rural South," where "cotton and other produce of the Negro could be bought, thereby preventing white capitalists from obtaining this produce at a ridiculously low figure, as was the case at present to the undoing of the farmer" (quoted in Harold 2007: 46). Significantly, Wimbs's commentary would have also enlarged the worldview of the *Cotton Farmer*'s readership. While it may seem unusual that black tenant farmers would have concerned themselves with the geopolitics of the cotton industry, especially given their limited education and often precarious living conditions under Jim Crow, their lives were in fact dictated by the vagaries and whims of the international cotton market. More than mere farmhands or a lumpenproletariat bereft of a sophisticated understanding of global markets, they would have at least had a rudimentary interest in and knowledge of cotton geopolitics and their place within this world industry.

Finally, Wimbs's editorials portended the *Cotton Farmer*'s possible trajectory to Panama, mapping a hemispheric periodical circulation route that, unlike the *Negro World*, did not travel through Harlem. "There is no sane reason why Greenville [Mississippi] should not be dotted with textile mills to spin and weave the cotton crop of its territory," he writes. "There we have the great Mississippi, the father of waters to carry the finished products to Mexican and South American ports" (*Cotton Farmer* 1921b). Given that DPL's properties sat along the Mississippi River for several miles, it would have been the most direct route by which the *Cotton Farmer* traveled to Bocas del Toro: down the Mississippi, through New Orleans, and on to Panama, likely aboard an UFCO steamship. Located at the mouth of the Mississippi, New Orleans was a "crucial geographical gateway between the Americas" (Gruesz 2001: 121). In the nineteenth and early twentieth centuries, it was the most important US city for shipping, trade, and print culture—including importing bananas and exporting cotton—and the Snyder Banana Company, acquired by UFCO in the 1890s, had a direct trade route between Bocas del Toro and New Orleans and Mobile (Gruesz 2008; Adams 1914). New Orleans was also home to an array of black diasporic social and political organizations, including a vibrant Garveyite community and the West Indian Seaman's Social, Benevolent, and Literary Association (Harold 2007; Harold 2013; Rolinson 2007). As the South's largest city and the locus of such dynamic global black south activity, New Orleans was almost certainly the crossroad linking the delta and Panama. Ultimately, by promoting a direct trade route between the delta and South America, Wimbs reveals how black agricultural workers actively negotiated and participated in transnational geographies. They held a range of diverse and often competing ideological commitments, variously resisting, accommodating, and adapting racial capitalist infrastructures. Taken together with Garveyism, periodical circulation, and labor migration and activism, Wimbs's hemispheric imaginary delineates sharecropper and tenant farmer transnationalism as a dynamic mode of black geopolitical practice and knowledge production.

The "strange career" of the *Cotton Farmer* presents the afterlife of the plantation in the global black south as a theoretical and methodological intervention within black transnational and diaspora studies. This obscure corporate plantation newspaper and its chance transnational circulation provide an alternative framework for interrogating the history of race, labor, and literacy by positioning sharecroppers and tenant farmers as chief architects of black geographic thought and practice. Situated within the local, domestic context of the Jim Crow South, the *Cotton Farmer* illustrates how the corporate plantation at once conformed to and departed from its colonial and antebellum antecedents. Instead of racial violence, deception, and coercion, DPL crafted welfare capitalist policies that created comparatively better working and living conditions and educational opportunities for black tenants, hence, Wimbs's establishment of a corporate plantation reading public and his efforts to promote DPL as a viable agrarian future for black southerners. Yet, company policies were still governed by paternalism, social control, and other racial capitalist logics, enabling a circumscribed future at best. Thus, in the Jim Crow South, the *Cotton Farmer* represents a rare and impressive instance of black institution building in the midst of corporate self-interest and racial retrenchment, as the gains of New Negro enterprise and self-determination eroded into widespread violence, dispossession, and disfranchisement.

The *Cotton Farmer*'s transnational circulation, however, inserts delta sharecroppers and tenant farmers into the dynamic hemispheric networks of the global black south. Linking DPL and UFCO illuminates how the corporate plantation in the US South emerged coterminously with European and US imperialisms in the Caribbean and Latin America, as both enterprises marshaled Jim Crow to produce a docile labor force and further grease the wheels of global capitalism. The *Cotton Farmer*, however, undercuts this hegemonic geography, by circulating along the subaltern routes and "lower frequencies" crafted by black sharecroppers, tenant farmers, and migrant laborers. By appropriating and reimagining corporate shipping and trade routes, Wimbs, Smith, Brown, and their contemporaries ruptured the rural-urban and local-global dichotomies that tend to delimit black transnational and diaspora studies. Alongside artists and intellectuals in Harlem and other urban metropoles, the *Cotton Farmer* shows how black agricultural workers were engaged in a transnational reading and writing public—forging a sharecropper and tenant farmer transnationalism from below in the midst of new and ever-evolving modes of domination and social control in the afterlife of the plantation.

Jarvis C. McInnis is the Cordelia and William Laverack Family Assistant Professor of English at Duke University. An interdisciplinary scholar of African American and African diaspora literature and culture, his teaching and research interests focus on the global south (primarily the US South and the Caribbean), sound studies, performance studies, and visual culture. He is currently at work on his first book manuscript, tentatively titled, "Afterlives of the Plantation: Aesthetics, Labor, and Diaspora in the Global Black South," which aims to reorient the geographic contours of black transnationalism and diaspora by elucidating the hemispheric linkages between southern African American and Caribbean writers, intellectuals, and cultures in the early twentieth century. His work appears or is forthcoming in journals and venues such as *Callaloo*, *MELUS*, *Mississippi Quarterly*, *Public Books*, the *Global South*, and *American Literary History*.

Notes

1   There is a significant discrepancy regarding DPL's size and number of black employees. Owens (1922) says it had 65,000 acres under development and employed approximately "10,000 negroes [*sic*] and 300 white people." The *Cotton Farmer* (1927a) says it owned "about 35,000 acres [of] fertile land." Dong (1993: 30–31) states that by 1937, DPL "owned 38,000 acres of land . . . and employed 1,000 black sharecropper families or 3,300 working hands; of this total acreage, 11,700 acres were planted in cotton."

2   I am deeply indebted to Mary G. Rolinson for sharing her copy of the single extant issue of the *Cotton Farmer* with me, which she found mixed in with the Marcus Garvey papers at the National Archives. I would not have been able to write this essay without her generosity.

3   On the "afterlife of slavery," see Hartman 2007: 6.

4   The US South has always been global, emerging out of the violent global processes of settler colonialism and transatlantic slavery. In African American studies, however, it is typically considered local and provincial, while the urban US North, especially Harlem, is deemed the locus of black diasporic activity. The "global black south," then, aims to demonstrate how the US South has remained an important locus of black transnational activity and diasporic practice well into the twentieth and twenty-first centuries.

5   The term New Negro, as I use it here, draws on recent scholarship that extends the New Negro era back into the nineteenth century and expands its geography beyond New York and the broader global north to encompass the US South, the Caribbean, and other parts of the black world. See Brittan 2013; Edwards 2003; Stephens 2005; Harold 2007, 2013; Briggs 2015; and Makalani 2013

6   These data may include the post-flood period, when the *Cotton Farmer* was defunct; contract renewal rates for the precise period of the paper's run are unavailable.

7   Working on "the halves" or "the fourths" refers to tenants' percentage of ownership and independence over their labor arrangement with the company (Nelson 1999: 95).

8   This was originally published in the *Mound Bayou Gazette* and republished in the *Cotton Farmer*. I interpret its republication as an endorsement by Wimbs and a reflection of his views on black newspapers.

9   This document, dated December 2, 1919, is located in Philippe Bourgois's personal, unpublished archive of UFCO business correspondence, which he discovered while conducting research in Bocas del Toro, Panama, in the 1980s. I am grateful to him for sharing his archive with me.

References

Adams, Frederick Upham. 1914. *Conquest of the Tropics*. Garden City, NY: Doubleday, Page, and Company.

Baldwin, Davarian L., and Minkah Makalani, eds. 2013. *Escape from New York: The New Negro Renaissance beyond Harlem*. Minneapolis: Univ. of Minnesota Press.

Bourgois, Philippe I. 1989. *Ethnicity at Work: Divided Labor on a Central American Banana Plantation*. Baltimore: Johns Hopkins Univ. Press.

Briggs, Gabriel A. 2015. *The New Negro in the Old South*. New Brunswick, NJ: Rutgers Univ. Press.

Brittan, Jennifer. 2013. "The Terminal: Eric Walrond, the City of Colón, and the Caribbean of the Panama Canal." *American Literary History* 25, no. 2: 294–316.

Colby, Jason M. 2006. "Banana Growing and Negro Management: Race, Labor, and Jim Crow Colonialism in Guatemala, 1884–1930." *Diplomatic History* 30, no. 4: 595–621.

Cotton Farmer. 1921a. "Encouraging Signs for Cotton." July 16. Tuskegee News Clippings File, 12:782.

Cotton Farmer. 1921b. "This Is Full of Hope for a Struggling People." August 13. Tuskegee News Clippings File, 12:783.

Cotton Farmer. 1923. "Why Read Colored Papers." September 1. Tuskegee News Clippings File, 18:933.

Cotton Farmer. 1927a. February 5.

Cotton Farmer. 1927b. "The Tenants' Response." February 5.

Darden, Gary Helm. 2009. "The New Empire in the 'New South': Jim Crow in the Global Frontier of High Imperialism and Decolonization." *Southern Quarterly* 46, no. 3: 8–25.

Delta and Pine Land Company Records. 1886–1982. Special Collections Department, Mississippi State University Libraries.

Detweiler, Frederick G. 1922. *The Negro Press in the United States*. Chicago: Univ. of Chicago Press.

Dong, Zhengkai. 1993. "From Postbellum Plantation to Modern Agribusiness: A History of the Delta and Pine Land Company." PhD diss., Purdue Univ.

Edwards, Brent Hayes. 2003. *The Practice of Diaspora: Literature, Translation, and the Rise of Black Internationalism*. Cambridge, MA: Harvard Univ. Press.

Grant, Colin. 2008. *Negro with a Hat: The Rise and Fall of Marcus Garvey*. Oxford: Oxford Univ. Press.

Gruesz, Kirsten. 2001. *Ambassadors of Culture: The Transamerican Origins of Latino Writing*. Princeton, NJ: Princeton Univ. Press.

Gruesz, Kirsten. 2008. "The Mercurial Space of 'Central' America: New Orleans, Honduras, and the Writing of the Banana Republic." In *Hemispheric American Studies*, edited by Caroline F. Levander and Robert S. Levine, 140–65. New Brunswick, NJ: Rutgers Univ. Press.

Harold, Claudrena N. 2007. *The Rise and Fall of the Garvey Movement in the Urban South, 1918–1942*. New York: Routledge.

Harold, Claudrena N. 2013. *New Negro Politics in the Jim Crow South*. Athens: Univ. of Georgia Press.

Harpelle, Ronald. 2000. "Radicalism and Accommodation: Garveyism in a United Fruit Company Enclave." *Journal of Iberian and Latin American Research* 6, no. 1: 1–28.

Harpelle, Ronald. 2003. "Cross Currents in the Western Caribbean: Marcus Garvey and the UNIA in Central America." *Caribbean History* 31, no. 1: 35–73.

Hartman, Saidiya. 2007. *Lose Your Mother: A Journey along the Transatlantic Slave Route*. New York: Farrar, Straus, and Giroux.

Manufacturer's Record. 1922. "Interesting Views on Law and Order Expressed by a Negro Paper of Mississippi." June 29: 44.

Manufacturer's Record. 1923. "Negro Workers on the World's Largest Cotton Plantation." October 25: 103–6.

McKittrick, Katherine, and Clyde Woods. 2007. "No One Knows the Mysteries at the Bottom of the Ocean." In *Black Geographies and the Politics of Place*, edited by Katherine McKittrick and Clyde Woods, 1–13. Toronto: Between the Lines.

Miller, Kelly. 1935. "The Farm—The Negro's Best Chance." *Opportunity: Journal of Negro Life* 13: 21–25.

Negro World. 1924. "Those Who Build Nothing." October 13.

Negro World. 1925. "The 'Cotton Farmer' Says President Coolidge Should Pardon Marcus Garvey." March 28.

Nelson, Lawrence J. 1984. "Welfare Capitalism on a Mississippi Plantation in the Great Depression." *Journal of Southern History* 50, no. 2: 225–50.

Nelson, Lawrence J. 1999. *King Cotton's Advocate: Oscar G. Johnston and the New Deal*. Knoxville: Univ. of Tennessee Press.

New Journal and Guide. 1923. "Inviting the Migrant to Stay Home." June 2.

Owens, Clarence J. 1922. "The Biggest Cotton Plantation in the World: A Romance of Achievement." *Durham (NC) Morning Herald*, March 30.

Prunty, Merle C., Jr. 1962. "Deltapine: Field Laboratory for the Neoplantation Occupance Type." In *Festschrift: Clarence F. Jones, Northwestern University Studies in Geography, No. 6*, edited by Merle C. Prunty Jr., 151–72. Evanston, IL: Northwestern Univ. Press.

Puri, Shalini. 2003. *Marginal Migrations: The Circulation of Cultures within the Caribbean*. Oxford: Macmillan Caribbean.

Putnam, Lara. 2013. *Radical Moves: Caribbean Migrants and the Politics of Race in the Jazz Age*. Chapel Hill: Univ. of North Carolina Press.

Quinn, Frank David. Papers, 1913–1971. Dolph Briscoe Center for American History, the University of Texas at Austin

Rolinson, Mary G. 2007. *Grassroots Garveyism: The Universal Negro Improvement Association in the Rural South, 1920–1927*. Chapel Hill: Univ. of North Carolina Press.

Smith, Jon, and Deborah Cohn, eds. 2004. *Look Away! The U.S. South in New World Studies*. Durham, NC: Duke Univ. Press.

Smith, Thomas Wright. 1923. "Welfare Work on America's Largest Cotton Plantation." *Manufacturer's Record*, September 20: 71–73.

Stephens, Michelle Ann. 2005. *Black Empire: The Masculine Global Imaginary of Caribbean Intellectuals in the United States, 1914–1962*. Durham, NC: Duke Univ. Press.

Taylor, Alexander O. 1935. "Ohio State News." *Chicago Defender*, July 20.

Taylor, Christopher. 2012. "Sharing Time: C. L. R. James and Southern Agrarian Movements." *Social Text* 30, no. 2: 75–98.

Walton, Lester A. 1929. "6000 Men and Women Enjoy Mammoth Feast of Barbecued Meats, Bread, Watermelon at Mound Bayou Holiday." *New York Age*, July 27.

Willis, John C. 2000. *Forgotten Time: The Yazoo Mississippi Delta after the Civil War*. Charlottesville: Univ. of Virginia Press.

Wimbs, Addison. 1927. "A Letter from Panama." *Cotton Farmer*, February 5.

Woodman, Harold D. 1982. "Postbellum Social Change and Its Effects on Marketing the South's Cotton Crops." *Agricultural History* 56, no. 1: 215–30.

Woodman, Harold D. 2001. "The Political Economy of the New South: Retrospects and Prospects." *Journal of Southern History* 67, no. 4: 789–810.

Woodruff, Nan Elizabeth. 2012. *American Congo: The African American Freedom Struggle in the Delta*. Chapel Hill: Univ. of North Carolina Press. First published 2003.

Woods, Clyde. 2017. *Development Arrested: Race, Power, and the Blues in the Mississippi Delta*. Brooklyn: Verso. First published 1998.

Benjamin Child

The Plantation Countermelodies of Dunbar and Du Bois: Writing Agropolitical Subjecthood in the Nadir

Abstract With attention to representations of the land and labor in the postslavery agricultural South of the nadir—a period when American apartheid was at its most violent—this essay uses Paul Laurence Dunbar's plantation poems and W. E. B. Du Bois's cotton novel, *The Quest of the Silver Fleece* (1911), to explore counternarratives of black subjecthood. Agriculture's focus on productive collaborations with the nonhuman, on cycles of decay and rebirth, and on the potential for self-determination provides a generative vocabulary for conceptualizing nadir-era experiences of the human. Under this model, literature provides a venue wherein the legacies of the plantation might be imaginatively transposed from a Jim Crow necropolitics of violent constraint and dispossession into vectors of agropolitical possibility. To that end, the essay uses Dunbar and Du Bois to propose potentially radical processes of black subject formation wherein physical and imaginative instances of reclamation give rise to fresh mergers of epistemic and embodied selfhood.

Keywords African American literature, ecocriticism, Post-Reconstruction, agriculture

Of all the public appearances and celebrity encounters recorded in Booker T. Washington's *Up from Slavery*, the most suggestive may be a benefit staged at Boston's Hollis Street Theatre in early 1899. According to the text, Washington made an address, W. E. B. Du Bois read an early version of *The Souls of Black Folk*'s profile of Alexander Crummell, and Paul Laurence Dunbar recited four poems (see Washington 1996: 123; and Du Bois Papers, Series 1A: General Correspondence, MS 312). The event was designed to pay tribute to the Tuskegee Institute, symbol of both Washington's educational philosophy and the system of labor that would soon emerge as a major point of contention with Du Bois. While none of

American Literature, Volume 91, Number 3, September 2019
DOI 10.1215/00029831-7722128 © 2019 by Duke University Press

the poems Dunbar read that afternoon ("When Malindy Sings," "The Party," "When de Co'n Pone's Hot," "An Antebellum Sermon") directly reference Tuskegee or Washington—his explicit tribute, "To Booker T. Washington," debuted a year later, at the Denver Ministerial Alliance—they are each celebrations and expressions of black achievement and the functions of double-voiced discourse. Most salient to my purposes are the opening lines of "When de Co'n Pone's Hot":

> Dey is times in life when Nature
> Seems to slip a cog an' go,
> Jes' a-rattlin' down creation,
> Lak an ocean's overflow. (1993e: 57)

The occasion for such disorder ("When yo' mammy says de blessin' / An' de co'n pone's hot") is less important than the poem's readiness to imagine a condition wherein "Nature"—reverently capitalized despite the otherwise nonstandard dialect—"[s]eems to slip a cog," to unfix and disastrously liquefy, throwing all expectations for the exterior world out of joint. Dunbar's keen sense of the untenable order of putatively elemental things—"Nature," but also history, culture, language, and race—allows him to triangulate the Washington–Du Bois continuum through the hermeneutic of imaginative literature. This is especially true of Dunbar's work that asserts forms of black agropolitics, a category emphasizing the emancipatory possibilities of agriculture and one that exists in concert with strains of black populism exemplified in the 1880s and 1890s by organizations like the Colored Farmers' Alliance and Cooperative Union and the Colored Agricultural Wheel (Ali 2010).[1]

With attention to representations of the land and labor in the postslavery agricultural South of the nadir—a period when American apartheid was at its most violent—I propose that literature provides a venue to envision counternarratives of black subjecthood.[2] Agriculture's focus on productive encounters with the nonhuman, on cycles of decay and rebirth, and on the chance for self-determination thus provides a generative vocabulary for conceptualizing nadir-era experiences of black humanity. Under this model, the legacies of the plantation might be imaginatively transposed from a Jim Crow necropolitics of violent constraint and dispossession into vectors of agropolitical possibility. Hence this essay explores how textual manifestations of black encounters with agriculture, so frequently construed as outmoded remainders of oppression via slavery or tenancy, both reflect and create forms of constructive defiance.

Questions about what agricultural labor could mean for black citizens in the new century were of high priority to many of the period's most prominent African Americans, including those mentioned above: Dunbar, Washington, and Du Bois. Rather than revisit the "debate" staged by Washington's *Up from Slavery* and Du Bois's *Souls*, I will consider ways in which Dunbar's poems of the plantation and Du Bois's 1911 novel, *The Quest of the Silver Fleece*, show how political subjecthood develops in combination with plant matter, particularly agricultural products. Such a view conveys potentially radical processes of black subject formation wherein the agricultural gives rise to new mergers of epistemic and embodied selfhood and where the sign "reclamation" reveals polysemous valences.

It is no surprise that the governing image in these projects is the plantation: it becomes a multidirectional current that drags the past into contemporary issues of labor, the southern landscape, and the competing trajectories of African American modernity. In black writing of the nadir, the plantation is deconstructed and reconstructed, evacuated and reoccupied; it is remembered, repudiated, sublimated, and ironized, often all in the same text. And it becomes not just a locus of the production of commodity crops that propelled capitalist modernity but also an imaginative matrix for black modernism.[3] To this end, my attention to cultures of black agriculture corresponds with Sven Beckert's (2014: 441) recent contention that "much of the emergence of the modern world occurred in the countryside." For his part, Walter Benjamin's image of nineteenth-century Paris as the hub of an irreducibly urban vision of *die Moderne*—"At one blow, [the arcades] became the hollow mold from which the image of 'modernity' was cast" (1999: 546)—is fueled by a "boom in the textile trade" (3). It is important to recognize the degree to which this account of Parisian modernity connects with the plantations of antebellum slavery. In the years leading up to the Civil War, France was one of several European countries dependent on raw cotton produced by slave labor in the US South: in 1859, for instance, 90 percent of the 192 million pounds used in France was supplied by US interests (see Fohlen 1956: 284, 514).[4] If, as Benjamin noticed, the arcades yielded particular forms and expressions of modern European consciousness in the nineteenth century, it is essential to recover iterations of the modern

African American consciousness that were forged in and through New World plantations, to hear the reverberations produced at these junctures of creolization, and to consider the new modes of being they engendered.

I argue here that black plantation countermelodies arose from multiple historical and material tensions, pressures that make comprehensible the ecocritical, even posthumanist, resonances of the depictions of rural landscapes and black bodies in Dunbar and Du Bois. None of this is without complication. Why, to draw on a famous phrase of Wendell Berry's (1972), is it so difficult to envision "a continuous harmony" for black agricultural subjects? Why do contemporary discourses of the posthuman and the biopolitical rest so uneasily alongside figurations of post-Reconstruction rural blackness? Although moves toward the posthuman have frequently touted the political possibilities of conceptually uniting abstract bodies with the landscape or with effacing differences between abstract humans and abstract animals, this is much less simply done when considering bodies historically coded black, bodies that centuries of racist thought and action have vigorously separated out as incompletely human. Zakiyyah Iman Jackson (2015: 215), for one, is rightly cautious about the possibility that "appeals to move 'beyond the human' may actually reintroduce the Eurocentric transcendentalism this movement purports to disrupt." Surveying the influence of Giorgio Agamben and Michel Foucault, Alexander G. Weheliye (2014: 4) makes a similar point: "Bare life and biopolitics discourse not only misconstrues how profoundly race and racism shape the modern idea of the human, it also overlooks or perfunctorily writes off theorizations of race, subjection, and humanity found in black and ethnic studies." My contention is that the master image of agricultural labor in the work of Dunbar and Du Bois allows a rethinking of relations between the body and the land that form the substrate of both slavery and tenancy, that they help demonstrate how in post-Reconstruction America imaginative engagement with the land made possible a more fully fleshed claim not just on citizenship but on subjecthood writ large. For whatever else it might signal in these texts, black agropolitics conjures spaces where the subject and the nation are inscribed on the ground itself, where people in their physical environments create new meaning and apprehend history afresh by discovering ontologically modern reflexes in the rural landscape.

Dunbar's "Plant of Freedom Upward Sprung"

Dunbar's agropolitical poems most frequently process the challenges of the present through the materials of the past, one saturated by memories of the plantation. While critics have often puzzled at the ambient nostalgia that permeates much of his work, one might also read these representations as a means of reshaping trauma and asserting a level of imaginative ownership over such spaces—to "brush history against the grain," as Benjamin (1968: 257) proposes. "To articulate the past historically," Benjamin holds, "does not mean to recognize it 'the way it really was.' It means to seize hold of a memory as it flashes up at a moment of danger" (255). The reconstructed plantation of Dunbar's poems reconceives both the space's historical significance and its meanings in the poet's own nadir moment of horrifying physical and psychological danger. More specifically, the past is rearticulated through images of the plantation itself as a zone of black appropriation. It becomes a poetic evocation of what Washington was aiming for with Tuskegee: the recuperation—indeed, the reclamation—of plantation space as an alternate "institute" and an alternate institution. If, as Marxist tradition is quick to remind us, working the land gives one greater claim to ownership than inheritance or legal deed, then all these nostalgic former slaves might be staking out a place in the social imaginary, unwriting plantation history by centralizing the labor of African Americans as a legitimate, if legally unbinding, deed.

Accordingly, Dunbar provides a rubric for remembering that identifies the undeniable relationships among southern soil, slavery, and freedom, effectively asking the questions: When a formerly enslaved person weeps at the site of a ruined plantation, can he reset his position in the historical narrative? Does she conjure up a differently signifying version of memory? It is tempting to dismiss these moves as blanching optimism or outright erasures, but they might also work a degree of parity into a sharply unbalanced arrangement of power. Arriving within the vicinity of what George B. Handley (2004: 28) identifies as the New World's "poetics of oblivion," we sense Dunbar's acknowledgment that, when representing traumatic histories, "language of necessity fails." This is not, Handley states, "cause for lamentation but rather an opportunity to pay homage to those histories that can never be summed up" (28). Adapting this model, the poems offer the empty plantation as a geography of oblivion, a site in which the silences of the historical record are borne out of the antebellum land-scape by generating opportunities for more emancipatory meanings.

One of Dunbar's most evocative poems, "The Haunted Oak," grimly indexes the geography of oblivion, lapsing into prosopopoeia to dra-matize dialogue between a tree that has recently served as the site of a lynching and a credulous observer, all while making the tree itself a victim of the horror: "why, when I go through the shade you throw, / Runs a shudder over me?" the passerby asks (1993d: 219). The tree answers by relating its distinct sensory reaction to the violent event: it "saw . . . [a] guiltless victim's pains" and it "hear[d] his sigh" (219). And though time has passed, the lingering corporeality of the lynching victim continually inscribes the "body" of the tree in the present tense:

> I feel the rope against my bark,
> And the weight of him in my grain,
> I feel in the throe of his final woe
> The touch of my own last pain. (220)

The victim's torture and his death are both shared by the tree in a remonstrance of mob violence that solidifies a bond, forged through suffering, between a black body and a fatally damaged plant. A spec-tral body killed by the "curse of a guiltless man" (220) held on rape charges ("the old, old crime" [219]), the tree is obligated to bear the man's weight forever as it watches the prominent citizens who car-ried out the deed enjoy their freedom—the judge and the doctor, the minister and his son. The tree is dead; it still speaks. By denying the silencing techniques of lynching, the poem becomes a postmor-tem monument to an unpunished, and epidemic, crime of the nadir, a countermonument to the (neo-)Confederacy at the very moment when "lost cause" memorials were proliferating. In Dunbar's ironic poetic economy, it falls on the tree—an object without language—to voice ghostly witness to ritual murder because, unlike black subjects in the period, its testimony to the terrors of white violence doesn't carry the threat of retaliation. The tree must speak in this poem because the human victims cannot. And a supernatural blend of human and plant matter, a scrambling of common separations of object and subject, becomes the most appropriate register through which to apprehend the fantastic brutality of Jim Crow.

"The Haunted Oak" also functions as a commentary on concepts of ownership that prevailed in plantation slavery and throughout its repetitions in post-Reconstruction tenancy: the slaveholder/planter violently presumes control over the enslaved/tenant body, the labor of the enslaved/tenant, and the landscapes they inhabit. This concatenation of body-labor-landscape is at the center of "The Haunted Oak," as it figures a collapsing distance between black bodies and the nonhuman world. In asking questions about what and how exactly the slaveholder/planter owns, the poem answers by pressuring the triad of body-labor-landscape, allowing the land—synecdochically present in the tree—a chance to protest in a startling voice. It summons, in other words, a legible archive for the nonhuman just as it achieves something like cross-species communication. Dunbar's human subject is not simply dissolved into "nature" so as to achieve new levels of (decidedly human) perception (e.g., the transparent eyeball that presides over Eurocentric American Romanticism): his powers of perception are extinguished along with his life in a burst of violence that imparts human forms of expression on the nonhuman. Plant and person combine in a jarring comment on the mutual exploitation of southern landscape and black body.

Similarly, Dunbar's Civil War rumination "The Colored Soldiers" presents the land as a venue for uncanny racial mixture in which the black speaker indicates to his white listener the precise spot where "their blood with yours commingling / Has enriched the Southern soil" (1993a: 51). To the elaborate social and legal boundaries established by paranoia about racial mixing in the white South—to the twin specters of "miscegenation" and "one-drop rule" that animated the lost cause—the poem offers the ultimate retort: the war itself produced these biracial sites of eternal (un)rest, battlefields that forever enshrine the impossibility of "pure" blood. "There is no holier spot of ground / Than where defeated valor lies, / By mourning beauty crowned" (Timrod 1872: 210). So wrote Henry Timrod in "Ode," an elegy sung during the 1867 decorating of Confederate graves at the Magnolia Cemetery in Charleston, South Carolina. The holiness isn't entirely effaced in Dunbar's poem; it is redrawn as biological regeneration, as the miracle of the soil. "The Colored Soldiers" thus concretizes a paradoxical relationship between dirt's reproductive properties and its burial function—its ability to assimilate life's material remainders and to create new life—by linking these to the combination of hope and hopelessness that marked the experiences of African Americans during the nadir. In refutation of what is perhaps Timrod's most famous work, "Ethnogenesis" (1861), "The Colored Soldiers" calls up a post-Reconstruction ethnogenesis, the birth of a new nation that denies the supremacy of whiteness by using unexpected material remnants of black lives (blood) to claim old landscapes and to represent ontologies of humanness that recognize the mutual constitution of organic matter.

This impulse toward reoccupation is treated in several Dunbar poems displaying an unsettled strain of southern homesickness. I will focus on two: "The Deserted Plantation" (1895) and "To the Eastern Shore" (1903), each of which locates a nucleus of African American life in the rural South and each of which seeks to remediate popular representations of plantation culture. In a celebrated appraisal of the poet, Henry Louis Gates Jr. (1988: 176) extols the rhetorical nimbleness with which Dunbar "signified upon the received white racist textual tradition and posited in its stead a black poetic diction." Such racist textual traditions, of course, include minstrelsy. Take Stephen Foster's ubiquitous "My Old Kentucky Home, Good-Night!" (1853): with crudely drawn racialisms and a heavy dose of Victorian sentimentalism, Foster's lyric mourned the absence of a plantation's black workers—their actions, their bodies, their voices:[5]

> They hunt no more for the possum and the coon
> On the meadow, the hill and the shore,
> They sing no more by the glimmer of the moon,
> On the bench by the old cabin door. (Foster 2010: 18)

Although in an early form ("Poor Uncle Tom, Good-Night!") the song functioned as a response to *Uncle Tom's Cabin* that showed Tom being sold away from the Shelby plantation, "Old Kentucky Home" never reveals the exact source of the absence. It is easy to presume that the speaker refers to separations caused by the slave trade ("The time has come when the darkies have to part, / Then my old Kentucky home, good-night!" [18]), but that doesn't do much to explain why an entire antebellum plantation seems emptied of its slaves. The absent referent in "Old Kentucky Home," in other words, is not the laboring black bodies but the cause of their absence. Eric Lott (1993: 189), discussing the function of Foster's plantation songs on the minstrel stage, has suggested that their persistent interest in the separations, deaths, and disappearances of the enslaved "supervised the elimination of black characters" to the extent that "what was being symbolically eliminated and put to rest was the whole lamented business of slavery in the United States, by means of the elimination of black people themselves." The plantation idyll is more than disrupted; it is dissolved, along with the peculiar institution and the people whose enslavement provided its peculiarity. And the vagaries of the plantation past—which was emphatically not past in Foster's 1853—are not so much enshrined as they are absorbed in melancholy's numbing embrace. Consequently, the song promotes a fixed and carefully staged peek at a past that consciously elides the traumas of the present.

At the center of Margaret Ronda's (2012) essential analysis of the georgic mode in Dunbar is an illuminating reading of "The Deserted Plantation," a piece she calls "the most controversial poem of Dunbar's oeuvre" (870). While she convincingly argues that the text's participation in the georgic mode consists in a "diagnostic frame" that is "ultimately tragic rather than accommodationist or subversive" (871), it is also possible to recognize that in picturing a plantation in decline, the poem deploys a series of rhetorical strategies that directly confront—and overturn—the pastoral conventions of minstrelsy's plantation melodies.[6] Indeed, the poem consciously reverses the tropes of the minstrel ballad so thoroughly that, as I argue below, it becomes a kind of modernist plantation countermelody, deliberately unstitching the seams that give the genre its distinctive shape.

Heard in this key, the sweet melodies of Dunbar's turn-of-the-century songs of the South take on a different tonality: ironic, earthy, and doubled—this is a music that one senses through its extramusical *absence* in the text rather than through the presence of sound. In its broadest dimensions, "The Deserted Plantation" is fundamentally formed by, and becomes a meditation on, (un)musical representations of slavery and its aftermaths. Alongside Ronda, we might recognize the silence that pervades "The Deserted Plantation" as a sign of its georgic commitments, for as Juan Christian Pellicer (2012: 3:293) claims, "There is no such thing as georgic song." In stony contrast to the pastoral's cheery music, the georgic refuses to sing.

While Foster's "Old Kentucky Home" introduces a scene in which the "corn top's ripe and the meadow's in the bloom," where "the birds make music all the day" (2010: 18), Dunbar's "The Deserted Plantation" reverses the scenario—all in the kind of dialect that provides minstrelsy its common currency: "In de furrers whah de co'n was allus wavin', / Now de weeds is growin' green an' rank an' tall" (1993b: 67).

The verdant expanse of the minstrel plantation, in short, is completely overrun by weeds. Perhaps the poem's firmest evocation of minstrelsy and its material culture arrives in the appearance of the banjo whose "voice is silent in de qua'ters" (67). A New World adaptation of stringed instruments traditional in Africa, the banjo's link to minstrelsy was solidified by the ascendancy of Dan Emmett's Virginia Minstrels in the mid-nineteenth century, when the instrument became a central element of that group and nearly every troupe that followed.[7] Its sound is conspicuously unheard in "The Deserted Plantation."

At every turn, in fact, the poem's soundscape denies sonic conventions, bringing its point of reference directly into the 1890s: "D' ain't a hymn ner co'n-song ringin' in de air" (67). Songs of spiritual consolation and endurance are missing but so, too, is the "coon song," a genre that infiltrated the American mainstream in the early 1880s and retained popularity through the first decade of the twentieth century. Composed by some of Tin Pan Alley's most celebrated songwriters— including a young Irving Berlin—the idiom drew heavily on racist caricature: watermelons and chickens, razors, dice, and whiskey all circulate fluidly in a still-vibrant plantation world. Why, then, does the speaker reference a genre that consciously performs anachronism if not to empty out its conventions in the contemporary moment? Here is a picture of the plantation that denies the representational authority of the coon song—it doesn't, it can't, exist on the grounds of the deserted plantation. If coon songs emasculate and humiliate in order to intimidate and coerce, then the speaker makes clear that their sound simply does not carry in Dunbar's post-Reconstruction imagination.

The loudest sound on the plantation, in fact, is the silence of emptiness and decay: the hoe "a-rustin' in de co'nah," the plow "a-tumblin' down in de fiel'" (67). Curiously here, the participial construction of the verbs, particularly in the image of the plow ("a-tumblin'"), freezes the process of decomposition, creating a scene in which the disintegration of the plantation happens—and continues to happen—in an unbroken series of present-tense repetitions. The vision of agropolitical subjecthood worked out in "The Deserted Plantation" is less about vaunting agricultural labor than proposing the phenomenological possibility of claiming lands formerly possessed by slaveholders through an agropoetics of waste and decay. The central conceit of "Old Kentucky Home" is that the plantation's slaves are, mysteriously, no longer present. But Dunbar's decision to revise that tableau in a post-emancipation context offers a peculiar instance in which the sole human inhabitant of the decaying plantation space is a (former) slave. Where the plantation of Foster's fantasy was oddly drained of blackness, Dunbar's lacks any defined trace of white influence or coercion to labor—so much so that the narrator redirects his attention and loyalty to "de othah Mastah," God, whose presence here is more apprehensible than that of the old plantation master (68).

Two years before he arrived at its conceptual counterpart "The Deserted Plantation" and forty years after "Old Kentucky Home" first appeared, Dunbar published "Goin' Back" (1893), a poem that explicitly signifies on Foster's work by using the prism of a past trained on emancipation to reimagine the overdetermined picture of a fecund southland with "bluegrass medders an' fiel's o' co'n" (1993c: 316). Distilling the plantation's legacies in the history of a single ex-slave, it draws on the vein of melancholy produced in Foster's song at the same time that it relocates its sources and tensions, effectively undoing the vague yearning of minstrelsy's environments. Dunbar writes black subjects back into the scene, picking up the story from their position by displaying an old man reminiscing on his time at a plantation while "standing beside the station rail" of a major city, preparing to board a train that will take him "[b]ack to my ol' Kaintucky home, / Back to the ol' Kaintucky sights" (317). He has been in the city for thirty years, having presumably fled the South after emancipation ("I caught the fever that ruled the day"), and although he admits that "thar was lots of things in the North to admire," the poem magnifies its speaker's doubleness, providing an extended rumination on the joys of his plantation youth and the drawbacks of city life:

They said that things were better North,
An' a man was held at his honest worth.
Well, it may be so, but I have some doubt,
An' thirty years ain't wiped it out. (317)

The poem also offers a glimpse into the moment just before the empty plantation of Foster's imagination, with its weeping mothers, hard times, and empty cabin doors, is about to be reanimated by an emancipated slave. But then, unlike "The Deserted Plantation," it pulls away. Deferring the triumph of an actual reoccupation, "Goin' Back" maps the geography of oblivion onto the old plantation, just as it implicates the North in both the suffering of ex-slaves and in the cruel discursive practices of the minstrel stage. By using black dialect to reclaim Foster's famed chorus as "My ol' Kaintucky home," the poem underscores Dunbar's larger project of showing that poetic ownership of these spaces belongs to the black southerners who endured slavery and benefited from emancipation and to those whose labor ushered the modern world into its current form.[8] Silences and hauntings, anthropomorphized trees and blood-fed plots of soil, a ground that coughs up voices: for Dunbar these openings expose the range of experiences—the overlapping planes of the psychic and the physical— that embody rural black lives in the nadir and that sculpt the possibilities of post-Reconstruction being and its claims on history.

"Bold Regeneration" in *The Quest for the Silver Fleece*

One of the major critiques leveled against Washington in *Souls* centers on the use and abuse of southern soil. In *Up from Slavery*, African American progress frequently manifests in agricultural terms, as when Washington (1996: 44–45) expresses a desire to "remove the great bulk of these people into the country districts and plant them upon the soil, upon the solid and never deceptive foundation of Mother Nature, where all nations and races that have ever succeeded have gotten their start." In *Souls*, however, earth most prominently inters broken bodies, suffocates educational opportunities, traps tenant farmers in endless cycles of debt. But that book does not contain Du Bois's last words on the matter during the nadir. Between 1898 and 1912, he contributed multiple articles on the conditions of black rurality to outlets such as the Department of Labor's *Bulletin* and *Publications of the American Statistical Association*.[9] And Du Bois's first novel, *The Quest of the Silver Fleece* (1911), uses the expressive latitude of fiction to reimagine the soil and toil of black folks in the agricultural South. Most importantly, as I argue below, it narrates an iteration of the modern that finds common ground between *Up from Slavery* and *Souls*, binding the physical reclamation of a plantation swampland to the rising agropolitical power of its black characters, thereby asserting the value of both agricultural labor *and* the liberal arts in the lives, histories, and imaginative possibilities of humanness for post-Reconstruction African Americans.

A densely plotted, thickly populated narrative, *Quest* centers on the relationship of two young black southerners, both, in the Du Boisian parlance, "gifted": Zora, a resident of Colonel Cresswell's tenant tract in the imagined town of Toomsville, Alabama, and the bearer of a "strange sixth sense" (2007: 163) that recalls both *Souls'* "gift of the Spirit" and its "second-sight" (1999: 162, 10); and Blessed "Bles" Alwyn, a transplant from Georgia whose "intelligence, broad sympathy, [and] knowledge of the world" position him as one of the "exceptional men" poised to lead the race (1903: 33–34). In the swamp at the edge of the Cresswell plantation, Zora and Bles collaborate to cultivate a preternatural cotton crop (the titular "silver fleece"), and although they briefly cohere romantically, Bles leaves when he learns that Zora was sexually abused by one of the Cresswells, whereupon they each exit Alabama—Bles, for Washington, DC, and Zora, for Atlanta, New York, and, finally, Washington. Alongside the actions of its black protagonists, the novel also narrates the machinations of two powerful white families—the Cresswells of Alabama and the Taylors of New England—who corner the global cotton market by promoting favorable political policy in Washington, managing the labor force in the South, and seeking to control production everywhere. The narrative concludes when Zora returns to Toomsville to complete her work in cooperative agriculture and education, a project that hastens the dissolution of the Cresswell Cotton Combine. With the help of Bles and Miss Smith, the white New Englander who runs a school for black students, as well as the local African American community, Zora buys the swamp, establishing it as a sovereign space of black economic production and cultural achievement. Buffeted by violent opposition from a white mob, Zora actualizes her vision just as she and Bles reconcile: he admits his mistake, and the narrative ends with her proposal of marriage.

The novel occupies a minor place in Du Bois's corpus. Even the author himself tended to minimize its importance: *Quest* warrants just a single sentence in his 1940 autobiography, *Dusk of Dawn*, and no mention at all in 1968's *Autobiography*. In the earlier book, Du Bois goes so far as to downplay *Quest*'s very status as a novel, insisting that it "was really an economic study" (2014: 134).[10] How can imaginative literature function as "economic study"? What is the precise relation of the fictional world of the text to the sociologist's world on the ground? *Quest* is tellingly not set in Georgia, the rural southern site most fully

scrutinized by Du Bois, but in a fictional town one state west—
Toomsville, Alabama. Since parts of both Alabama and Georgia fall
within the Black Belt, and under the same regime of cotton tenancy,
the decision to swap one for the other may seem fairly unremarkable.
Yet it is difficult to deny the significance of Alabama's ironclad association with Washington and Tuskegee. In fact, the historical basis for
Miss Smith and her school is likely unimaginable without Washington. As Herbert Aptheker (1974: x–xi) observed, the novel's fictional
geographies expanded on Du Bois's own 1906 fieldwork studying the
conditions of black citizens in Lowndes County, Alabama (see also
Farland 2006: 1017–19; and McInnis 2016: 91). Here Du Bois found
the prototype for Miss Smith's project in the Calhoun Colored School,
an institution founded on the Hampton-Tuskegee model in 1892 by
Charlotte Thorn and Mabel Dillingham, two white New England women
operating under Washington's direction.[11] With this unexpectedly
favorable portrayal of a school committed to industrial education as
just one example, *Quest* sweeps across the partitions so often ascribed
to Du Bois's thinking; it offers vivid images of a politically productive
engagement with capitalist modernity and black modernism by following it across environments of both blackness *and* rurality.[12]

Quest's figurations of the rural modern come into earshot in the
novel's opening scene. While searching for Miss Smith's school, with
night falling around him, Bles stumbles into a "strange land," crossing
into the Cresswell swamp and finding himself frightened when "of a
sudden up from the darkness came music" (2007: 1). It is not just the
unexpected intrusion of sound but also the music's sonic qualities—
its "wildness and weirdness" (1)—that disquiet Bles, a repetition of
Du Bois's own account in the Sorrow Songs of *Souls*. Explaining
the hybrid epigraphs that open each chapter, Du Bois describes the
"haunting echo of these weird old songs in which the soul of the black
slave spoke to men" (1999: 154–55). But since Du Bois sets himself up
as an avatar of American blackness and since he proposes these songs
as the black *folk*'s most important legacy, it is fair to ask, Whence the
weirdness?

For one thing, in Du Bois's reading, these melodies originate in
slavery, an institution he—unlike Washington—never experienced
firsthand. Second, and more importantly, the songs "came out of
the South unknown to me, one by one, and yet at once I knew them
as of me and mine" (1999: 155). They are at once indispensable to

Du Bois's sense of black self ("at once I knew them") and "unknown"—distant in both geography and culture, since given Du Bois's background and training he stands, in Eric J. Sundquist's (1993: 466) memorable phrase, as something of a "folk parvenu." Writing of the affective consequences of the Sorrow Songs, Jonathan Flately (2008: 147) holds that they "signal missing histories, absent worlds." I contend that these histories go missing and worlds become absent because the songs themselves—even when dressed up by the Fisk Jubilee Singers—remain imbricated in forms of rural southern labor to which Du Bois had only partial access. While forwarding the "Negro folksong" as "the singular spiritual heritage of the nation," he still experiences it through a veil of weirdness (1999: 155).

Du Bois's task in *Souls* was to promote, from his own position, the Sorrow Songs as world historical art. In *Quest* he uses Zora, who thoroughly exemplifies Achille Mbembe's (2003: 22) description of the plantation subject who is "able to demonstrate the protean capabilities of the human bond through music and the very body that was supposedly possessed by another." Consequently the novel—an extended, imagined narrative instead of a sociological or historical study—allows Du Bois to propose a direct, untranscribed encounter with the source of the sound itself, a sound as trance inducing as it is startling. One point of apparent paradox is that the noise emanating from Zora / the swamp, the "formless, boundless music," affiliates fairly easily with a modernist soundscape, with the experiments in tonality and compositional structure associated with the concert music of, say, Anton Webern, Charles Ives, and Arnold Schoenberg, all of whom were in the avant-garde in the early twentieth century. The implication here is that the "folk"—so often made synonymous with rural blackness—might effectively double, parallel, and perhaps even give rise to certain aesthetic innovations of sonic modernism.

Thus the music rises, unbidden, "up from the darkness" (Du Bois 2007: 1)—from spaces (the swamp) and bodies (Zora's) distinctly coded black. The significance of darkness here introduces a motif developed throughout *Quest*: plantation darkness and blackness serve as an experiential register that allows for new opportunities of communication and community building. So where Bles expresses fear of the "black dark" in the novel's opening pages, Zora "love[s] night" (3)—she is most at peace in an environment where her own complexion matches the complexion of the atmosphere itself. There are also, the novel explains, practical advantages to blackness. In a scene from the penultimate chapter, when a violent mob attempts to intimidate Toomsville's increasingly assertive black population by attacking the schoolhouse under the cover of night, a mob member exclaims, "I wish I could see a nigger" (232). Although phenotypic differences worn on the skin often cause "race" to manifest as a kind of hypervisibility in the light of day, this scene runs that familiar formation backward, in a proto-Ellisonian turn whereby blackness makes possible a strategic invisibility.

Moreover, in contrast to the counterpoint of whiteness, modes of rural blackness given body, voice, and movement by *Quest*'s characters—by Zora in particular—come to represent an alternate, radical epistemology and a new strain of political subjecthood. The novel consistently explores what the characters know, how they know it, and the material, political consequences of these distinct canons of knowledge. So much so, in fact, that one effect *Quest* creates—and one allowed by the novel as a medium more broadly—is a series of conversations between these competing epistemologies and literacies. When Zora dances into the novel's frame in the opening scene, the narrator comments approvingly on the "poetry of her motion" (2), forwarding a poetics that depends on embodied rhetoric rather than language alone. Yet the difficulty of sounding—or visualizing—this poetry across hermeneutic divisions poses often-insurmountable problems. John Taylor, the Yankee businessman oriented by calculations, capital, and chronometric time, is blind to the "poetry of Toil . . . in the souls of the laborers" (25), while his sister, Mary, is temporarily transfixed when Bles introduces her to the intricate beauties of labor and the growing cycle: "The poetry of the thing began to sing within her" (12). However, none of this is enough to change Mary's notions of what counts as culture: "Culture and work—were they incompatible? At any rate, culture and *this* work were" (34).

Under Mary Taylor's definition, then, culture is a single thing—it is reliably white and concomitant with modes of labor decidedly not agricultural. One feels the novel's radical impulses most acutely, then, when it stages expressions of black rural culture that are empowering and productive rather than oppressive and alienating, cultures of black agriculture that pose a direct challenge to the white overclass. The severity of the challenge is evident in an exchange between Harry Cresswell and his sister, Helen. Harry is hoping to make Helen's introduction to Mary:

"By the bye, Sis, there's a young lady over at the Negro school whom I think you'd like."
"Black or white?"
"A young lady, I said. Don't be sarcastic."
"I heard you. I did not know whether you were using our language or others'." (51)

Our language, our culture, our land, our image of "lady"—each demands protection.

The key to African American advancement, Bles quickly intuits, is to break the stranglehold through education. Hence Bles insists that Zora's own grammar of expression and communication—her own nonstandard literacy—meet the dominant forms. For her part, Zora needs convincing: "Don't white folks make books? . . . I knows more than they do now—a heap more" (20). This isn't a statement the novel seeks to overturn. In fact, Mary Taylor, warning Miss Smith of Zora's disruptive potential, makes essentially the same case: "she knows quite too much" (33). Yet Zora evinces a different sense of what counts as power: "No, no. They don't really rule; they just thinks they rule. They just got things—heavy, dead things. We black folks is got the *spirit*. We'se lighter and cunninger; we fly right through them; we go and come again just as we wants to. Black folks is wonderful" (20). Bles does not disagree, but still he holds to the importance of standard literacies and formal education: "Even if white folks don't know everything they know different things from us, and we ought to know what they know" (20). In its concluding chapters, the narrative bears out Bles's intuition: Zora's full capability can arrive only through a merger of "things" and "spirit" that reveals the interpenetrating spirit of book learning and the thingness of physical labor at the same time that it valorizes the object matter of education and the very poetry of work.

For Zora, the space between things and spirit is apprehensible in the swamp's oneiric qualities. While Bles spends his first night near the swamp in a "dreamless sleep" (2), Zora lapses into a "daydream," speaks "dreamily" (3), and asserts that "behind the swamps is great fields full of dreams" (4). Later, she and Bles pull that future a little closer as they prepare to put out a cotton crop, allowing Zora to claim the swamp itself as the place "where the Dreams lives" (38). For the narrator, though, the "black swamp" (183) appears in a consistently achromatic color, with its "black lake" and soil "virgin and black" (38); elsewhere we glimpse the "black waters of the lagoon" alongside a "black patch of rich loam" (47). Likewise, the uncanny cottonseeds the couple obtains from Zora's mother—a conjure woman, the novel is at pains to point out—are not "the green-white seed which Bles had always known, but small, smooth black seeds" (50). Dreams are converted into reality-shifting material in a black space charged with oppositional energies. The representation of this liminal territory is illuminated by Monique Allewaert's (2008) handling of "ecologies of resistance" in the swampy "plantation zone" of the late eighteenth century. Building on Michael Warner's concept of the "citizen-subject of print culture," Allewaert argues, "Instead of simply producing subjects who gained power through an abstract and abstracting print culture, the plantation zone witnessed the emergence of agents who gained power by combining with ecological forces" (341). Zora becomes a hybrid citizen-subject / ecological collaborator, both arbiter and epitome of "translation"—a central tenet of Bruno Latour's (1993: 10) model of modernity, one that "creates mixtures between entirely new types of beings, hybrids of nature and culture." Her translation happens in a physical landscape, much like the postbellum racial landscape, marked by almost pure potential, an observation that neatly aligns with economic reality since when it comes to cotton production, as one antebellum commentator wrote, "two millions of acres of swamplands are worth four millions of upland," providing one "take *time and expense* of cultivation into account" (Emmons 1860: v).

While Dunbar poetically reclaims plantation grounds, Du Bois's novel stages a more literal reclamation, enacted in the mode of Progressive Era reformers for whom, in Jedediah Purdy's (2015: 164) words, "Conservation was the principle and technique of eliminating waste." In 1908, as horticulturalist Liberty Hyde Bailey was convening the Country Life Commission—a Roosevelt-administration group designed to improve the circumstances of US rurality—Du Bois (2004) corresponded with Bailey, stressing "the extreme importance that the real condition of Negro farmers be gotten at" and warning of the excessive power of "the great landlords." If the commission's report, issued the same year as *Quest*, wasn't exhaustive on the troubled states of race and tenancy in the rural United States, it had plenty to

say about swamp reclamation, particularly as it relates to the interde-
pendence of humans and nonhuman environments (*Report of the Commission on Country Life* 1911: 62–64). It is worth noting here, then,
that *Quest*'s "bold regeneration of the land" proceeds in the rational-
ized style of Progressive conservationists: it must be "carefully studied out, long thought of and read about," and submitted to a "plan of
wide scope" (Du Bois 2007: 218). Tellingly, however, the manipulation
and recomposition of a plantation's waste places are achieved not
through governmental intervention but through the subnational
efforts of Toomsville's black citizens, as the novel affiliates the reclamation of black land—from "swamp" to "swamp in name only" (234)—
with the reclaiming of black lives.

The most pointed example, of course, is Zora, whose full capability
as an expressive figure and as a political agent takes shape in another
dreamworld, this one rising through her immersion in northern libraries: "She was in dreamland; in a world of books" (136). Counterintui-
tively, to redeem the plantation's disregarded margins Zora must absorb
the traditions of a print-culture public. Through a sequence of para-
graphs outlining Zora's education via reading, the narrator scans the
breadth of Western history and mythology, making Zora both witness
to and participant in the creation of archetypal narratives of North
Atlantic identity. And in a provocative gesture, an African American
woman reared in plantation environments of abuse and neglect serves
as testimony, repository, and culmination of Western culture: "She
gossiped with old Herodotus across the earth to the black and blame-
less Ethiopians"; she is on the scene with Demosthenes, Cornelia,
"the drunken Goths"; visits "the Paris of Clovis, and St. Louis"; weeps
with the prophet Jeremiah; and clasps hands with Mary of Scotland
and Joan of Arc (136).

Subsequently, in what is perhaps the novel's most direct address of
Souls' criticisms of the Washingtonian model, *Quest* stages several
scenes that pointedly allow for the value of both physical labor *and*
the liberal arts. For instance, after Zora and Bles reunite at the swamp
in the narrative's final act, she gives him a tour that includes "the
proposed farm sites" and her "den" (218), a separate building hosting
volumes that could have lined Du Bois's own shelf in 1911—Plato's
Republic; Maxim Gorky's 1906 call for broad-based collectivism,
"Comrade"; a "Cyclopaedia of Agriculture"; Honoré de Balzac novels;

Herbert Spencer; and a volume of Tennyson. Political and economic theory, poetry, fiction, and an agricultural resource mingle freely.

Given the breadth of texts mentioned by the narrator, I want to suggest that the bookcase metaphorizes the novel's larger commitments to the dialectic as a driver of political and intellectual development. The obvious clue may be *Republic*, a pioneering model of dialectical inquiry, but even beyond that the separate volumes display internal contradiction re-created as forward action—the "concrete" in the Hegelian triad. For instance, although Spencer's interest in the economic and social power of vivid individualism is antithetical to Gorky's (1906: 509) flinty critiques of a world where the "strong were the rich" and "the weak should, without murmuring, submit themselves to the strong," the narrative resolves this disagreement in the figure of Zora, whose strength as an individual is undeniable but who never spends her energy toward personal gain alone. Just as, while temporarily working as an assistant to the wealthy white Mrs. Vanderpool, Zora masters the manners of the upper class—Vanderpool has recently asked Zora, with no apparent irony, if "she'd like to be ambassador to France" (Du Bois 2007: 136)—she declares, "I'm going back South to work for my people" (161). An "educated woman" who doesn't just return to the rural South but to hands-on cotton farming (216), Zora represents a constructive step beyond the *Up from Slavery–Souls* continuum. Pace Washington, there is nothing absurd about a young black farmworker studying French grammar. But neither is there anything tragic about working one's way out of an oppressed position through agricultural labor. "This is my university," Zora explains, in a statement that demonstrates how thoroughly she has "transformed [the] swamp" (218). She has transformed it through physical labor, through the courts, through confrontation with an angry mob, through Miss Smith's school: transformed it into the loftiest plane of higher education. The novel's discrete dreamworlds combine in its image of the cabin's library, as the spirit flows through the material object of the text and texts themselves rise from the dirt floor. Taking in Zora's accomplishments and the full spectrum of her experience, Bles realizes that, by following her lead, he was "being revolutionized" (218); he is "startled" over and over again by the continual "newness of the girl" (13). Although the novel emphasizes *becoming* across a range of characters, it is Zora who most fully defies "classification" (34); she is its most complete embodiment of newness.

Zora's constitution as an idealized social and political energy remains central to Du Bois's novelistic project. Pointedly, it is one key feature fiction affords. In "The Negro Landholder of Georgia," Du Bois (1901: 666) approvingly comments on "socialistic experiments" among black farmers in the rural districts but notes, "There was too little experience and intelligence to allow such experiments to be successful generally." Fiction, then, builds Du Bois's visions of agropolitical possibility by conjuring a character with the exact experience and intelligence it would take to pull off such an endeavor. Imaginative literature bridges a gap in the archive, allowing Du Bois to create a new kind of political actor within the plantation-as-proscenium, a protagonist so dynamic as to appear "inhuman" to one of her white observers (Du Bois 2007: 211). Du Bois's novel isn't didactic in any simple or final way, however. In dramatizing its solutions, *Quest* never fails to acknowledge the conflict, the profound risk, carried in the settlement's establishment. What Zora creates in the Toomsville swamp is nothing less than a sovereign black agricultural collective. And though this emphasis on collectivity is not altogether surprising given Du Bois's embrace of socialism and, later, the Communist Party, the geographic setting is.[13] Measured against the bloodred, ravaged ground of Georgia surveyed in *Souls*, *Quest*'s black soil is a fecund source of strength and independence. Yet, despite its focus on the commons, collectivity is possible in the novel's post-Reconstruction Alabama only through land ownership: "We must have land—our own farm with our own tenants—to be the beginning of a free community," Zora proclaims (198). Proposing to break the spirals of debt and rent, the community will mix privately held parcels of twenty acres with a "central plantation of one hundred acres for the school," land preserved "for the public good" (221). Here again is an oblique point of agreement with Washington, who repeatedly argued for the abolishment of the croplien system and for the centrality of black ownership; it also stands as a prediction of Fanonian emphasis on the revolutionary capacity of agriculture: "For a colonized people, the most essential value, because it is most meaningful, is first and foremost the land" (Fanon 2005: 9).[14] Bles, pitching the idea to Cresswell's African American tenants, emphasizes the richness of the physical environment ("the best land in the county") and the autonomy of the swamp, promising a "little hospital," a "cooperative store for buying supplies," a "cotton-gin and a saw-mill," all under control of the collective, with every member—including

"the women and girls and school children" (Du Bois 2007: 221)—
redeemed through labor.

"Rescue your own flesh and blood—free yourselves—free yourselves!" (202–3), Zora importunes in an impassioned speech at a local
church. Free yourselves through labor, land ownership, *and* education? Through participation in national and transnational markets?
Consciously or not, the overlap with Washington's Tuskegee—in
geography, in concept, in rhetoric—runs deep as Zora's swamp signals a chance to create a space of self-rule, dependent on agriculture,
with a school at the center. To Arnold Rampersad (1990: 129), the
novel reveals Du Bois's "ideal state" as fundamentally "agrarian in its
economic and social base"—a vision that transmits fairly smoothly
with Washington's. As does *Up from Slavery*, the novel recognizes the
need for participation from women and children, as well as a necessary diversity of tasks—"we want all sorts of industries," Bles explains
(Du Bois 2007: 221). Zora herself appears drawn up to realize Anna
Julia Cooper's (1988: 28) contention—made in a metaphor that matches
Quest's tropology—that "the regeneration, the re-training of the race,
as well as the ground work and starting point of [the race's] progress
upward, must be the *black woman.*"

Even as it promotes diverse "industries," the novel remains com-
mitted to exploring the characteristics and consequences of what
Sven Beckert (2014: 70) calls the "global cotton production complex."
Rather than promoting alternatives to cotton, as Washington does in
Working with the Hands (1904) and to a lesser extent *Up from Slavery*,
Quest forwards images of racial redemption that centralize cotton.
Critics often place the novel within a genealogy of Progressive realist
fictions designed to expose the casualties of early twentieth-century
extractive industries (Aptheker 1974: iv; Rosetti 2012): Frank Norris's
depictions of wheat (*The Octopus* [1901] and *The Pit* [1903]); Upton
Sinclair on meat, coal, and oil (*The Jungle* [1906], *King Coal* [1917],
and *Oil!* [1927]); and James Lane Allen on hemp (*The Reign of Law: A
Tale of the Kentucky Hemp Fields* [1900]). Of all these, Du Bois's attention to cotton is perhaps most significant, for as Beckert has demonstrated, cotton was ab initio the raw material that catalyzed the Industrial Revolution and solidified the bond among modern global
markets. To calibrate these scalar relationships, the novel pans out to
the macrocosm—underlining cotton's place in a tightly woven transnational network of capital flows and unprocessed materials—just as it

zooms in on the micro, presenting a social and ecological condition wherein everything is reducible to cotton: "Cotton was currency; cotton was merchandise; cotton was conversation" (Du Bois 2007: 99); it was "the very life and being of the land" (16). Such descriptions ascribe cotton a dimensionality that meets Timothy Morton's (2013: 1) explanation of the "hyperobject": it is "massively distributed in time and space relative to humans." While the growing cycle of any individual crop obviously falls well within a single human lifespan (well within a single year, in fact), the aggregate "cotton" "involve[s] profoundly different temporalities than the human-scale ones we are used to" (1). It arcs across capitalist modernity in a way that eludes containment within any one place or time.

Cotton necessitates a searching, global perspective, then, just as surely as it demands the exploitation of land and the manipulation of laborers, for any benefit produced by the cotton industry in the nineteenth century could be realized only through force. In 1853 the *American Cotton Planter* put it this way: "It is idle to talk of producing Cotton for the world's supply with free labor. It has never yet been successfully grown by voluntary labor" (quoted in Beckert 2014: 119). If postbellum tenancy represents the possibility of making free labor *un*free, then the *American Cotton Planter*'s antebellum formula carries through to *Quest*'s historical setting at the turn of the twentieth century. Miss Smith, for one, recognizes that "the bounty of Southern hospitality" (Du Bois 2007: 54) on exhibit at the Cresswell mansion was "built on a moan" (73). Yet the novel's basic premise holds that even as cotton can oppress, it might also be turned upside down toward freedom (compare McInnis 2016: 80). Such a turn, however, is possible only through unbending toil, through victory in the courts, and through canny defense against the realities of white violence.

Quest's investments in the reparative politics of representation and narrative arrive most fully in its point-by-point responses to two contrapuntal genres popular to the period. Many critics have noticed Du Bois's opposition to the conventions of the plantation romance (see, for example, Byerman 1992; Farland 2006; and McInnis 2016). Yet as Maurice Lee (1991: 391–92) has suggested, Du Bois's treatment of the double-marriage plot also denies a "central device of reconciliation romances," or what Nina Silber (1993: esp. 112–23) has aptly called the nadir-era "romance of reunion." Specifically, the double wedding that pairs Harry Cresswell–Mary Taylor and John Taylor–Helen

Cresswell is a clear revision of a similar device organizing Thomas Nelson Page's *Red Rock* (1898).[15] In *Red Rock*, the unions of both the ex-federal officer and Southern belle and of the Confederate gentleman and northern lady signal not just the national unification of formerly warring factions but also the adoption, by right-minded northerners, of "southern" values like the naturalization of Jim Crow racial codes and a general amiability about the war's causes. (In a passage satirizing the necessity of "mutual understanding," for example, Harry claims, "Both [sides] were right" [78].) These marriages make up *Red Rock*'s conclusion, acting as resolution of both narrative and national conflict. In *Quest*, by contrast, the double marriage occurs at the end of the first act, bringing into focus a different set of interests: speculative finance of the North and the declining social-cultural order tied to the cotton aristocracy of the South. Where *Red Rock* used the marriage plot to create harmony within the families and between regions, *Quest*'s marriages ultimately sow discord and dissolution. Both Cresswell and Taylor grow rich in the Cotton Combine, but the union radically alters the social, domestic, and physical landscape: John Taylor betrays Colonel Cresswell in his legal dispute with Zora; Harry is unfaithful to Mary throughout their marriage; industrialized mills overrun and ruin the local environment. Even the prospect of unification through new birth is frustrated, as the process of delivering a stillborn child renders Mary infertile, revealing the extent to which the rise of a modern nation belongs to Zora and Bles—African Americans from and of the rural South.

The Quest of the Silver Fleece, a book scarcely claimed by its own author and rarely considered by contemporary readers, confounds the discursive split that so often attends to accounts of Du Bois and Washington. And in its fictive presentation of farming in the Black Belt, it recasts as politically radical an old and familiar relationship to the earth. Understood correctly, understood as another branch of the liberal arts, agriculture offers an unpredictably productive way of inhabiting and producing modern black subjecthood. Though posthuman models of "transversal subjectivity" may well "restructure the processes of . . . racialization" (Braidotti 2013: 98), such projects meet their limits when faced with circum-Atlantic histories that cannot justly overlook the indissoluble realities of racialized violence. These realities are the New World plantation's steepest legacy. In Houston A. Baker Jr.'s (2001: 83) singular definition, "United States black modernism" is achievable only through "black public-sphere mobility and fullness of United States black citizenship rights of locomotion." The plantation, by contrast, is a deliberate zone of "designated black or African *immobilization*" that leads directly to the carceral structures that continue to flourish in the present day (84). While I don't dispute Baker's definitions or the range of his analysis, I have argued that the agropolitical texts of Dunbar and Du Bois discussed here figure something different: modes of resistance, liberatory subjectivities, and affective responses that rise from the plantation itself. They acknowledge that in attending to problems ordered to the magnitude of slavery's life and afterlives, imaginative literature's highest calling is to cultivate our sense of what is possible—both within and beyond the human—from the ground up.

Benjamin Child is an assistant professor of English at Colgate University. His articles have appeared in journals such as *Modern Fiction Studies, American Studies,* and *Southern Cultures,* and his book, *The Whole Machinery: The Rural Modern in Cultures of the US South, 1890–1946* (2019), is part of the University of Georgia Press's New Southern Studies series. Child's current research addresses literary productions and interpretations of US populism.

Notes

My thanks to Katie Child, Leigh Anne Duck, Linck Johnson, Kenneth Warren, and Jay Watson for essential advice on this material.
1   I am grateful to John Connor for help with the term *agropolitical.*
2   I follow historians of the twentieth century in using *nadir* as shorthand for the period when lynching and other acts of race-based terrorism occurred with greatest frequency, from the end of Reconstruction (1877) through the 1920s. This usage originates in Logan 1954.
3   On African American literature as a primary source for broader configurations of modernism, see Smethurst 2011. For an incisive account of rurality and African American masculinity, see Richardson 2007.
4   Acknowledgments are due to Beckert (2014: 243) for uncovering Fohlen 1956.
5   For a suggestive examination of Dunbar's relation to the signifying practices of the minstrel stage, see Carr 2010. The politics of Foster's dialect lyrics have been subject to several revisions: Steven Saunders (2012: 286) contends, "Foster's plantation melodies embody his own conventional, Democratic, middle-class values more than any progressive, utopian views about the politics of race."

6   I follow Saunders (2012: 286) in using the term "plantation melodies" since it points to pieces, such as "Old Kentucky Home," that "straddle the line between parlor song and minstrel song."

7   According to Laurent Dubois's (2016: 194) survey of the banjo's New World histories, the "instrument came to the [minstrel] stage in the hands of Virginian Joel Walker Sweeney," who first appeared with the banjo at the Old Italian Opera House, in New York, in 1839.

8   For two brilliant accounts of slavery's role in the creation of the modern world, see Baptist 2014 and Johnson 2013.

9   See Du Bois 1898, 1899, 1901, and 1912. The reason for Du Bois's interest in the issue is plain in the opening line of "The Negro Landholder": "One of the greatest problems of emancipation in the United States was the relation of the freedman to the land" (1901: 647).

10   Among the small but robust body of *Quest* criticism, Jarvis McInnis's (2016) wonderful contribution—which I didn't encounter until after having completed this essay—deserves special mention here. McInnis is also interested in the novel as an economic study. But he is primarily concerned with analyzing *Quest*'s "aesthetics" so as "to leverage a moral and economic critique of the plantation romance and plantation modernity" (74) and, to a lesser extent, with connecting the novel's "economic study" to Du Bois's unfinished project of the 1950s, "The Cotton Slave/ The Slave and the Cotton" (94). See also Oliver 2014: 63–64.

11   On Washington's involvement with the Calhoun School, see Ellis 1984.

12   Maria Farland (2006: 1036) notes that the novel "marked [Du Bois's] surprising affinities with the industrial and manual training association with Booker T. Washington" but says nothing further on the topic.

13   On the novel's tabulations of Du Bois's 1910s socialism, see Wienen and Kraft 2007.

14   Washington's (1904: 139) goal for black agriculture, laid out in a declaration of principles adopted by the Annual Negro Farmers' Conference, encapsulates exactly this point: "To abolish and do away with the mortgage system just as rapidly as possible." On the issue of land ownership, compare McInnis 2016: 90–91.

15   "Arguing with Mr. Thomas Nelson Page," Du Bois (1999: 44) famously claims in *Souls*, is an "imperative duty of thinking black men."

References

Ali, Omar H. 2010. *In the Lion's Mouth: Black Populism in the New South, 1886–1900*. Jackson: Univ. Press of Mississippi.

Allewaert, Monique. 2008. "Swamp Sublime: Ecologies of Resistance in the American Plantation Zone." *PMLA* 123, no. 2: 340–57.

Aptheker, Herbert. 1974. Introduction to *The Quest of the Silver Fleece*, by W. E. B. Du Bois, i–xvi. Mineola, NY: Dover.

Baker, Houston A., Jr. 2001. *Turning South Again: Re-Thinking Modernism / Re-Reading Booker T*. Durham, NC: Duke Univ. Press.

Baptist, Edward E. 2014. *The Half Has Never Been Told: Slavery and the Making of American Capitalism*. New York: Basic Books.

Beckert, Sven. 2014. *Empire of Cotton: A Global History*. New York: Knopf.

Benjamin, Walter. (1942) 1968. "Theses on the Philosophy of History." In *Illuminations: Essays and Reflections*, translated by Harry Zohn, 253–64. New York: Schocken.

Benjamin, Walter. 1999. *The Arcades Project*. Translated by Howard Eiland and Kevin McLaughlin. Cambridge, MA: Belknap Press of Harvard Univ. Press.

Berry, Wendell. 1972. *A Continuous Harmony: Essays Cultural and Agricultural*. New York: Harcourt, Brace.

Braidotti, Rosi. 2013. *The Posthuman*. Malden, MA: Polity.

Byerman, Keith. 1992. "Race and Romance: *The Quest of the Silver Fleece* as Utopian Narrative." *American Literary Realism* 24, no. 3: 58–71.

Carr, Elston L., Jr. 2010. "Minstrelsy and the Dialect Poetry of Paul Laurence Dunbar." In *We Wear the Mask: Paul Laurence Dunbar and the Politics of Representative Reality*, edited by Willie J. Harrell Jr., 49–58. Kent, OH: Kent State Univ. Press.

Cooper, Anna Julia. (1892) 1988. *A Voice from the South*. New York: Oxford Univ. Press.

Du Bois, W. E. B. 1898. "The Negroes of Farmville, Virginia: A Social Study." *Bulletin of the United States Department of Labor* 14: 1–38.

Du Bois, W. E. B. 1899. "The Negro in the Black Belt: Some Social Sketches." US Bureau of the Census, *Bulletin* 4: 401–17.

Du Bois, W. E. B. 1901. "The Negro Landholder of Georgia." US Bureau of the Census, *Bulletin* 35: 647–777.

Du Bois, W. E. B. 1903. "The Talented Tenth." In *The Negro Problem: A Series of Articles by Representative American Negroes of To-day*, edited by Booker T. Washington, 31–76. New York: James Pott and Company.

Du Bois, W. E. B. 1912. "The Rural South." *Publications of the American Statistical Association* 13, no. 97: 80–84.

Du Bois, W. E. B. (1903) 1999. *The Souls of Black Folk*. New York: Norton.

Du Bois, W. E. B. (1908) 2004. "Letter to Liberty Hyde Bailey." *Liberty Hyde Bailey: A Man for All Seasons*. Ithaca, NY: Cornell Univ. http://rmc.library .cornell.edu/bailey/commission/commission_3.html/.

Du Bois, W. E. B. (1911) 2007. *The Quest of the Silver Fleece*. New York: Oxford Univ. Press.

Du Bois, W. E. B. (1940) 2014. *Dusk of Dawn*. New York: Oxford Univ. Press.

Du Bois Papers. Special Collections and University Archives, University of Massachusetts Amherst Libraries.

Dubois, Laurent. 2016. *The Banjo: America's African Instrument*. Cambridge, MA: Belknap Press of Harvard Univ. Press.

Dunbar, Paul Laurence. (1895) 1993a. "The Colored Soldiers." In *The Collected Poetry*, edited by Joanne M. Braxton, 50–52. Charlottesville: Univ. of Virginia Press.

Dunbar, Paul Laurence. (1895) 1993b. "The Deserted Plantation." In *The Collected Poetry*, edited by Joanne M. Braxton, 67–68. Charlottesville: Univ. of Virginia Press.

Dunbar, Paul Laurence. (1893) 1993c. "Goin' Back." In *The Collected Poetry*, edited by Joanne M. Braxton, 316–17. Charlottesville: Univ. of Virginia Press.

Dunbar, Paul Laurence. (1903) 1993d. "The Haunted Oak." In *The Collected Poetry*, edited by Joanne M. Braxton, 219–20. Charlottesville: Univ. of Virginia Press.

Dunbar, Paul Laurence. (1895) 1993e. "When de Co'n Pone's Hot." In *The Collected Poetry*, edited by Joanne M. Braxton, 57–58. Charlottesville: Univ. of Virginia Press.

Ellis, R. H. 1984. "The Calhoun School, Miss Charlotte Thorn's 'Lighthouse on the Hill' in Lowndes County, Alabama." *Alabama Review* 37, no. 3: 183–201.

Emmons, Ebenezer. 1860. *Agriculture of North Carolina, Part 2: Containing a Statement of the Principles of the Science upon Which the Practices of Agriculture, as an Art, Are Founded*. Raleigh: W. W. Holden.

Fanon, Frantz. (1961) 2005. *The Wretched of the Earth*. Translated by Richard Philcox. New York: Grove.

Farland, Maria. 2006. "W. E. B. Du Bois, Anthropometric Science, and the Limits of Racial Uplift." *American Quarterly* 58, no. 4: 1017–45.

Flately, Jonathan. 2008. *Affective Mapping: Melancholia and the Politics of Modernism*. Cambridge, MA: Harvard Univ. Press.

Fohlen, Claude. 1956. *L'industrie textile au temps du Second Empire*. Paris: Librairie Plon.

Foster, Stephen. (1853) 2010. "My Old Kentucky Home, Good-Night!" In *Stephen Foster and Co.: Lyrics of America's First Great Popular Songs*, edited by Ken Emerson, 18–19. New York: Library of America.

Gates, Henry Louis, Jr. 1988. *The Signifying Monkey: A Theory of African-American Literary Criticism*. New York: Oxford Univ. Press.

Gorky, Maxim. 1906. "Comrade." *Social Democrat* 10, no. 8: 509–12.

Handley, George B. 2004. "A New World Poetics of Oblivion." In *Look Away! The US South in New World Studies*, edited by Jon Smith and Deborah Cohn, 25–51. Durham, NC: Duke Univ. Press.

Jackson, Zakiyyah Iman. 2015. "Outer Worlds: The Persistence of Race in Movement 'Beyond the Human.'" *GLQ* 21, nos. 2–3: 215–18.

Johnson, Walter. 2013. *River of Dark Dreams: Slavery and Empire in the Cotton Kingdom*. Cambridge, MA: Belknap Press of Harvard Univ. Press.

Latour, Bruno. 1993. *We Have Never Been Modern.* Translated by Catherine Porter. Cambridge, MA: Harvard Univ. Press.

Lee, Maurice. 1999. "Du Bois the Novelist: White Influence, Black Spirit, and *The Quest of the Silver Fleece.*" *African American Review* 33, no 3: 389–400.

Logan, Rayford. 1954. *The Negro in American Life and Thought: The Nadir, 1877–1901.* New York: Dial.

Lott, Eric. 1993. *Love and Theft: Blackface Minstrelsy and the American Working Class.* New York: Oxford Univ. Press.

Mbembe, Achille. 2003. "Necropolitics." Translated by Libby Meintjes. *Public Culture* 15, no. 1: 11–40.

McInnis, Jarvis C. 2016. "'Behold the Land': W. E. B. Du Bois, Cotton Futures, and the Afterlife of the Plantation in the US South." *Global South* 10, no. 2: 70–98.

Morton, Timothy. 2013. *Hyperobjects: Philosophy and Ecology after the End of the World.* Minneapolis: Univ. of Minnesota Press.

Oliver, Lawrence J. 2014. "W. E. B. Du Bois and the Dismal Science: Economic Theory and Social Justice." *American Studies* 53, no. 2: 49–70.

Page, Thomas Nelson. 1898. *Red Rock: A Chronicle of Reconstruction.* New York: Charles Scribner's Sons.

Pellicer, Juan Christian. 2012. "Pastoral and Georgic." In *The Oxford History of Classical Reception in English Literature*, edited by David Hopkins and Charles Martindale, 3:287–322. New York: Oxford Univ. Press.

Purdy, Jedediah. 2015. *After Nature: A Politics for the Anthropocene.* Cambridge, MA: Harvard Univ. Press.

Rampersad, Arnold. (1976) 1990. *The Art and Imagination of W. E. B. Du Bois.* New York: Schocken.

Report of the Commission on Country Life. (1911) 1917. New York: Sturgis and Walton.

Richardson, Riché. 2007. *Black Masculinity and the US South: From Uncle Tom to Gangsta.* Athens: Univ. of Georgia Press.

Ronda, Margaret. 2012. "'Work and Wait Unwearying': Dunbar's Georgics." *PMLA* 127, no. 4: 863–78.

Rosetti, Gina M. 2012. "Turning the Corner: Romance as Economic Critique in Norris's Trilogy of Wheat and Du Bois's *The Quest of the Silver Fleece.*" *Studies in American Naturalism* 7, no. 1: 39–49.

Saunders, Steven. 2012. "The Social Agenda of Stephen Foster's Plantation Melodies." *American Music* 30, no. 3: 275–89.

Silber, Nina. 1993. *The Romance of Reunion: Northerners and the South, 1865–1900.* Chapel Hill: Univ. of North Carolina Press.

Smethurst, James. 2011. *The African American Roots of Modernism: From Reconstruction to the Harlem Renaissance.* Chapel Hill: Univ. of North Carolina Press.

Sundquist, Eric J. 1993. *To Wake the Nations: Race in the Making of American Literature.* Cambridge, MA: Belknap Press of Harvard Univ. Press.

Timrod, Henry. 1872. "Ode." In *The Poems of Henry Timrod*, 209–10. New York: E. J. Hale and Son.

Washington, Booker T. 1904. *Working with the Hands: Being a Sequel to "Up from Slavery" Covering the Author's Experiences in Industrial Training at Tuskegee*. New York: Doubleday, Page, and Company.

Washington, Booker T. (1901) 1996. *Up from Slavery*. New York: Norton.

Weheliye, Alexander G. 2014. *Habeas Viscus: Racializing Assemblages, Biopolitics, and Black Feminist Theories of the Human*. Durham, NC: Duke Univ. Press.

Wienen, Mark Van, and Julie Kraft. 2007. "How the Socialism of W. E. B. Du Bois Still Matters: Black Socialism in *The Quest of the Silver Fleece*—and Beyond." *African American Review* 41, no. 1: 67–85.

Julius B.
Fleming Jr.

Transforming Geographies of Black Time:
How the Free Southern Theater Used
the Plantation for Civil Rights Activism

Abstract This essay examines the cultural and political work of the Free Southern Theater, specifically how this company used plantations, porches, and cotton fields in order to build a radical black southern theater in the civil rights movement. Staging plays like Samuel Beckett's
Waiting for Godot for black southern audiences, the theater challenged a violent structure of
time at the heart of global modernity that I call *black patience*. By this I mean an abiding historical demand for black people to wait: whether in the hold of the slave ship, on the auction block,
or for emancipation from slavery. Focusing on the centrality of the plantation to the spatializing
logics of black patience, I consider how the Free Southern Theater used performance
to demand "freedom now" and to revise the oppressive histories of time rooted in the material
geographies of the US South. Mounting time-conscious plays, the theater used temporal aesthetics to transform the region's historical geographies of black time (e.g., the labor time of
black slaves and sharecroppers working in cotton fields) into radical sites of black political
action, aesthetic innovation, and embodied performance. Engaging and reinvesting the meanings of the South's plantation geographies, the theater revealed how one hundred years after
emancipation, time remained essential to procuring the afterlives of slavery and colonialism and
to shoring up the region's necropolitical attachments. Examining these aesthetic and political
experiments illuminates the importance of time to the emerging field of black geographies and
to the field of black studies more broadly.
Keywords black geographies, performance, US South, afterlives of slavery

In this essay, I examine the historical relationship
between blackness and time and the role of this relation in the making
of slavery and its afterlives. In the broadest sense, my ambition here
is to urge a greater critical attention to time in black studies and social
theory. More specifically, though, this essay is about how time has

American Literature, Volume 91, Number 3, September 2019
DOI 10.1215/00029831-7722140   © 2019 by Duke University Press

operated as a historical weapon of antiblack violence and a charged arena of necropolitical maneuver.[1] Unfurling the historical significance of time to the organizing of a world firmly rooted in antiblackness and white supremacy, it contributes to an area of critical inquiry literary theorist Saidiya Hartman (2007) has called "the afterlives of slavery." On this front, Hartman explains, "If slavery persists as an issue in the political life of black America, it is not because of an antiquarian obsession with bygone days or the burden of a too-long memory, but because black lives are still imperiled and devalued by a racial calculus and a political arithmetic that were entrenched centuries ago. This is the afterlife of slavery—skewed life chances, limited access to health and education, premature death, incarceration, and impoverishment" (6). As Hartman points out, even in the wake of emancipation, descendants of enslaved Africans continue to navigate the ongoing perils of transatlantic slavery and their lingering effects on the nature of black being. Taking these instructive observations as a point of departure, I argue that time is a key variable in the "racial calculus" and "political arithmetic" that generate the afterlives of slavery—the "skewed life chances" of black being.[2] Further, I contend that even as the civil rights movement is widely celebrated for its commitment to the political logic of "freedom now," we have yet to detail thoroughly how this radical time-based political ideology helped to revamp the racial timescapes of US democracy and to shape the aesthetic and political contours of global modernity. Put differently, the staple presence of this refrain has engendered a certain taken-for-grantedness that obscures the degree to which this radical grammar of the present—of the here and now—was pivotal to black people's efforts to exist and imagine otherwise.

In the prologue to his 1967 novel 'Sippi, black writer and activist John Oliver Killens highlights the significance of race and time to the making of slavery and its afterlives. In the novel readers encounter Jesse Chaney, a black Mississippi sharecropper in his late fifties, in the throes of what can seem a curious performance of running. This act certainly puzzles Jesse's longtime "friend," plantation owner, and white employer, Charles Wakefield (Killens 1967: ix). "That black bastard is hauling," Wakefield exclaims. "What in the hell was anybody doing running like that in all this God-forsaken heat[?] . . . Especially a poor-ass Negro? . . . Must be the devil chasing him" (ix). To Wakefield's surprise, Jesse is hardly retreating from the "devil." Rather, his performance of running was sparked by the US Supreme Court's 1954 decision that found segregation in public schools unconstitutional and its provocative mandate for states to comply with "all deliberate speed" (*Brown v. Board of Education* 347 U.S. 483 [1954]).[3] Emboldened by the court's seemingly urgent investment in dismantling the spatial infrastructure of Jim Crowism, Jesse used the black body in performance to translate the court's time-space imperative into a radical act of civil rights protest. Abandoning his work "in the cotton field of . . . Wakefield's plantation," the sharecropper "didn't stop running till he reached the Big House more than a mile and a half away" (Killens 1967: vi). Opting to snub the racial protocol of entering through the back door, Jesse infiltrates the segregated space of the Wakefields' front porch, staging a courageous performance of protest that flouts the doctrines and decrees of racial-spatial segregation while worrying the structures of "racial time" that have historically shaped Mississippi's "plantation geographies" (McKittrick 2013: 4).[4] In other words, by untethering his body from the exploitative labor time of sharecropping, and then utilizing that body to mount a performative enactment of "all deliberate speed," Jesse stakes an embodied claim to a different time-space horizon: one that is both a saying and a doing of "freedom now," staged on the very grounds of a Mississippi plantation.

I begin with Killens's novel because it illuminates how, during the civil rights movement, black people used their bodies to challenge the conventions and constraints of racial time. More specifically, Jesse's performance of running unsettles a structure of racial-temporal violence I call *black patience*. By this I mean a racialized system of waiting that has historically produced and vitalized antiblackness and white supremacy by compelling black people to wait and to capitulate to the racialized terms and assumptions of these forced performances of waiting. Whether in the barracoon or the dungeon of the slave castle, in the hold of the slave ship or atop the auction block, whether waiting for emancipation or being cautioned to "go slow" in the pursuit of full citizenship, black patience was as pivotal to transatlantic slavery and colonialism as it remains to procuring their afterlives in the wake of emancipation.

And yet, black people have historically recast black patience as a tool of black political and ontological possibility. We can glean the significance of these radical rearticulations of black patience in Jesse's performance of standing-in on the segregated porch of the Wakefield plantation house. Like scores of activists in the sit-in movement, Jesse's stand-in highlights the centrality of embodied stillness—a performative mode of black patience—to the choreographies of civil rights activism. Ultimately, this willingness to wait moves within the same economy of protest as Jesse's revolutionary performance of running. It is, in other words, a challenge to black patience qua black patience— a performative attempt to unsettle "the wait" in and through a radical performance of waiting.[5]

To more carefully consider these relationships between blackness and time, movement and stillness, politics and embodied performance, I turn here to the cultural and political work of the Free Southern Theater, a vibrant grassroots theater that emerged from the storied geographies of Mississippi. Founded in 1963, the Free Southern Theater was crucial to the cultural and political fronts of the civil rights movement. As the theater's more well-known and celebrated counterparts were marching, sitting-in, and using other modes of embodied performance to demand "freedom now," the Free Southern Theater was likewise harnessing the power of bodies in performance to contest the structures of racial time invigorating the repeating violence of antiblackness and white supremacy. I argue that they did so in two primary ways. First, the theater's repertoire creatively exposed and critiqued the violent operations of black patience. Second, the materiality of the theater's productions—specifically, its symbolic settings— re-elaborated the violent histories of racial time archived in Mississippi's plantation geographies. From the fields in which black sharecroppers (like Jesse Chaney) worked at exhausting speeds to lynchings and segregation signs that were nothing other than demands for black patience, this assemblage of material relations between blackness and time fueled the economies and ecologies of plantation slavery and remains critical to contemporary schemes to foist the plantation form on black lives lived in the wake of slavery.

Killens's depiction of the Wakefield plantation house captures the lasting effects of slavery's singular violence. When staging his stand-in, Jesse positions his body under one of the four electric ceiling fans that had been installed in the plantation house. According to the narrator, "[e]ven before the Supreme Court decision," Wakefield had come to the conclusion that "it was not slavery time anymore, and you could not expect Negroes to pretend it was and stand around and do your fanning for you" (Killens 1967: viii). In addition to retrofitting the plantation house with modern cooling technologies, Wakefield had also added "all the modern amenities" (viii). In its material configuration, then, the Wakefield plantation house stands as a shining emblem of modern progress. Further, as the narrator notes, Wakefield's wife is an avid reader of "modernistic novels" (x). Still, even in this context of high southern modernity, the very existence of the Wakefield plantation house, the sharecropping economy it supports, and the relations of racial violence it engenders reveal how almost a century after emancipation black life was still endangered by the brutal operations of slavery and its afterlives.

Like Jesse, the Free Southern Theater used embodied performance to articulate a powerful demand for "freedom now" and to revise the racial meanings of the South's plantation geographies. Staging and repurposing plays like Samuel Beckett's *Waiting for Godot* (1954) — often on the back porch of a shack or in a cotton field—the theater's performances firmly critiqued the violent cultures of black patience while inviting black southerners to forge a new temporal relationship to the region's plantation geographies. In the final analysis, my argument is threefold: (1) theater, like photography and television, was a key, if understudied, technology of civil rights activism; (2) the Free Southern Theater's repertoire was keenly attuned to, and intervened in, the global history of blackness and time, and more specifically the racial project of black patience; and (3) the theater's inspired transmutation of Mississippi's plantation geographies into radical sites of performance illuminates time's constitutive role in shaping the afterlives of slavery and thus the importance of time as a conceptual object in the emerging field of black geographies.[6] Focalizing the interconnection of race, time, performance, and geography, my argument therefore builds on Christina Sharpe's idea of "living in the wake." According to Sharpe (2016: 2), to live in the wake is to experience the "still unfolding aftermaths of Atlantic chattel slavery." But it is also to "resist, rupture, and disrupt" the threat of black death the aftermath continues to generate (13). This dynamic process of living in the wake—of navigating the "still unfolding aftermaths" of slavery—is evident in black people's encounters with time in the wake of transatlantic slavery.[7]

Black Time/Black Geography

In 1964, when Free Southern actress Denise Nicholas arrived in Mississippi "alone and scared," she felt as if she had "landed on another planet or stepped back in time" (Holsaert et al. 2010: 259). For Nicholas, Mississippi was an abject geography that existed outside the normative time-space of the modern world. This is likely what Free Southern Theater cofounder Doris Derby had in mind when declaring, "If theatre means anything anywhere, it certainly ought to mean something here [in Mississippi]!" (O'Neal 1968: 71). And there is no doubt that the state registered in this way for black singer and civil rights activist Nina Simone. In her now-classic civil rights anthem "Mississippi Goddam," Simone sings: "Alabama's gotten me so upset / Tennessee made me lose my rest / And everybody knows about Mississippi goddam" (Simone 1964). In Simone's civil rights song, Mississippi emerges as the exceptional site of antiblack violence, what we might call the ur-scene of subjection (see Hartman 1997). Whereas Alabama and Tennessee are villainous geographies that leave Simone restless and "upset," in the final analysis it is Mississippi that assumes the role of accursed titular character, of eponymous star, in Simone's Deep South drama of antiblackness and white supremacy. These designations ultimately lend meaning to the song's title and refrain, "Mississippi, Goddam."

This paradigmatic rendering of Mississippi as a trope of racial violence has pervaded the global imagination. As the civil rights movement developed, the state became a vital element of political discourse and a touchstone in the global geopolitical imagination. Consider, for example, Malcolm X's (1965: 90) claim that the United States should "get Mississippi straightened out before we worry about the Congo." On yet another occasion, the leader argued that Mississippi is "anywhere south of the Canadian border" (Haley 1964: 479).

As Simone's "Mississippi, Goddam" and Malcolm X's remarks suggest, during the civil rights movement Mississippi was a well-trod metaphor and material referent for depicting the scale of antiblack violence plaguing the Jim Crow South and the US nation-state more broadly. In framing Mississippi as the ground zero of antiblack violence, Simone and Malcolm X gesture toward a wider structure of feeling that developed and thrived within the discursive process of producing Mississippi as geographic fact. Rooted in a deep history of racial violence and a powerful set of ideological assumptions, this geography-based feeling has wrought Mississippi into a knowable and commonly known geographic being. As Simone puts it: "everybody knows about Mississippi, goddam." Along these lines, we might usefully rearticulate Frantz Fanon's (1952: 91) now-classic postulation, "Look, a Negro," as "Look, Mississippi." In this revised scene of hailing, fantasies of geographic otherness—and the structures of imaginative geography that produce them—form a compelling analogue for understanding how power and discourse collaborate to engender difference and, in this instance, to render Mississippi an unusually "abjected regional other" (Baker and Nelson 2001: 236).[8] In a word, this convergence of geography and semiotics, of power and epistemology, of repetition and the performative production of geographic being, has imbued Mississippi's material geographies with ontological meaning: a mode of geographic being that epitomizes what it means to be "back in time."

Here the insights of scholars working in the interdisciplinary field of time geography are instructive. As these scholars point out, the lived experience of time and space is crucial to the making of the social world, and it informs possibilities for being human. At the intersections of time and geography, we can glean the importance of time in defining Western conceptions of the human—and orchestrating transatlantic slavery and its afterlives. Zooming in on the temporal dimensions of physical environments, the time-geographic framework foregrounds "the conditions which space, time and environment impose on what the individual can do" (Thrift 1977: 4). For geographer Torsten Hägerstrand, widely credited as the architect of the time-geographic approach, the "life-paths" objects and humans take as they move from one point in space to another influence the experience of social life. But these paths or movements between "stations" are affected by "constraints," which not only impede travel through space but also control and limit one's ability to access stations. On this front, Hägerstrand outlines three categories of constraints: capability, coupling, and authority. Whereas capability constraints emphasize the limits biology might pose (e.g., one needs sleep), coupling constraints acknowledge "where, when, and for how long, the individual has to join other individuals, tools, and materials in order to produce, consume, and transact" (Hägerstrand 1970: 14). And, finally, authority constraints account for those "domains" or "control areas" in which travels through time-space are regulated by law and social custom, for instance. When considered through the valence of black life, each of these restrictions on movement through time-space is always already encumbered by the weight of an authority that finds its muscle in the production and preservation of racial difference and in the social transformation of that difference into uneven distributions of power and capital. When distilled to their most basic social operations, Hägerstrand's categories of constraint for black people are inextricably linked to the proscriptions of racial authority. Taking the constraining capabilities of biology as an example, the possession of black flesh—more than a lack of sleep—is the most limiting biological constraint one encounters while navigating the social fiction of race and the "stations" this biologized fiction creates. To be sure, it would be a grave oversight to disregard how, under modernity's extractive regimes of labor domination, sleep deprivation pressures and strains black lives. But it bears emphasizing that even sleep deprivation, a "capability constraint," is at the same time also an authority constraint—one inseparable from, and indeed attributable to, the fact of blackness and the structures of racial authority that ground that fact in the material geographies of black flesh. We can say, then, that within the racial order of global modernity, black flesh is rendered a constraint that impinges on the time-space experiences and life paths of black people throughout the African diaspora.

In this regard, Mississippi's material geographies serve as an illuminating case study. That is, the state's social, political, and economic conditions have effectively established a prohibitive relationship between black people and Mississippi's plantation geographies.[9] This affiliation between the geographies of black flesh and the material geographies of the US South is what Wakefield hoped to solidify in his hard-edged reminder to Jesse Chaney: "Nigger, don't you know you're in Mississippi?" (Killens 1967: xiii). And it is ultimately what Mississippi writer William Faulkner (1956) hoped to reinforce in warning black southerners to "go slow" (51) and to "wait" (52) in their pursuit of full citizenship.

All this considered, I would argue that Mississippi exists as a geographical instantiation of what performance theorist Robin Bernstein (2011: 11) has called a "scriptive thing." According to Bernstein, material objects often contain a set of culturally specific "invitations" that affect—or script—how individuals relate to a given object. Expanding Bernstein's perceptive observations into the realm of Mississippi's plantation geographies, I want to suggest that under the historical conditions of slavery and its afterlives, Mississippi's physical landscapes have functioned as scriptive things. Conditioned by the state's racialized modes of governmentality and the pillars of antiblackness that support them, Mississippi's material geographies have historically been shaped by the laws and customs of racial-spatial segregation. These structures of spatial division have effectively prescribed relations between the land and those racial subjects who desire and pursue an encounter with the (geographical) object.

These relational dynamics among race, time, and geography were certainly alive when the Free Southern Theater pitched its tent in Mississippi in the thick of the civil rights movement. During a performance at Mississippi's historically black Tougaloo College, these interconnections were apparent to Free Southern Theater actor Robert Costley. As the actor stood on the grounds of the campus—which were also the grounds of the Boddie cotton plantation—he was in awe of a tree rumored to be eight hundred years old. For Costley, the tree conjured up the ghostly presence of black slaves who had once lived on and worked the land under the excruciating rhythms of racial capitalism: "It stood straight and tall while hundreds of slaves bent under the lash. . . . As I stood sheltered by its great arms, in my mind's eye a panorama of days long gone rushed by me and for a few moments I could hear the sound of the lash, the singing and crying of those in bondage." This performance, he notes, was "the best yet" (quoted in Dent, Schechner, and Moses 1969: 81). Moreover, Costley's encounter with the land signals the importance of Mississippi's plantation geographies to the Free Southern Theater's political visions, aesthetic preoccupations, and efforts to unsettle the violent cultures of black patience. It sheds light on the theater's attempt to transform Mississippi into a radical geography of black freedom (Now!).

"They'll Take Drama into the South"

Motivated by a shared commitment to the movement, a mutual passion for theater, and a set of complex investments in the US South, when Doris Derby, Gilbert Moses, and John O'Neal founded the Free Southern Theater they added a new weapon—perhaps an unlikely one—to the arsenal of civil rights activism in Mississippi: black theater. Like scores of college students and recent graduates, they embarked on a risky journey into the belly of the Jim Crow South, lending their time and bodies to the movement.[10] With scarce financial resources and theater accoutrements, in 1963 the founders transformed their dreams of a radical black southern theater into a fledgling but ambitious grassroots company that would eventually become the Free Southern Theater. In addition to drafting a "General Prospectus for the Establishment of a Free Southern Theater," the founders began to recruit participants and to host workshops in the Tougaloo College playhouse (Free Southern Theater Papers, box 6, folder 12). Tougaloo was certainly an auspicious site for the Free Southern Theater to launch its operations. In addition to having a vibrant theater program and a rich legacy of civil rights activism, the college was also a private institution, which allowed it to exist—as one Free Southern Theater playbill put it—"outside the jurisdiction of the state legislature" (Free Southern Theater Papers, "Free Southern Theater Acting Brochure: Interested?" box 33, folder 2). Unlike its public peers, Tougaloo was not funded by the state government in Mississippi and was therefore relatively less vulnerable to the legislature's habit of using its purse to suppress civil rights activism on college campuses.

In 1964 the Free Southern Theater began to solicit participation in its Summer Stock Repertory Theater, announcing calls for actors, dancers, singers, directors, technicians, designers, and "angels" (people with money). On this front, one of the theater's brochures notes: "Checks should be made payable to Theater Project, Tougaloo College. We still need $15,000" (Free Southern Theater Papers, "Free Southern Theater Acting Brochure: Interested?" box 33, folder 2). As the Free Southern Theater negotiated its own fiscal uncertainty, it recognized that black Mississippians' financial resources were often as scarce as their own. Thus, the theater decided as a general practice to forgo fees for admission. The theater knew, too, that these financial realities would impact the nature of their stages and sites of performance. A far cry from the lush theater houses of Broadway, their stages, one brochure announced, would be the "community centers, schools, churches, and fields of rural Mississippi and of the South" (Free Southern Theater Papers, "Free Southern Theater Acting Brochure: Interested?" box 33, folder 2). Though influenced by economic constraints, these performance spaces reflected and embraced the spatial realities of black southern life, while putting these plantation geographies in the service of radical performance. As I argue in this essay, the theater's considered and inventive approach to setting was as seminal to challenging the South's violent cultures of black patience as the radical aesthetics of time at the heart of the theater's repertoire. By examining these relations of theatrical production alongside the Free Southern Theater's temporal aesthetics, we gain a clearer sense of the histories of racial time (e.g., the time of black patience and the labor time of slavery and its afterlives) contained in the shacks, cotton fields, plantations, bombed freedom schools, and many other sites that composed Mississippi's plantation geographies. Transmuting these spaces of black abjection into staging grounds for its radical expressions of "freedom now," the Free Southern Theater used embodied performance to rewrite the histories of racial time archived in the land and to alter the normative time-space of Mississippi's material geographies.

The Free Southern Theater kicked off its pilot project by touring Martin Duberman's award-winning documentary play, *In White America* (1964). While the theater found *In White America* a "funny" choice — likely realizing the irony of inaugurating a black southern theater with a play by a white northern man — a key motivation for its decision was the play's thoughtful engagement with the long history of black patience. In this tenor, Denise Nicholas recalls that *In White America* "was such a profound experience." It enabled the audience to "see today's struggle as an *old* fight, and they recognized that people had been fighting much the same way, all over the country, for a long time: for *all the time*" (Moses et al. 1965: 68; emphasis mine). As Nicholas indicates, *In White America* offered a dramatic critique of black patience, providing theater members with an aesthetic instrument through which they could fashion a regionally specific critique of this global phenomenon, which, in their words, had left black people "suffer[ing] for recognition for three hundred years" (68).

Opening in the thick of the transatlantic slave trade and culminating with the civil rights movement, *In White America*'s vast temporal setting accrues epistemological importance insofar as it produces knowledge about slavery and its afterlives, about the limits of waiting in a world where the repetition of antiblack violence constantly subtends the flows of historical time. Therefore, the play's temporal setting exemplifies the transhistorical character of black patience, or the long history of black people waiting in white America. On this front, the opening scene is telling. Set on January 12, 1964, the action begins when one of two characters named White Man retrieves a newspaper from a table. Reading the date aloud, White Man proclaims: "If God had intended the races to mix, he would have mixed them himself" (Duberman 1964: 2). In the wake of this provocative but all-too-familiar claim, other characters begin to chime in. A vital dimension of the dialogue that ensues pivots around the violent cultures of black patience. For instance, according to the other character named White Man, "Negro impatience can be readily understood." Just moments later, Negro Man adds: "After 400 years of barbaric treatment, the American Negro is fed up with the unmitigated hypocrisy of the white man" (4). When the curtain opens on *In White America*, then, audiences are faced with the dilemma of black patience and its origins in transatlantic slavery.

In this vein, the play makes an analeptic leap from 1964 to the transatlantic slave trade. Duberman culls this early segment of the script from the notes of a doctor who worked aboard a slave ship in the 1700s. Describing the interval prior to leaving the coast of Guinea to start "the middle passage," the doctor explains:

The slave ships lie a mile below the town, in Bonny River, off the coast of Guinea. . . . Scarce a day passes without some negroes being purchased and carried on board. . . . The wretched negroes are immediately fastened together, two and two, by handcuffs on their wrists and by irons riveted on their legs. They are then sent down between the decks and placed in a space partitioned off for that purpose. They are frequently stowed so close as to admit of no other position than lying on their sides. Nor will the height between decks allow them to stand. (5)

The doctor's observations highlight the centrality of time and space to the making of transatlantic slavery. At the same time, they underscore the significance of the slave trade to the racialized production of time and space. In other words, during this inceptive phase of global modernity, the transatlantic slave trade persisted as a horrific venture in organizing black bodies' relationships to time and space and rooting that association in the time-space logics of black patience.

As *In White America* makes clear, the hold of the slave ship was critical to establishing and codifying these relations. With hands and legs fettered by irons and cuffs, in the hold of the slave ship newly enslaved Africans were being primed to wait and suffer the restrictive spatialities that would come to characterize black people's experiences in the New World, whether in slave cabins or legally segregated schools. Moreover, that the doctor uses the diurnal cycle ("scarce a day passes") to relate these conditions of suffering underscores the everyday nature of the slave trade's extravagant violence, while gesturing toward a movement of natural time counterpoised to the slave's compulsion to remain still in the hold of the ship. In this way, the "relentless rhythm of the slave ships," much like the rhythms of time, stood in sharp contradistinction to the slave's compulsory stasis (Smallwood 2007: 7). These time-space conditions—that is, the forced stillness of black bodies within environments of rapid motion—inaugurated a paradigmatic relationship among black bodies, time, and space within the context of global modernity: a relationship that continues to thrive in the wake of slavery.

While *In White America* opens with images of black bodies waiting in the hold of the slave ship, it goes on to chronicle black people's centuries-long wait for emancipation and the entitlements of full US citizenship. Along these lines, in the play's final moments, audiences encounter a young black girl being taunted by a recalcitrant white mob, whose members avow with sharp venom: "No nigger bitch is going to get in our school. Drag her over to this tree! Let's take care of the nigger" (Duberman 1964: 66). The girl's offense: like Jesse Chaney, the Free Southern Theater, and scores of civil rights activists, she dared to take seriously the US Supreme Court's (prima facie) directive to alter the prevailing racial order of the US nation-state and to do so with "all deliberate speed."

Considered together, these scenes index the long history of black patience and highlight time's constitutive role in the making of transatlantic slavery and its afterlives. As the play reveals, one dimension of black patience entails the historical use of "the wait" as a mechanism for deferring and denying black freedom. Such oppressive manipulations of time are accompanied, nonetheless, by a powerful set of affective protocols that aim, in the final analysis, to produce "docile" black bodies.[11] Black patience is, then, not only about the wait, or deferral, or time, even. It is grounded also in a violent affective logic that strives to discipline black bodies through the strategic management of black affective expression. The *Oxford English Dictionary* defines *patience* as a mode of "calm, self-possessed waiting," an "uncomplaining endurance of pain."[12] Situated at this intersection of time and affect, black patience is invested in coercing black bodies to wait but is, at the same time, concerned with the affective tenor of the wait and the implications of black people's refusal to wait. To this end, the mob's tempestuous outrage for the black girl stems not only from her refusal to wait but also from the mob's perception of this refusal as a sign of black impudence and, therefore, an affective affront to the violent impositions of black patience.

As *In White America* shows through its depictions of "negro impatience," during the civil rights movement black people were becoming increasingly averse to waiting. Armed with centuries of evidence that the deceptive logics of black patience—and its tactical uses of the future—ultimately fuel antiblackness and white supremacy, Negro Man and Negro Woman close the play with a vision of black life unencumbered by the strictures of black patience:

NEGRO WOMAN: We can't wait any longer.
NEGRO MAN: *Now* is the time. (Duberman 1964: 68–69)

Rescripting Mississippi's Plantation Geographies

If the founders of the Free Southern Theater worked to invent aesthetic forms rooted in black southern culture, their settings were equally grounded in the South's physical geographies and built environments and thus in the configurations of racial power these spatialities signified and reinforced. This was certainly true for the company's 1964 performances of *In White America*. Throughout the opening season, productions were generally "simple—with a few lights and one platform" (Dent, Schechner, and Moses 1969: 17). And because the theater often used outdoor, afternoon settings, even these lights were sometimes unnecessary. This was the case at a Holmes County, Mississippi, performance, where audience members had come "from the farms" to attend a production of *In White America* but wanted to "get back home by dark" (63).

Such vibrant synergies between performance and geography, theater and environment, were also apparent at a lively production of *In White America* in the small town of Ruleville, Mississippi. The stage for this performance was the back porch of a shack, a space that surely resonated with the theater's largely poor black southern audiences. Conjuring up memories of the slave cabin and signifying the stark economic inequalities black southerners have historically faced, the porch of a shack might seem an unlikely and even undesirable site of performance. But in reinvesting this historical spatiality, the Free Southern Theater creatively wove the architecture of black southern life into the setting of the live performance. In the US South, moreover, porches have historically functioned as a valuable arena for black cultural production and communal formation. In addition to serving as "stages for interactive storytelling" (Harris 1996: xii) or a "gallery seat" (Hurston 1979: 49) for watching the goings-on of a town, porches have also been critical to developing an "alert political community" (Davis 2011: 81), an outcome that was pivotal to the Free Southern Theater's founding vision. Seen from this vantage point, the back porch is something more than a makeshift stage. It exceeds the results of any calculus that would constrain its being to a material sign for black deprivation. In transforming the back porch of a shack into a radical site of performance, of black political participation and community engagement, the Free Southern Theater converted this historical site of inequality into a generative space of "radical openness" (hooks 1990: 145).[13] Thus, even as the porch continued to conjure up the specters of plantation slavery and to embody capitalism's uneven and racialized distribution of wealth, the social meanings and the ontology of the porch were transformed in the act of live performance, affording the porch, the shack, and black southern audiences alike another way of being in the world and of relating to Mississippi's traumatic plantation geographies.

If the stage for this performance was unconventional, the seating was as improvisational and attuned to the material geographies of the US South. In fact, audience members not only sat on cots, benches, and folding chairs but some even watched the production while sitting on the ground. Here I want to linger for a moment on this seemingly benign but supremely evocative performance of *sitting on the ground.* To sit on the ground in this instance—whether sitting on a bench, a cot, or directly on the land—is to stage a haptic encounter between black southern bodies and southern land, to gather the signs and histories of these material geographies into an important relational proximity, one that disturbs the historically violent relationship between black-south bodies and Mississippi's plantation geographies.[14]

According to philosopher Bruno Latour (1993: 82), "History is no longer simply the history of people, it becomes the history of natural things as well." Extending Latour's thinking to Mississippi's plantation geographies, I am interested in the histories of antiblack violence and, more specifically, the histories of racial time enfolded in the material geographies of the US South. Here I want to zoom in on a key dimension of this particular history of the natural thing, one that exposes the role of race and time in that historicity: that is, the laboring black body within the South's plantation economy.

Under the brutal conditions of slavery, sharecropping, the chain gang, and other racialized regimes of labor domination, the black-south body has consistently been forced to work quickly—to move to the crushing clock of racial capitalism. Theorizing what he calls "clock-regulated slave labor," historian Mark M. Smith (1997: 2) explains that the clock became "the planters' weapon of choice in their ongoing battle with their chattel" (5). In this sense, clock time operates as a modern "weapon" of antiblack violence; it hardens the master-slave binary while fortifying the dynamics of racial power that define this relation. When seen from this perspective, "all deliberate speed" is better regarded as a guiding principle of black labor exploitation than juridical liberal-democratic intervention into the United States' racialized politics of time and space. What I am suggesting is that Mississippi's material geographies are key repositories for racialized histories of time and the lived experiences of black-south bodies that have been forced to work and move to the extractive rhythms of racial capitalism—to the tempos of slavery and its afterlives. Therefore, we might amend Latour's claim to emphasize how in the context of plantation slavery the history of people is always a history of natural things, and the history of natural things is always a history of people.

And yet, it is my contention that the act of sitting on the ground during the Free Southern Theater's performances unsettled these historical entanglements of race, time, and geography. In this suggestive convergence of dark matter—of dark southern soil and black southern flesh—the subject who sits on the ground rubs up against and revamps the racial histories of time archived in Mississippi's plantation geographies.[15] To put a finer point on this claim, though occupying grounds beleaguered by oppressive histories of racial time, the moment of live performance enabled black southern audiences to inhabit and enjoy what I term the *time of black leisure*.

Considered alongside histories of slavery and colonialism and their substantive constraints on possibilities for black leisure, the willful act of sitting on the ground to experience a play is a meaningful and politically significant form of leisure that troubles and recasts the racial project of black patience.[16] In this moment of live performance, the audience suspends labor, body, and reality to linger in the theater's imaginative flights. Like the performance of sitting-in at a lunch counter, sitting on the ground was a radical reinterpretation of black patience. This exercise in waiting and deferral creatively reinvested the wait. In a labor economy that overrepresented black Mississippians in jobs that required long hours and physically exhausting work (like sharecropping), time was a valuable resource. Thus, attending a Free Southern Theater performance meant that laundry was deferred. Cooking had to wait. Managing the garden was delayed. Unsettling the historical aversion to black bodies in leisure, audiences staged an embodied intervention into the time-space of the South's plantation geographies, the clock time of racial capitalism, and the repeating temporalities of slavery and its afterlives. Black southerners' attendance at these performances, then, were willful uses of black time.

According to Walter D. Mignolo (2002: 67), since the Renaissance "time has functioned as a principle of order that increasingly subordinates places, relegating them to before or below from the perspective of the holders of time." I would add that time likewise subordinates people. The designation "holders of time," then, names a historical contingent of power holders that routinely manipulate time as a way of dominating places and people, landscapes and flesh. For these "holders of time"—Wakefield and Faulkner among them—time operates as a resource of social power and, in this instance, impacts racial formation and the structures of racial power this process engenders. However, in sitting on the ground for the theater's performances, black southern audiences managed to become "holders of time."

To be sure, the performance of black leisure does not wholly disassemble the violent infrastructure of racial time or the sturdy mechanisms of antiblackness. On this front, we might recall the Holmes County, Mississippi, performance where the audience expressed desires to "get back home by dark." For many of them, this wish to return home before "dark" was likely rooted in having to begin the taxing work of sharecropping early the next morning or, worse, in being conscious of the imminent threats of racial violence that routinely surfaced in the dark. This threat was heightened on the heels of attending the Free Southern Theater's performances. Thus, in the hours following *In White America*, the grounds of black leisure would soon become a theater of black labor exploitation and quite possibly a stage for murder.

Acknowledging this connection between black death and Mississippi's plantation geographies, noted civil rights activist, sharecropper, and Free Southern Theater audience member Fannie Lou Hamer (2011: 58) dubbed Sunflower County "the land of the tree and the home of the grave." As the Free Southern Theater would learn, Hamer's adage was as true for other regions in Mississippi as it was for Ruleville or any other town in Sunflower County. The theater gained a clearer sense of this stark reality when civil rights activists James Chaney, Andrew Goodman, and Michael Schwerner were murdered and found buried ("home of the grave") near a Mississippi dam. Not only did the theater cancel its performance on August 7, 1964, to observe the slain activists, but it added a section to its production of *In White America* that wove these murders into the plot. Following a performance in Beulah, Mississippi, the company was again reminded of the dangers animating Mississippi's plantation geographies. Here an interracial coterie of Free Southern Theater actors was forced to the local police station and bombarded with questions like: "What are you doing down here, Pretty Boy?"; "How is that black pussy?"; and "How does it feel to screw a white woman?" Finally releasing the group at approximately 2 a.m., the police alerted the Ku Klux Klan that "two nigger lovers and a nigger were loose"—"so pick them up for us." For three hours, the actors endured "abject terror," crawling along country roads, hiding in weeds, dodging the beams of the Ku Klux Klan's flashlights (Dent, Schechner, and Moses 1969: 86). Like hundreds of other activists who put their bodies on the line for the movement, these actors endured violence, terror, and imprisonment for performing in the drama of civil rights activism. Their stages and performances, however, are practically invisible in conventional histories and memories of the movement. By some act of fate, the actors managed to elude physical harm, though not without a visceral reminder of the dangers haunting the plantation geographies the Free Southern Theater had chosen as a site of performance and a radical stage of civil rights activism.

When the theater staged *In White America* in Milestone, Mississippi, the community center hosting the production was missing its walls, and the stage stretched out into a cotton field. Like the porch, fields were a staple site of performance for the theater. This was especially the case for its productions of Ossie Davis's 1961 satiric comedy, *Purlie Victorious*. Like *In White America*, *Purlie*'s temporal and spatial settings are key to understanding the transhistorical workings of black patience, the time-space of geographical matter, and their relationships to the afterlives of slavery. The place, the script notes, is the "cotton plantation country of the *Old South*," while the time is "the *recent past.*" Further, most of the action takes place within "an *antiquated*, run-down farmhouse," while stage props like "an old dresser" likewise evoke and create a setting in which the past lingers (Davis 1961: 5; emphasis mine). As the plot develops, the temporal setting "recent past" comes to highlight the proximities between slavery and its afterlives nearly a century after emancipation.

The first actor whom the audience meets is the eponymous protagonist, Purlie Judson, who later renames himself Purlie Victorious. "Tall, *restless*, and commanding," Purlie is "consumed with . . . *divine impatience*" (5–6; emphasis mine), a relationship to racial time that recalls the "Negro impatience" at the center of *In White America* (Duberman 1964: 4). Davis's stage directions, then, attach to Purlie's character an aversion to waiting, signaling his staunch resistance to the violent enclosures of black patience. Set in fictional Cotchipee County in the "cotton plantation country" of Georgia, *Purlie Victorious* bears a striking resemblance to Killens's *'Sippi*. In both works, the plantation form continues to structure society in the wake of plantation slavery. Moreover, both works spotlight sharecropping as an especially brutal form of slavery's afterlives. Whereas Charles Wakefield was the boss of Wakefield County in *'Sippi*, in Davis's play Ol' Cap'n Cotchipee is similarly the master of Cotchipee County. "You see that big white house, perched on top that hill with them two windows looking right down at us like two eyeballs?" Purlie asks. "That's where Ol' Cap'n lives." "And that ain't all," he continues. "Hill and dale, field and farm, truck and tractor, horse and mule, bird and bee and bush and tree—and cotton!—cotton by bole and by bale—every bit o' cotton you see in this county!—Everything and everybody he owns!" (Davis 1961: 9). That nearly the entirety of Cotchipee County's material geographies is owned and controlled by one man is striking. Even more shocking is Purlie's claim that Cotchipee owns "everybody." During a postslavery moment in which trafficking in human bodies was outlawed, such a statement might seem hyperbolic. But one cannot ignore the ruses of power and the tricky calculus that kept scores of black sharecroppers indebted to landlords, and thus confined to peonage, well into the middle of the twentieth century. As Purlie so aptly puts it: "The longer you work . . . the more you owe at the commissary; and if you don't pay up, you can't leave" (8–9). These conditions of entrapment worry any neat division between slavery and freedom. And they illuminate how such violent suspensions of black people in time and space ("the longer you work . . . you can't leave") endure across the time-space of modernity to (re)produce the South's plantation geographies.

So grim and heavy were these conditions, they prompted Purlie's decision to migrate from Georgia twenty years prior. However, the lure of reclaiming Big Bethel—a historical black church that was pilfered by Ol' Cap'n Cotchipee—inspired his return. On the heels of Purlie's failure to recover Big Bethel, Charlie, Ol' Cap'n Cotchipee's liberal-leaning son and civil rights sympathizer, registers the deed to Big Bethel in the name Purlie Victorious Judson. Disrupting the patrilineal lines of inheritance that nourish the afterlives of slavery, Charlie's act of betrayal dealt a lethal blow to his father. On the one hand, Cotchipee's death could signal a vanishing of the South's plantation geographies; an incipient dismantling of the "big white house" and the plantation society it represented and struggled to preserve. According to Purlie's brother, Gitlow, however, Ol' Cap'n Cotchipee was "the first man [he] ever seen in all this world to drop dead standing up" (80). That Cotchipee dies while standing up hints at the possibility of a resurrection—the prospect of a renewal that would breathe new life into the South's plantation geographies and thus into the afterlives of slavery.

With its fusion of political awareness, black sermonic aesthetics, slapstick comedy, gospel music, and a setting that was intimately familiar for black southerners, *Purlie Victorious* was a hit among Free Southern Theater audiences. In the words of Gilbert Moses, *Purlie* "laid the audience in the aisles with laughter" (Dent, Schechner, and Moses 1969: 52–53). As was often the case, the Free Southern Theater found itself performing *Purlie* outdoors in makeshift theaters. This decision was sometimes not by choice but made out of necessity when the original site of performance was eviscerated by violent acts of white terror. These acts were nothing less than savage demands for black patience. In a 1964 letter to its New York fundraising committee, the Free Southern Theater writes of one such instance:

Last month in Indianola we gave an outside performance of PURLIE VICTORIOUS. We set up our playing area on a field next to the Indianola Freedom School which had recently been condemned by city officials due to a fire which had "mysteriously" broken out in the building. COFO workers say that firemen watched the building burn, and that after finally deciding to put the fire out, they destroyed a lot of equipment in the building with water hoses and axes. (55)

This mysterious destruction of the freedom school creates another scenario in which material spaces, like the cotton field and the shack, help to reinforce and sustain the afterlives of slavery. The destruction and subsequent condemning of this freedom school–cum–radical site of performance was a material injunction for black people to wait—a vicious reminder for them to adhere to the violent protocols of black patience.

Still, the Free Southern Theater transformed this scene of racial terror into a site of empowering, comedic performance. In its letter to the fundraising committee, the theater notes that the outdoor setting was "especially appropriate for the character Gitlow who . . . literally ran on stage from the cotton field spewing cotton from his pockets" (55). Recalling this particular performance, Denise Nicholas (2010: 263) writes: "In one town we performed the play right next to a cotton field. There's a scene where a character comes running through the rows of cotton pitching cotton bolls into the air. It was real cotton." She goes on to note that the theater, and "Purlie in particular, allowed for another way of venting—through comedy—and people loved it. They laughed and laughed." Not only does this performance revamp the meaning of the cotton field by challenging the "exchange-value/ use-value binary" (McInnis 2016: 74). But this access to laughter and political awareness afforded by sitting on the ground rubbed up against and unsettled the exploitative histories of black time etched into the cotton fields and cotton bolls that served as stage and prop for the theater's performances.[17] Recalling civil rights protests that used embodied performance to revamp the meanings of buses, segregated lunch counters, streets, and other dimensions of the South's plantation geographies, the Free Southern Theater's performances posed a similar challenge to the region's orthodox conceptions of how black people could relate to the South's plantation geographies. Like these more celebrated and carefully documented geographies of civil rights activism, the theater's performances imbued Mississippi's plantations, cotton fields, porches, and shacks with new meaning and radical possibility. Further, as the theater used performance to demand freedom now, its audiences' own acts of sitting on the ground transformed the wait into an instrument of black leisure and black political possibility, thereby redirecting normative relationships between black bodies and the time-space of Mississippi's plantation geographies. These efforts mark a creative intervention into the violent cultures of black patience while, at the same time, showing how such radical rearticulations of black patience have been central to the grammars of black political protest. This is the making of revolution. It is a sitting, a laughing, and a practice of *communitas* that move over and against modernity's historical regulation of black leisure—and more broadly of black time.

"They Are Waiting for Godot in Mississippi, Too"

As I move toward closing this essay, I want to pivot to what was perhaps the Free Southern Theater's most explicit engagement with black patience: its production of Samuel Beckett's 1954 classic, *Waiting for Godot*. The time-conscious dynamics of Beckett's plot accorded with and underscored the game of waiting for full citizenship black southerners had been playing for more than a century. As many of us will remember, the central conceit of *Waiting for Godot* is that Vladimir and Estragon, Beckett's two campy protagonists, are trapped in a cycle of waiting for the arrival of one Godot:

> ESTRAGON: He should be here.
> VLADIMIR: He didn't say for sure he'd come.
> ESTRAGON: We'll come back tomorrow.
> VLADIMIR: And then the day after tomorrow.
> ESTRAGON: Possibly.
> VLADIMIR: And so on. (Beckett 1954: 6)

Interestingly, the duo is anticipating the arrival of a person who has made no promises to come. But even in the face of their uncertainties about his impending arrival, they agree to return "tomorrow . . . [a]nd then the day after tomorrow . . . [a]nd so on," entering a seemingly interminable cycle of patience that holds no guarantees for Godot's arrival.

The Free Southern Theater's production of Beckett's *Waiting for Godot* baffled and even bored some of the theater's audiences. Penny Hartzell, a Free Southern Theater actor, notes in her journal that *Godot* "mystified, amused, bored, [and] shocked" many of those who experienced the play (Dent, Schechner, and Moses 1969: 53). In fact, some audience members registered their dissatisfaction by walking out before the play ended. And at a performance in Greenville, Mississippi, a group of children even threw spitballs at the stage. Paying attention to these disapproving acts of audience reception illuminates how the practice of reinvesting black patience through sitting on the ground did not unfold without nuance and complexity. Whether leaving a performance early or throwing spitballs at the stage, these responses index how audiences sometimes grew impatient with the Free Southern Theater's critiques of black patience. Further, this willful decision to use one's time as one wishes is as much a temporal claim of authority over the self as an act of sitting on the ground to enjoy a Free Southern Theater performance and the time of black leisure.

For many members of the theater's black southern audiences, Estragon and Vladimir's fruitless patience symbolized how the US nation-state manipulated time to defer black people's access to full citizenship. The play's larger themes of waiting, violence, and power were certainly not lost on Fannie Lou Hamer. At a 1964 Ruleville performance of *Godot*, Hamer (2011: 53) exclaimed: "You can't sit around waiting. . . . Ain't nobody going to bring you nothing. You got to get up and fight for what you want. Some people are sitting around waiting for somebody to bring in freedom just like these men [Vladimir and Estragon] are sitting here. Waiting for Godot." Echoing these sentiments in a talk that followed on the heels of this performance, Hamer urged the nearly all-black audience to "pay strict attention to the play because it's due to waiting that the Negro is as far behind as he is" (53). This forceful rejection of black patience accords with Vladimir's call to action in the play's final moments: "Let us not waste our time in idle discourse! [*Pause. Vehemently.*] Let us do something, while we have the chance! . . . Let us make the most of it, before it is too late!" (Beckett 1954: 70).

As this essay has demonstrated, the temporal aesthetics of plays like Beckett's *Waiting for Godot* exposed and critiqued the project of black patience. At the same time, this essay has demonstrated how the Free Southern Theater was engaged in a radical new materialist project, namely, its relations of theatrical production, and more specifically, its innovative use of setting. If, as new materialist thinking has posited, matter "matters," Mississippi's plantation geographies are forms of geographic matter that have historically been as open to processes of racialization and performativity as human identity itself (Ahmed 2010: 234). Thus, in making the back porches of shacks, cotton fields, and former plantations some of its primary sites of performance, the Free Southern Theater embraced performance geographies that were teeming with histories of antiblack violence. The theater adopted stages chock-full of ontological meaning. It planted roots in grounds that had long "scripted" the ways black people could inhabit these restrictive spatialities. Time, as we have seen, is vital to producing and preserving these racially uneven geographies.

As Vladimir and Estragon ponder whether Godot actually intends to come, Vladimir begins to "look wildly about him, as though the date was inscribed in the landscape" (Beckett 1954: 7). In this gesture of "looking" at the landscape, Vladimir searches, in effect, for a history of time in the land. Such a performance of looking for time in the grounds of Mississippi's plantation geographies reveals histories of blackness and time that are firmly rooted in the violences of plantation slavery and its afterlives. It illuminates black southern futures that are as uncertain and precarious as the futures of Beckett's protagonists. It would illuminate how the conventional "holders of time" have historically forced black people—whether slaves, sharecroppers, or members of the chain gang—to work southern geographies with "all deliberate speed," while being ordered to go slow in their historical fights for full citizenship. This temporal paradox between the quick time of black labor and the slow time of black freedom was a driving force of slavery and continues to shape the racial order of the modern world. The Free Southern Theater's critique of black patience and its radical engagements with the histories of black time stored in Mississippi's plantation geographies were pivotal to the civil rights movement's campaigns to curate new materialisms, to engender new political possibilities, and to cultivate new modes of sociality that were grounded in the revolutionary demand for "freedom now." Using theater to unsettle the racial project of black patience, the Free Southern Theater altered the violent enclosures of racial time that continue to energize the still-unfolding aftermath of slavery in the postemancipation and postcolonial presents.

Postscript: Toward a Theory of Afropresentism

In mounting exhilarating, sometimes confusing, but always community-centered performances, the Free Southern Theater furnished a cultural conduit through which black southerners could challenge the historical regime of black patience and inhabit a radical structure of black time I want to term *Afropresentism*. By this I mean a political, affective, and philosophical orientation toward enjoying and demanding the "good life" in the here and now, in the present. As the performances in this essay have demonstrated, rather than capitulating to the violent impositions of black patience, black people have routinely engineered a range of creative strategies to enjoy the affordances of the good life by unlocking the latent possibilities of the here and now. Excavating the radical potential of the present, these engagements with, and experiences in, the Afropresent both critique and refuse the West's wily attempts to quarantine black people's access to the good life to an always arriving, and often unarrivable, black future. Seen from this vantage point, Afrofuturism is less a future-oriented practice of black freedom and self-making and more a tactical form of delay and a racialized experiment in duration. As I have tried to show, white supremacy has routinely claimed the future as a wheelhouse for manufacturing deceptive tools of delay that ultimately advance the cause of white supremacy.

Recent scholarship in Afropessimist thought has emphasized these transhistorical continuities of racial violence and has mapped their lasting impact on black being and on the structural conditions of the modern world. As the examples in this essay demonstrate, far from a cure-all for the violences of black patience, or antiblackness more generally, Afropresentism is instead about seizing and enjoying the good life in the here and now, knowing that in the context of antiblackness the future is always a zone of precarity, as Afropessimist thinking reminds us. And yet, access to a different way of being in the world—however fleeting—puts pressure on prescriptions for black racial being that take teleology's force of finality, or white supremacy's violence, as their chief grounds of critical imagination.

In the physical act of sitting on the ground, these relational tensions among black pasts, black presents, and black futures are dramatized in and through the black body's communion with the land and the differential histories of time—the time of slavery and racial capitalism, the time of black leisure and black aesthetics, the time of black political discourse—this communing assembles and allows. In other words, when black southern audiences sat on the ground to experience the Free Southern Theater's performances, the exploitative quick time of black labor stored in the geographies of southern land and black-south bodies converged with the time of black patience, black leisure, and the play's radical temporal aesthetics to create a multilayered assemblage of time. This fraught palimpsest of black time exposes how any line of flight made possible in the Afropresent always unfolds in relation to the racial traumas of the past and the precarities of black futures. Thus, far from a flight from history, or a pessimistic rejection of the future, or a naive celebration of the present, Afropresentism is instead a heightened attunement to black possibility in the here and now, knowing that in the face of antiblackness the enjoyment of these possibilities will likely be as fleeting and ephemeral as the Free Southern Theater's live performances or, more broadly, the very ontology of performance itself.[18] What to Afropessimism is the moment of the present?

Julius B. Fleming Jr. is an assistant professor of English at the University of Maryland, College Park. Specializing in African diasporic literatures and cultures, he has particular interests in performance studies, black political culture, decolonial theory, and diaspora—especially where they intersect with race, gender, and sexuality. Julius is currently completing his first book manuscript, tentatively titled "Black Patience: Performance and the Civil Rights Movement." His work appears in *Callaloo*, *American Literary History*, *Text and Performance Quarterly*, *College Literature*, the *James Baldwin Review*, and the *Southern Quarterly* and has been supported by the Mellon Foundation, the Woodrow Wilson Foundation, and the Carter G. Woodson Institute for African American and African Studies at the University of Virginia.

Notes

1   Achille Mbembe (2003: 39) calls into question the ancillary position that theories of biopower assign to death. Centering death in his analysis, Mbembe proposes a model of necropolitics to theorize the ways in which sovereignty is deployed toward the goal of destroying certain members of society.

2   Whereas black studies and social theory take space as key critical concerns, this article aims to make time more central to these discourses. It contributes to a burgeoning field I have called elsewhere "black time studies" (Fleming 2019).

3   Legal scholar Charles Ogletree (2004: 299) notes that when civil rights lawyers consulted the dictionary to uncover the meaning of "all deliberate speed," they concluded that the court's phrase meant "slow."

4   I borrow the term "racial time" from political scientist Michael Hanchard (1999: 252). According to Hanchard racial time is "the inequalities of temporality that result from power relations between racially dominant and subordinate groups" (253).

5   I borrow the concept of "the wait" from performance studies scholar Harvey Young (2010: 42–43). Young is likewise interested in how the process of waiting animates the various segments of the transatlantic slave trade and black life more broadly.

6   The field of black geographies has begun to emphasize the role of black racial identity in the production of space and geography. See, for example, Davis 2011; McKittrick 2006; Shabazz 2015; and McKittrick and Woods 2007.

7   On this front, if we return to the context of postemancipation Mississippi, it was not by accident that sharecropping's corrupt manipulations of black labor time both mirrored and replaced the cruel regime of black labor that had been the motor of Atlantic chattel slavery, creating what historian Douglas A. Blackmon (2008) calls "slavery by another name."

8   Constructions of the South as a distinctively problematic region are often an exercise in "imaginative geography"—that is, a practice of "designating in one's mind a familiar space which is 'ours' and an unfamiliar space beyond 'ours' which is 'theirs'" (Said 1978: 54–55).

9   As Thadious M. Davis (2011: 2–4) has argued, even as the South has, in many ways, been a closed society for people of African descent, black southerners have nonetheless managed to use the very space of the US South to curate empowering forms of being, creativity, and sociality.

10   While Derby and O'Neal worked as field secretaries for the Student Nonviolent Coordinating Committee, Moses was a writer for the *Mississippi Free Press*, a weekly civil rights newspaper.

11   I borrow the concept of docile bodies from Michel Foucault (1977: 136), who captures how modernity uses discipline as a means to subject bodies to "constraints, prohibitions, and obligations" that render them docile— or in the "grip of very strict powers."

12   *Oxford English Dictionary Online*, s.v. "patience," www.oed.com/view /Entry/138816?rskey=gefoWY&result=1&isAdvanced=false#eid (accessed May 12, 2018).

13   According to bell hooks (1990), sites of "radical openness" are spaces that enable an opportunity to "redeem and reclaim the past, legacies of pain, suffering, and triumph in ways that transform present reality" (147).

14 I borrow the term "black-south body" from literary critic Houston A. Baker Jr. (2001: 81).
15 According to theater historian Bruce McConachie (1992: 169), theater history has routinely privileged the "means" over the "relations" of theatrical production, engendering a critical tendency to "separate the aesthetic from the practical." Further, in tracing the etymology of theatrical production to discourses surrounding political economy in the eighteenth century, namely, to Adam Smith's *The Wealth of Nations* (1776), McConachie draws a striking connection between the linguistic genealogy of theatrical production and global genealogies of industrial capitalism. This relation is certainly apparent when plantation geographies are transformed into sites of black theatrical performance.
16 As scholarship on race and leisure has demonstrated, slaves were given limited amounts of time for black leisure. But this time was often filled with personal chores like gardening and washing and was often under surveillance. See, for example, Holland 2002. Also, scholars like Hartman (1997) remind us that leisure itself has often been a site of antiblack violence.
17 For concepts of "black time" and "white time," see Warren 2016 and Mills 2014, respectively.
18 The very nature of performance has been a point of serious discussion throughout performance studies discourses. See, for example, Taylor 2003 and Phelan 1993.

References

Ahmed, Sara. 2010. "Orientation Matters." In *New Materialisms: Ontology, Agency, and Politics*, edited by Diana Coole and Samantha Frost, 234–57. Durham, NC: Duke Univ. Press.

Baker, Houston A., Jr. 2001. *Turning South Again: Re-Thinking Modernism / Re-Reading Booker T.* Durham, NC: Duke Univ. Press.

Baker, Houston A., Jr., and Dana D. Nelson. 2001. "Preface: Violence, the Body, and 'The South.'" *American Literature* 73, no. 2: 231–44.

Beckett, Samuel. 1954. *Waiting for Godot*. New York: Grove Press.

Bernstein, Robin. 2011. *Racial Innocence: Performing American Childhood from Slavery to Civil Rights*. New York: New York Univ. Press.

Blackmon, Douglas A. 2008. *Slavery by Another Name: The Re-Enslavement of Black Americans from the Civil War to World War II*. New York: Random House.

Davis, Ossie. 1961. *Purlie Victorious*. New York: Samuel French.

Davis, Thadious M. 2011. *Southscapes: Geographies of Race, Region, and Literature*. Chapel Hill: Univ. of North Carolina Press.

Dent, Thomas C., Richard Schechner, and Gilbert Moses, eds. 1969. *The Free Southern Theater by the Free Southern Theater: A Documentary of the South's Radical Black Theater, with Journals, Letters, Poetry, Essays, and a Play Written by Those Who Built It.* New York: Bobbs-Merrill.

Duberman, Martin B. 1964. *In White America: A Documentary Play.* Boston: Houghton Mifflin.

Fanon, Frantz. 1952. *Black Skin, White Masks.* New York: Grove.

Faulkner, William. 1956. "A Letter to the North." *Life,* March 5: 51–52.

Fleming, Julius B., Jr. 2019. "Sound, Aesthetics, and Black Time Studies." *College Literature* 46, no. 1: 281–88.

Foucault, Michel. 1977. *Discipline and Punish: The Birth of the Prison.* New York: Vintage.

Free Southern Theater Papers. 1960–1978. Amistad Research Center, Tulane University, New Orleans.

Hägerstrand, Torsten. 1970. "What about People in Regional Science?" *Papers in Regional Science* 24, no. 1: 7–24.

Haley, Alex. 1964. *The Autobiography of Malcolm X.* New York: Ballantine.

Hamer, Fannie L. (1964) 2011. "I'm Sick and Tired of Being Sick and Tired." In *The Speeches of Fannie Lou Hamer: To Tell It like It Is,* edited by Maegan Parker Brooks and Davis W. Houck, 57–64. Jackson: Univ. Press of Mississippi.

Hanchard, Michael. 1999. "Afro-Modernity: Temporality, Politics, and the African Diaspora." *Public Culture* 10, no. 2: 245–67.

Harris, Trudier. 1996. *The Power of the Porch: The Storyteller's Craft in Zora Neale Hurston, Gloria Naylor, and Randall Kenan.* Athens: Univ. of Georgia Press.

Hartman, Saidiya V. 1997. *Scenes of Subjection: Terror, Slavery, and Self-Making in Nineteenth-Century America.* New York: Oxford Univ. Press.

Hartman, Saidiya. 2007. *Lose Your Mother: A Journey along the Atlantic Slave Route.* New York: Farrar, Straus, and Giroux.

Holland, Jearold W. 2002. *Black Recreation: A Historical Perspective.* Chicago: Burnham.

Holsaert, Faith S., Martha P. N. Noonan, Judy Richardson, Betty G. Robinson, Jean S. Young, and Dorothy M. Zellner, eds. 2010. *Hands on the Freedom Plow: Personal Accounts by Women in SNCC.* Urbana: Univ. of Illinois Press.

hooks, bell. 1990. *Yearning: Race, Gender, and Cultural Politics.* Cambridge, MA: South End Press.

Hurston, Zora N. (1928) 1979. "How It Feels to Be Colored Me." In *I Love Myself When I Am Laughing . . . and Then Again: A Zora Neale Hurston Reader,* edited by Alice Walker, 152–55. New York: Feminist Press at the City Univ. of New York.

Killens, John O. 1967. *'Sippi.* New York: Trident.

Latour, Bruno. 1993. *We Have Never Been Modern.* Cambridge, MA: Harvard Univ. Press.

Malcolm X. 1965. "At the Audubon." In *Malcolm X Speaks: Selected Speeches and Statements,* edited by George Breitman, 88–104. New York: Grove.

Mbembe, Achille. 2003. "Necropolitics." Translated by Libby Meintjes. *Public Culture* 15, no. 1: 11–40.

McConachie, Bruce A. 1992. "Historicizing the Relations of Theatrical Production." In *Critical Theory and Performance,* edited by Janelle G. Reinelt and Joseph R. Roach, 168–78. Ann Arbor: Univ. of Michigan Press.

McInnis, Jarvis C. 2016. "'Behold the Land': W. E. B. Du Bois, Cotton Futures, and the Afterlife of the Plantation in the US South." *Global South* 10, no. 2: 70–98.

McKittrick, Katherine. 2006. *Demonic Grounds: Black Women and the Cartographies of Struggle.* Minneapolis: Univ. of Minnesota Press.

McKittrick, Katherine. 2013. "Plantation Futures." *Small Axe* 17, no 3: 1–15.

McKittrick, Katherine, and Clyde Woods. 2007. *Black Geographies and the Politics of Place.* Toronto: Between the Lines.

Mignolo, Walter D. 2002. "The Geopolitics of Knowledge and the Colonial Difference." *South Atlantic Quarterly* 101, no. 1: 57–96.

Mills, Charles W. 2014. "The Chronic Injustice of Ideal Theory." *Du Bois Review* 11, no 1: 27–42.

Moses, Gilbert, John O'Neal, Denise Nicholas, Murray Levy, and Richard Schechner. 1965. "Dialogue: The Free Southern Theatre." *Tulane Drama Review* 9, no. 4: 63–76.

Nicholas, Denise. 2010. "A Grand Romantic Notion." In Holsaert et al. 2010: 257–66.

Ogletree, Charles. 2004. *All Deliberate Speed: Reflections on the First Half Century of "Brown v. Board of Education".* New York: W. W. Norton.

O'Neal, John. 1968. "Motion in the Ocean: Some Political Dimensions of the Free Southern Theater." *Drama Review* 12, no. 4: 71.

Phelan, Peggy. 1993. *Unmarked: The Politics of Performance.* New York: Routledge.

Said, Edward. 1978. *Orientalism.* New York: Vintage.

Shabazz, Rashad. 2015. *Spatializing Blackness: Architectures of Confinement and Black Masculinity in Chicago.* Urbana: Univ. of Illinois Press.

Sharpe, Christina. 2016. *In the Wake: On Blackness and Being.* Durham, NC: Duke Univ. Press.

Simone, Nina. 1964. "Mississippi Goddam." On *Nina Simone in Concert.* Phillips PHM 200-135.

Smallwood, Stephanie E. 2007. *Saltwater Slavery: A Middle Passage from Africa to American Diaspora.* Cambridge, MA: Harvard Univ. Press.

Smith, Mark M. 1997. *Mastered by the Clock: Time, Slavery, and Freedom in the American South.* Chapel Hill: Univ. of North Carolina Press.

Taylor, Diana. 2003. *The Archive and the Repertoire: Performing Cultural Memory in the Americas*. Durham, NC: Duke Univ. Press.

Thrift, Nigel. 1977. "An Introduction to Time-Geography." *Concepts and Techniques in Modern Geography*, no. 13.

Warren, Calvin. 2016. "Black Time: Slavery, Metaphysics, and the Logic of Wellness." In *The Psychic Hold of Slavery: Legacies in American Expressive Culture*, edited by Soyica D. Colbert, Robert J. Patterson, and Aida Levy-Hussen, 55–68. New Brunswick, NJ: Rutgers Univ. Press.

Young, Harvey. 2010. *Embodying Black Experience: Stillness, Critical Memory, and the Black Body*. Ann Arbor: Univ. of Michigan Press.

Roberta
Wolfson

Race Leaders, Race Traitors, and the Necropolitics of Black Exceptionalism in Paul Beatty's Fiction

Abstract This essay examines two oppositional figures in Paul Beatty's debut novel, *The White Boy Shuffle* (1996), and most recent novel, *The Sellout* (2015): the exalted race leader and the excoriated race traitor. Positioned at extreme ends of the spectrum of exceptionalism, these figures function to perpetuate a phenomenon that the essay's author terms the necropolitics of black exceptionalism, the paradox of justifying the violent oppression of the majority of black people by celebrating or censuring a single black figure. In exploring the absurd dimensions of these extreme figures through the lens of satire, both novels denounce black exceptionalism as a necropolitical tool of oppression that entrenches the social death and civic exclusion of black people in a modern US society that purports to be color-blind and postracial. Emerging within the postmodern turn of the African American literary tradition, these novels take on a nihilistic tone to raise questions about how the black community might effectively (if at all) achieve civil progress in the contemporary age. Ultimately, these satirical novels reimagine historically necropolitical spaces, such as the basketball court, the plantation, and the segregated urban neighborhood, as potential, albeit vexed sites of black agency, empowerment, and community building.
Keywords social death, (anti)racism, satire, black postmodernism, bare life

> Scoby's eyes reddened and he started to sniffle. He was crack-
> ing under the pressure. Watching his hands shake, I realized
> that sometimes the worst thing a nigger can do is perform
> well. Because then there is no turning back. We have no place
> to hide, no Superhuman Fortress of Solitude, no reclusive
> New England hermitages for xenophobic geniuses like Bobby
> Fischer and J. D. Salinger. Successful niggers can't go back
> home and blithely disappear into the local populace. American
> society reels you back to the fold.
> —Paul Beatty, *The White Boy Shuffle* (1996)

American Literature, Volume 91, Number 3, September 2019
DOI 10.1215/00029831-7722152   © 2019 by Duke University Press

In this revelatory moment from Paul Beatty's first novel, *The White Boy Shuffle* (1996), the narrator Gunnar Kaufman gives voice to the burden of racial exceptionalism placed on standout figures in the black community in modern US society. This passage describes the nervous breakdown of Nicholas Scoby, Gunnar's best friend in the predominantly black and Latinx Los Angeles neighborhood of Hillside. Due to their extraordinary basketball skills, both Gunnar and Scoby have experienced a meteoric rise to fame within their high school community. This attention soon becomes a source of affliction when they realize that being categorized as exceptional black figures comes with a heavy price—as paragons of black success, Gunnar and Scoby are no longer allowed to enjoy the simple freedom of anonymity; instead, their every move is scrutinized as representative of the larger black population. This burden enslaves them to the demands of a modern US society that justifies the systematic mistreatment of black people by pointing to a few token success stories. In this pivotal moment of the novel, Gunnar's meditation on the perils of achieving success as a young black man serves to critique the oppressive narrative of black exceptionalism. Performing well, as Gunnar sees it, marks a point of no return for a reigning hero of the black community, beyond which the exceptional black figure will be subjected to the capitalist whims of white America, which sees his body, much like the bodies of his slave ancestors, as a source of spectacle and commodification. The exceptional black figure, then, can be understood as a tokenized pawn of white America, permitted to enjoy success only insofar as such success reinforces the specious narrative that the United States has achieved racial equality in the post–civil rights era.

Published nearly twenty years after *The White Boy Shuffle*, Beatty's most recent novel, *The Sellout* (2015), further critiques this narrative of black exceptionalism by creating a narrator who stands in direct opposition to the exalted Gunnar. This narrator, who calls himself Me, is also an exceptional black man, yet he gains recognition not for bringing honor to the black community but for "selling out" his people by reinstating slavery and segregation in his hometown, a predominantly black and Latinx Los Angeles neighborhood called Dickens. Although Me's efforts to reinstate slavery and segregation actually succeed in unifying his black community, mainstream US society scapegoats him as a race traitor because he threatens to disrupt the racist status quo by exposing the fact that the legacies of these racist institutions still circumscribe black lives in the twenty-first century. Like Gunnar, then, Me is categorized as an exceptional black figure because white America refuses to acknowledge the continued existence of racism in the twenty-first century. This refusal reflects an investment in color-blind neoliberal multiculturalism that ignores black people's subjection to systematic surveillance, policing, and murder by state agents.[1]

In this essay, I examine the positioning of Gunnar and Me at two extreme ends of the spectrum of black exceptionalism—the former lauded as a race leader and the latter denounced as a race traitor—in order to trace an ideological arc in Beatty's fiction that condemns what I term the *necropolitics of black exceptionalism*. I define this as a phenomenon rooted in the paradox of justifying the violent oppression of the black majority by celebrating or excoriating a single black figure. I argue that black exceptionalism functions as a necropolitical narrative because it entrenches the "social death" (Patterson 1982: 38) of black people, the essential condition of slavery characterized by a loss of individuality, most notably in the form of "natal alienation" (7), in which the enslaved individual is "alienated from all 'rights' or claims of birth" (5) and excluded from belonging "to any legitimate social order" (5). While African Americans are no longer literal slaves today, they are still subjected to oppressive structures (mass incarceration, political disenfranchisement, antiblack law enforcement) that deny them legitimate inclusion in the nation's social order.[2] The narrative of black exceptionalism functions as yet another antiblack structure by drawing public attention to a few exceptional black figures in order to justify the oppression of the black majority. In exploring the absurd consequences of Gunnar's and Me's establishment as tokens of black exceptionalism, *The White Boy Shuffle* and *The Sellout* denounce black exceptionalism as a necropolitical tool of oppression that dictates how and when black people should live and die.

In critiquing this narrative of black exceptionalism, Beatty's novels demand a new understanding of the state of exception that Giorgio Agamben (1998: 4) calls "bare life," the status of being stripped of political significance and rendered susceptible to erasure without protection from the state. The operative word here is *stripped*, as it defines bare life as the loss of civic status. But this definition fails to consider the historical reality that people of color have been denied civic status since the formation of the US nation, in keeping with the terms of the "racial contract" (Mills 1997) that established whiteness as a necessary criterion for civic inclusion.[3] According to the terms of this racial contract, black slaves in the antebellum period were relegated to an in-between category of personhood that Monique Allewaert (2013: 6) terms "parahuman" or "beside the human," given that black slaves were "not legally or conceptually equivalent to human beings while at the same time not precisely inhuman." This concept of parahumanity forms the backbone of black people's categorization as bare life, since their variable status throughout US history as slaves, incarcerated criminals, and disenfranchised nonconstituents has consistently ensured their exclusion from full political participation in the civic order alongside their necessary inclusion as second-class subjects in order to validate the nation's white supremacist racial hierarchy. By demonstrating that bare life has always been a designated status for people of color through an exploration of the necropolitics of black exceptionalism, Beatty's novels engage with recent critiques that bare life discourse "largely occludes race as a critical category of analysis" (Z. Jackson 2015: 8) and "misconstrues how profoundly race and racism shape the modern idea of the human" (Weheliye 2014: 4). Beatty's novels bring racial politics to the center of bare life discourse by condemning the necropolitical narrative of black exceptionalism that reads the black body as parahuman and therefore always and already categorized as bare life.

In exploring the necropolitics of black exceptionalism in these novels, Beatty highlights the troubling fact that this phenomenon has endured, rather than diminished, over nearly two decades. By the time *The White Boy Shuffle* was published in 1996, the backlash to the civil rights and black power movements of the 1960s had manifested in the war on drugs, which led to increased policing in black neighborhoods and an upsurge in black incarceration rates; further, attendant moralizing rhetoric attributed racial disparities in income, housing, and health to the cultural failures of black people and found expression in terms like the "welfare queen," "career criminal," and "deadbeat dad" (Carpio 2008: 4). Given that such policies and rhetoric only increased throughout the 1970s and 1980s, it is not surprising that the 1992 acquittal of Rodney King's police abusers ignited multiple days of civil unrest in Los Angeles, testifying to black people's frustration at the state's continued failure to recognize their humanity. Yet far from succeeding to advance black civil rights, this protest only further entrenched black people's oppression by serving as fodder for conservative claims about the moral deficiencies of the black community. Such claims have endured into the twenty-first century, which has seen a resurgence in white supremacist ideology and antiblack police brutality in the 2010s, the decade of *The Sellout*'s publication. These trends have unfolded against a backdrop of national discourses that construct the United States as postracial.

Racial exceptionalism plays a critical role in maintaining this false veneer of postraciality and justifying the continued oppression of black people. According to Utz McKnight (2013: 20), in an effort to "create a racially neutral public space" in the aftermath of the civil rights movement, US society experienced a shift in racial politics represented by two figures of exception: the white racist, which functions to "absolve the remainder of the White community of culpability in ongoing social descriptions of racial inferiority" (20), and the exceptional black subject, which "has been taken as a mark of the success in public discourse of both equality legislation and of the aims of the Civil Rights Movement" (24). Indeed, the post–civil rights era has seen a proliferation of exceptional black figures in many public spheres, including politics (Clarence Thomas, Condoleezza Rice, Barack Obama), entertainment (Oprah Winfrey, Will Smith, Beyoncé), and sports (Mike Tyson, Michael Jordan, Kobe Bryant). Beatty himself could be included in this list of exceptional black people, given his international acclaim after *The Sellout* became the first US novel to win the Man Booker Prize in 2016. Beatty's status as an exceptional black author is not without significant irony, as his newfound fame only serves to advance the very necropolitics of black exceptionalism that his novels are invested in critiquing. Black exceptionalism is inherently necropolitical because it reinforces white supremacy by permitting tokenized black celebrities to rise to the limelight in order to "obscure the reality of ongoing institutional white control while reinforcing the ideologies of individualism and meritocracy" (DiAngelo 2018: 26). By diverting attention away from the fact that an overwhelming majority of black people still struggle to make economic, social, and political gains in contemporary US society, "black celebrities have sold the idea that America is no longer manacled to its history" (Cashmore 2012: 2). In this way, contemporary white America's insistence on propping up select figures of black exception can be understood as a new form of racism that Tim Wise (2009: 9) calls "Racism 2.0, or enlightened exceptionalism, a form that allows for and even celebrates the achievements of individual persons of color, but only because those individuals generally are seen as different from a less appealing, even pathological black or brown rule."

The shared investment of both *The White Boy Shuffle* and *The Sellout* in exploring racial exceptionalism serves not only to expose the state's continued necropolitical treatment of black people across two decades but also to highlight the challenge faced by black people of achieving true liberation within a white supremacist framework that refuses to recognize their full humanity. In order to understand this move, we must situate Beatty's work within the postmodern turn of the African American literary tradition, which Madhu Dubey (2003: 5) traces back to the 1970s, when demographic shifts made urbanity "the given condition of black social life," giving rise to a "sense of crisis in the category of racial community." According to Dubey (6), a defining characteristic of postmodern African American literature is a concern with "tackling the difficulties of imagining racial community within contemporary urban conditions." Beatty's novels reflect this impulse by asking how today's black population might effectively—if at all—achieve civil progress within necropolitical urban spaces that are controlled by white supremacist structures. In doing so, Beatty's works join a rich cohort of contemporary black artists who are concerned with processing the continued oppression of black people even after the passing of the Civil Rights Act of 1964 and Voting Rights Act of 1965. Since these landmark acts of legislation, many black artists have turned away from the rhetoric of black pride voiced by their predecessors from the Black Arts movement to explore themes of nihilism and social death that showcase the limited gains of the civil rights and black power movements. Such themes can be found in the neo-slave narrative genre, which first emerged in the second half of the twentieth century with the publication of novels like Margaret Walker's *Jubilee* (1966), Octavia E. Butler's *Kindred* (1979), and Toni Morrison's *Beloved* (1987); this genre still finds representation in twenty-first-century works like Noni Carter's novel *Good Fortune* (2010) and Steve McQueen's film *12 Years a Slave* (2013).[4] These themes are also reflected in the continuities between "hood" films from the 1990s, such as John Singleton's *Boyz n the Hood* (1991) and Allen and Albert Hughes's *Menace II Society* (1993), and many films produced by black directors in the twenty-first century, such as Lee Daniels's *Precious* (2009), Barry Jenkins's *Moonlight* (2016), and Jordan Peele's *Get Out* (2017).

Beatty's postmodern exploration of the challenges of constructing black community within the necropolitical framework of white supremacy is rooted in the satirical premises of both novels—that black people's liberation can be found in either their suicide (*The White Boy Shuffle*) or their return to slavery and segregation (*The Sellout*). This technique is called reductio ad absurdum, a strategy designed to reveal the "foolishness of a concept or idea by taking it to its apparent logical—and most outrageous—conclusion" (Dickson-Carr 2001: 26). Beatty's use of reductio ad absurdum in these novels is two-pronged. First, he explores the absurd consequences of Gunnar's establishment as a race leader and Me's establishment as a race traitor in order to expose the damage caused by the necropolitics of black exceptionalism. Second, he reveals the foolishness of the idea that black people can effectively protest their oppression within a necropolitical US society that has always treated (and will continue to treat) them as bare life by exploring the black community's absurd attempts to find liberation in suicide, slavery, and segregation. This second critique finds particular purchase in light of the fact that the many different forms that black protest has taken throughout US history, including the abolitionist movement, the accommodationist strategies of black uplift, the New Negro movement, and the black power and civil rights movements, have ultimately all failed to unfetter black people fully from the necropolitical chains of social death.

Although Beatty has stated that he does not consider himself a satirist,[5] his works utilize satirical strategies that would place him within a long line of African American writers who use humor to advance social commentary, including W. E. B. Du Bois, Charles W. Chesnutt, Zora Neale Hurston, Wallace Thurman, George Schuyler, Ralph Ellison, Ishmael Reed, John Edgar Wideman, Colson Whitehead, Dave Chappelle, Keegan-Michael Key, and Jordan Peele. As a subversive genre that possesses a "Janus-face identity" (Carpio 2008: 5) because it can disrupt the white supremacist status quo while nevertheless appearing nonthreatening to white people, satire has served as a critical platform for social protest within the black community since the antebellum period, when slaves created "various complex coded languages and expressions that allowed for the indirect expression of their frustration" (Dickson-Carr 2001: 3). These satirical codes became a "staple of African expressive culture" that "functioned as a kind of 'communal psychological medicine'" (Caponi 1999: 27). This palliative function of satire is captured succinctly by Beatty's own words in the introduction to his edited collection, *Hokum: An Anthology of African-American Humor* (2006b: 12): "If you're laughing, then you ain't hurt." Writing within this tradition, Beatty uses humor in both *The White Boy Shuffle* and *The Sellout* to explore what it might mean to laugh at the paradoxes of the postmodern black existence, in which a few exceptional black figures are thrust into the limelight even as the majority of black lives are seen as expendable.

Gunnar as the Exceptional Race Leader in *The White Boy Shuffle*

The White Boy Shuffle follows Gunnar's experiences as he struggles to find his place in a late twentieth-century US society that insists on categorizing him as a paragon of black success. The novel traces Gunnar's journey from elementary school to college, throughout which he is variously celebrated as a basketball star, a renowned urban poet, and a leader of the black people. This last status is conferred on him by both black and white people, who are motivated—for entirely different reasons—to "fill the perennial void in African-American leadership" (Beatty 1996: 1) left open after the passing of Martin Luther King Jr. While the divided black community yearns for a leader who can rebuild the unity of old, the white community seeks to identify a token black success story to prove once and for all that the nation has achieved racial equality. When, in his newfound status as a race leader, Gunnar inspires the suicides of black people across the nation by suggesting that self-destruction is the ideal form of protest against antiblack racism, the novel's biting satire crystallizes. By exposing the absurdity of a US society that has no qualms about celebrating a single black man while ignoring the erasure of a majority of black lives, *The White Boy Shuffle* simultaneously critiques the state's necropolitics of black exceptionalism and the black community's hopelessly misguided pursuit of liberation.

The Hypocrisy of Color-blindness

The White Boy Shuffle critiques the necropolitics of black exceptionalism by juxtaposing two racial landscapes: first, the elementary school that Gunnar attends in Santa Monica and, second, the neighborhood of Hillside that Gunnar moves to at the start of middle school. The Santa Monica elementary school espouses a philosophy of color-blind multiculturalism that Gunnar quickly learns is artificial. While racist jokes proliferate on the playground, color-blind ideology dominates in the institutionalized space of the classroom. Such contradictions are modeled by the figurehead for this institutionalized space, the humorously named teacher Ms. Cegeny, who has adorned the space above her blackboard with "multiculturalist propaganda" (29). On a surface level, this classroom seems to fit Elijah Anderson's (2011: xiv) description of a "cosmopolitan canopy," which he defines as a "pluralistic space . . . where people engage one another in a spirit of civility, or even comity and goodwill." In the post–civil rights era, these cosmopolitan canopies are institutionally regulated to ensure that US society appears racially integrated. However, they problematically cultivate an illusion of interracial unity that belies the racism still simmering beneath the facade of civility. Anderson (253) points out that even in these spaces of civility, racism can surface in what he calls the "nigger moment," a "time in the life of every African American when he or she is powerfully reminded of his or her putative place as a black person." Gunnar is subjected to this phenomenon every time Ms. Cegeny singles him out in ways that reveal her underlying prejudices, such as when she openly questions his intelligence and work ethic. Such biased treatment of Gunnar, the token black student, stands as a subtle vestige of the more overt racism of previous decades.

In contrast to the "cosmopolitan canopy" of the elementary school, Gunnar's new neighborhood, Hillside, is heavily surveilled by a police force whose racism is anything but discreet. After only a week in his new home, two police officers pay a visit to interrogate Gunnar about his gang affiliation on the grounds that they are practicing "preventative police enforcement" (Beatty 1996: 47). Although Gunnar handles the grilling with poise, he is incredulous about the encounter, remarking to himself, "Gang affiliation? I didn't even have any friends yet" (48). This interaction exposes Gunnar to the disturbing experience of being profiled by authorities who see him as a potential threat because they read black teenage boys as exceptionally dangerous. The Hillside police's assumption that Gunnar must possess criminal tendencies contrasts starkly with the discourse of racial civility touted in Ms. Cegeny's classroom. By juxtaposing these different institutional treatments of race, the novel exposes the hypocrisy of color-blind ideology, which purports to champion a new era of race relations in the post–civil rights era, even as race-based profiling continues to control black bodies in certain spaces.

Commodifying the Exceptional Black Body

The White Boy Shuffle further critiques the necropolitics of black exceptionalism by satirizing Gunnar's establishment as a token figure of black success. Gunnar's ascent to fame begins when he is discovered— quite accidentally—to possess remarkable skills on the basketball court shortly after moving to Hillside. After suffering for a few weeks as a social pariah in his new school, Gunnar makes a tentative friend in Scoby, who informs him, "If you want to hang with me, you're gonna have to play ball" (73). Although Gunnar has never played basketball before, his desire for social acceptance compels him one day to join a game with Scoby. During this game, Gunnar manages to perform a spectacular feat of athleticism:

> I caught the ball, took the one dribble my coordination allowed, then jumped as hard as I could, my eyes closed tight. . . . I must have stopped breathing, because I could feel my legs kicking in midair as if I were suspended from an invisible noose. What the fuck was I doing with a basketball in my hands? I opened my eyes and saw that my momentum was hurtling my fragile body toward the basket and the steel rim was closing in on the bridge of my nose. I raised my arms in self-defense and crashed into the basket, the ball slamming through the hoop with an authoritative boom. Instinctively, I grabbed onto the rim to stop myself from flying into the pole. When I slowed to a gentle sway, I let go and dropped to the ground with a soft thud. (75)

Gunnar's achievement in dunking the ball, despite being presented as an accident after a series of missteps, earns him the admiration of his fellow players, who immediately stop playing and burst into a "frenzy of high-pitched whooping, high fives, and high-stepping jigs" (75).

Their delight reveals their investment in the narrative of black exceptionalism that establishes successful black athletes as symbols of hope for the rest of the black population. Reuben A. Buford May (2008: 160) critiques this investment as woefully misguided, claiming that the belief in athletics as a viable means of social mobility is a "dirty trick" played on low-income communities of color by US society. This dirty trick is highlighted by the strategic use of lynching imagery in the description of Gunnar's miraculous ball dunking ("suspended from an invisible noose"), which draws an explicit connection between basketball and black erasure. Although Gunnar's schoolmates view his basketball talent as a sure ticket to fame and fortune, this ominous imagery foreshadows a crueler outcome.

Sure enough, Gunnar's athletic talent eventually leads to his exploitation by white basketball scouts and university recruiters, who view him as a "spectacular commodity" (Murray 2008: 225) and potential source of profit. Gunnar's standing as a basketball star directly exposes him to the contemporary US paradox of celebrating black athletes as idols while simultaneously policing, commodifying, and fetishizing their bodies. When Gunnar is invited to attend Nike Basketball Camp as one of the top one hundred high school basketball players in the nation, he encounters white coaches and scouts who reduce his value to his ability to make a basket, effectively exchanging his humanity for his exceptionalism. In several emails written from camp, he complains to his mother, "Ma, I swear they look at you like they want to fuck you, using every and any excuse to slap your butt" (Beatty 1996: 143), and he informs Scoby, "This place makes me feel like a racehorse. Every morning I get up at six o'clock to get weighed, fed, and put through my paces" (145–46). These words demonstrate Gunnar's awareness that his status as a basketball star has not earned him respect and autonomy but has rendered him a commodity to be cultivated and consumed in a capitalist US society that has profited from the labor and sexualization of black bodies since slavery. Gunnar's exceptionalism-turned-commodification, then, can be understood as an outgrowth of a historically capitalist US culture that profits from black people's labor and dehumanization. In comparing himself to a racehorse, Gunnar exposes the fine line between being exalted as an exceptional black subject and being exploited as a prize pet, thereby giving voice to the assumption of black alterity that lies at the heart of discourses of black exceptionalism, which finds historical precedence in the national myth that black people are inherently "dysfunctional" (Kelley 1997: 3). Throughout US history, this myth has been used to define a white standard of normalcy that "relies on the idea of black abnormality for its cultural capital" (Ikard 2013: 10). In keeping with this discourse of black abnormality, the narrative of black exceptionalism can be understood as yet another mechanism of white supremacy used to justify the systematic persecution of black subjects. Gunnar's establishment as an exceptional black subject, then, functions *by design* to further perpetuate the oppression of black people.

Perhaps no other character reveals how the narrative of black exceptionalism can be used to entrench black oppression more clearly than Scoby, another remarkable basketball player whose "uncanny ability to put a ball in the basket" (Beatty 1996: 192) invites both awe and fear from mainstream US society. Eventually Scoby is recruited along with Gunnar to play basketball for Boston University, where his exceptional talent is routinely broadcast on sports television channels. Whereas in high school Scoby's basketball skills were celebrated by adoring members of his community, in college these same skills are viewed as threatening by a predominantly white audience because they throw "every theory, every formula, every philosophical dogma out of whack" (192). Scoby is alarming to white America because he is *too* skilled; his excellence disrupts a US racial hierarchy built on the national myth that "American exceptionalism, as the expression is conventionally employed, means *white* American exceptionalism" (Stewart 2011: 167). Consequently, the nation responds with outrage at Scoby's basketball prowess by subjecting him to immense scrutiny, as hundreds of sportswriters, university professors, and scientists stalk and study Scoby at all times of the day in the hopes of learning the secret of his perfection and exposing his hidden flaws. Many people attend Scoby's games simply to pray that his "next attempt will roll in and out of the rim and the universe will return to normal" (Beatty 1996: 192). When each game ends with these anticheerleaders in tears because Scoby's record has remained unblemished, Gunnar reflects, "They would be a lot better off if they simply called Scoby a god and left it at that, but no way they'll proclaim a skinny black man God" (192). These words suggest that US society will not permit black exceptionalism if it threatens to dismantle white supremacy. This fact is reinforced by the audience's routine efforts to make Scoby aware of their displeasure by throwing symbolically racist objects, such as "bananas, coconuts, nooses, headless dolls, and shit" (193), at Scoby when he runs onto the court at the start of every game. This gesture sends a menacing message: Scoby may continue to make money for the university and provide entertainment for the public, but he may never be allowed to forget that his status as a black man renders him susceptible to the necropolitics of a racist US society that sees him as worthy of living only so long as he serves the needs of the white majority.

"Sometimes Hara-Kiri Makes You Win"

According to Therí A. Pickens (2014: 3), many works of African American literature showcase the fragility of the black body as a way to counteract racist sociopolitical discourse that depicts "the raced and gendered body as exclusively able, exceptionally strong, or visibly threatening." In keeping with this trend, *The White Boy Shuffle* establishes Gunnar's obsession with death as a counterpoint to his seemingly superhuman abilities in order to further the novel's critique of the necropolitics of black exceptionalism. After dwelling for years on thoughts of his own mortality, Gunnar eventually advocates for suicide as the ultimate form of protest against antiblack racism. Gunnar makes his obsession with death public when he speaks at a political protest rally at Boston University during a pivotal scene that ends with his being anointed "king of the blacks" (Beatty 1996: 200). After being introduced to the crowd as a "star athlete, accomplished poet, black man extraordinaire, [and] voice of a nation" (198), Gunnar steps up to the podium and quotes the words that are engraved on the plaque at the base of the campus's Martin Luther King Jr. sculpture, "If a man hasn't discovered something he will die for, he isn't fit to live" (199–200). Having invoked the spirit of the renowned civil rights leader, Gunnar continues:

> So I asked myself, what am I willing to die for? The day when white people treat me with respect and see my life as equally valuable to theirs? No, I ain't willing to die for that, because if they don't know that by now, then they ain't never going to know it. Matter of fact, I ain't ready to die for anything, so I guess I'm just not fit to live. In other words, I'm just ready to die. I'm just ready to die. . . . What we need is some new leaders. Leaders who won't apostatize like cowards. Some niggers who are ready to die! (200)

These words ignite the crowd, prompting the audience to point at Gunnar and chant, "You! You! You!" (200) in unanimous agreement that he should be the next black leader. This plot twist comes across as ironic, given that the crowd is establishing Gunnar as a race leader despite—or perhaps because of—his public call for the death of black people.

While Gunnar's advocacy for mass suicide can be understood as misguided (Grassian 2009) and pathological (Ikard 2013), I contend that this move can also be understood as a generative act of community building.[6] I base this argument on the fact that Gunnar's call for mass suicide takes inspiration from the ancient Japanese tradition of hara-kiri, a ritual act of suicide that absolves the self of shame and reintegrates the self into the larger community. Gunnar learns about hara-kiri from his Japanese wife, Yoshiko, who introduces him to literature that describes this ancient practice as a radical act of self-advocacy. This understanding of hara-kiri inspires Gunnar's statement during an interview on *Good Morning, America*: "It is as Mishima once said: 'Sometimes hara-kiri makes you win.' I just want to win one time" (Beatty 1996: 202). Although this comment is largely dismissed by the show's hosts, it reveals Gunnar's understanding that "Japanese tradition has long regarded suicide as a purposeful act, which may be and often is, honorable" (Hayakawa 1957: 48). When Gunnar explains that hara-kiri does not conform to "the Western idea of suicide—the sense of the defeated self" (Beatty 1996: 202), he demonstrates that he understands suicide as an act of self-determination, which is the English translation for one of the Japanese words for suicide, *jiketsu* (Rankin 2011: 19). For Gunnar, then, committing suicide can be understood as a radical act of agency that may allow black people to determine the conditions of their lives and deaths and thereby defy the necropolitics of a racist US society.

As black people around the country begin killing themselves at alarming rates, however, the idealized notion that suicide might serve as the ultimate expression of self-determination begins to fall flat. When white America responds to these mass suicides with delighted fascination, viewing the loss of black life as the ultimate form of entertainment, it becomes painfully clear that these deaths will not disrupt the racial hierarchy.[7] If, as Judith Butler (2004: 20) argues, one's status as human depends on whether one's life is considered "grievable," then white America's refusal to acknowledge these deaths as

worthy of mourning reflects its continued disavowal of black humanity. Given US society's longstanding tradition of reading blackness as
inherently pathological (Scott 1997: xi), white America's reaction to
these deaths is not surprising. In fact, white America's dismissal of
the gravity of these mass suicides finds precedence in the arguments
of antebellum slave owners who claimed that slaves did not kill themselves to escape the dehumanizing conditions of slavery but because
they "were ethnically predisposed to suicide, superstitious and fearful, or temperamental and stubborn" (Snyder 2015: 12), as well as
of white Southerners who depicted black people as psychologically
degenerate in order to justify Jim Crow segregation (Scott 1997: xii).
In keeping with this tradition of justifying black people's oppression by
reading their psychology as pathological, white people in *The White
Boy Shuffle* grossly misinterpret the black community's collective
embrace of suicide as a spectacle designed exclusively for their viewing pleasure. Ironically, then, despite Gunnar's idealized notions of
hara-kiri, these acts of suicide are ultimately more self-defeating than
self-determining.

Perhaps no suicide is as tragic as that of Scoby, who jumps off a
roof after growing increasingly disillusioned in his role as Boston University's most hated and celebrated basketball player. Scoby's death
profoundly affects Gunnar, prompting him to drop out of college and
return with his wife to Hillside, where they choose to make the birth
of their child public as a way of honoring Scoby and "giving something back to the community" (Beatty 1996: 217). One warm Friday
night in Reynier Park, Yoshiko enters labor while surrounded by hundreds of people, effectively transforming an intimate experience into a
public affair. Positioned against a constant backdrop of death, the
birth of Yoshiko and Gunnar's daughter represents the possibility of
renewal within the Hillside community. Yoshiko's labor also produces
communal life by inspiring a weekly series of "outdoor open mikes,
called the Black Bacchanalian MiseryFests" (219), which feature
poetry readings, car shows, and song and dance performances put
on by members of the Hillside community and soon become a time-
honored neighborhood tradition. These gatherings pulse with life,
capturing the resilience of a black population that refuses to be controlled by the necropolitics of a racist US society. At the same time,
they reflect the limits of black resistance, as they are co-opted by
mainstream television networks, which recognize them as a potential

source of profit and broadcast them across the nation so that white America can continue to enjoy the spectacle of black misery and black celebration. The MiseryFests thus become a contested site of meaning, as they help generate a sense of community for the black attendees even as they subject them to commodification by the white majority. In this way, the MiseryFests can be understood as an outgrowth of what Saidiya V. Hartman (1997) identifies as a longstanding white American practice of reading black expressions of contentment, enjoyment, and celebration in terms of both black abjection and black empowerment. Just as expressions of pleasure within slave populations in the antebellum period simultaneously enabled slave owners to "secure the submission of the enslaved" (43) and allowed slaves to generate "supportive, enjoyable, and nurturing connections" (60), so, too, do the MiseryFests serve to both entrench the black participants' subjection to white supremacy and build camaraderie within their community. As a site of contradiction where mourning and merriment merge, the MiseryFests can be understood as an inevitable byproduct of Gunnar's call for mass suicide, in which the black community seeks to heal from its losses by reaffirming the value of black lives through a collective display of solidarity. In creating community out of tragedy, the Hillside residents demonstrate a remarkable ability to reconstruct the necropolitical space of the urban ghetto as a site of black agency.

Me as the Exceptional Race Traitor in *The Sellout*

The narrator of *The Sellout*, Me, shares much in common with Gunnar. Both protagonists endure abuse by violent fathers, grow up in Los Angeles, and are categorized as exceptional black figures. However, they differ in a critical capacity: Gunnar is considered exceptional for being a race leader, whereas Me is considered exceptional for being a race traitor. Me earns this denunciation after reinstating slavery and segregation in twenty-first-century US society, an absurd act that garners the attention of the Supreme Court. His censure, like Gunnar's celebration, functions to further the necropolitical acts of a racist US state that would rather lambaste a scapegoat than acknowledge the continued existence of racial oppression. The legacies of slavery and segregation endure in twenty-first-century forms of state-sanctioned violence that control black bodies, such as stop-and-frisk law enforcement practices that fuel the mass incarceration of people of color, demands from lawmakers for harsher sentences for nonviolent offenders, and the continued loss of black lives at the hands of police. Such violence has gained only more traction alongside the resurgence of white nationalism after Barack Obama's 2008 election to the presidency, which reveals many white Americans' renewed investment in subduing black people in order to maintain their racial hegemony. In establishing Me as a race traitor, then, Beatty satirizes the ways in which the necropolitics of black exceptionalism have endured in the nearly twenty years since the publication of *The White Boy Shuffle* to ensure black people's continued status as bare life. With this move, Beatty critiques the contemporary US racial climate that demands that exceptional black figures who become too vocal about racial injustice be excoriated, rather than exalted, as a way to divert attention from the routine violence committed against black bodies in the twenty-first century.

Part of the novel's satirical humor stems from the irony that the mainstream US public misunderstands the motivations behind Me's behavior—he does not want to bring back the historically racist institutions of slavery and segregation to further oppress black people but to disrupt the continued legacies of these institutions. In fact, in reinstating slavery and segregation, Me ironically performs the most radical act of protest against antiblack racism by highlighting black people's continued subjection to contemporary forms of slavery and segregation. The absurdity of this move is powerful because it subverts the racist logic on which black oppression is based. Reinstating slavery and segregation might seem outrageous, but this act simply extends the current necropolitical practices that already subjugate black communities, thereby exposing and critiquing the continued maintenance of black people's social death.

When Me describes himself as a *"Chamaeleo africanus tokenus"* (Beatty 2015: 20), adding the Latinized word *tokenus* to the scientific name for the African chameleon, he identifies his status as a tokenized figure whose role is to take on the vitriol of a US public deeply invested in the fantasy that it has moved beyond race. Me makes this comparison while sitting before the Supreme Court and enduring the scathing glare of the only black justice. The metaphor of a chameleon is fitting in this moment, as it speaks to Me's understanding that the public conceives of him as an untrustworthy individual who manipulates his image according to the demands of the situation. Me recognizes that this public perception is necessary for the continued maintenance of a racial system that cannot afford to acknowledge the true inequities hidden beneath the veneer of racial equality. Unlike the black justice, who is described as "believ[ing] in the system" (23) largely because it has benefited him personally, Me understands that the system does not work for the majority of black people but ensures their continued oppression. Both the white majority and black elite need to skewer Me, a black man who dares to defy the system, because they collectively want to ignore the country's failure to make significant racial progress nearly half a century after the end of the civil rights movement. In acknowledging his status as a tokenized race traitor, Me criticizes both contemporary black America's insistence on seeking liberation through adopting bourgeois values (a remnant of the flawed accommodationist strategies of turn-of-the-twentieth-century black uplift ideology) and contemporary white America's strategic refusal to recognize the ways in which the legacies of slavery and segregation continue to entrench black people's second-class status.

Black Erasure and Social Death

The plot of *The Sellout* is set into motion with the erasure of two sets of black lives—first, that of Me's father, and second, that of an entire city of people when Me's neighborhood, Dickens, is removed from the map of Los Angeles. The death of Me's father occurs at the hands of the police, despite the fact that he is a prominent social scientist who often works closely with members of the Los Angeles Police Department to prevent suicide attempts in Dickens.[8] In making the inciting incident of its plot the police murder of a black man, *The Sellout* echoes one of the central messages of the Black Lives Matter movement that launched in 2013: antiblack racism in the supposedly postracial contemporary moment continues to allow state agents to murder black people with impunity. When Me endeavors to learn how the shooting happened, Captain Murray Flores informs him that it was purely "accidental" (50), thereby refusing to admit any guilt on the part of the police department. Flores goes on to explain that after being issued a traffic ticket, Me's father made some remark to two police officers that prompted them to take "exception" (50) by pulling their guns on him and firing four shots into his back when he attempted to leave. The use of the word *exception* here is notable, given that it gestures to the fact that even though Me's father was known in the community for being exceptional, this status could not save him from a violent end at the hands of state agents. When Flores tells Me, "You just have to allow me to do my job. You have to let the system hold the men responsible for this accountable" (50), he reveals an inability to recognize the flaws of a criminal justice system that does not protect black lives. Me responds, "In the history of the Los Angeles Police Department, do you know how many officers have been convicted of murder while in the line of duty? . . . The answer is none, so there is no accountability" (50–51).[9] These words demonstrate Me's refusal to participate in Flores's fantasy that the criminal justice system is impartial and denounces the racist police state that routinely kills black people.

Five years after Me's father's death, Dickens also perishes, albeit symbolically, in a hushed-up affair that Me attributes to a "blatant conspiracy by the surrounding, increasingly affluent, two-car-garage communities to keep their property values up and blood pressures down" (57). The metaphorical murder of Dickens occurs suddenly one morning, when its residents awake to find that "the signs that said WELCOME TO THE CITY OF DICKENS were gone" without "an official announcement, an article in the paper, or a feature on the evening news" (58). This erasure of Dickens mirrors the erasure of Me's father, whose death also transpired without fanfare or significant media attention, setting the stage for Me's later rise to public prominence to appear even more satirical by exposing the paradoxes in US culture of making visible a few exceptional black people while rendering invisible the black majority. These dual erasures are psychologically traumatizing for Me, who mourns these losses as a loss of the self: "Dickens was me. And I was my father. Problem is, they both disappeared from my life, first my dad, and then my hometown, and suddenly I had no idea who I was, and no clue how to become myself" (40). These losses are psychologically distressing to Me because they produce a sense of isolation that harks back to the natal alienation of slavery. The ease with which Me's father and hometown are erased reflects the extent to which African Americans are and have always been categorized as socially dead since their introduction to the nation as slaves. If, as Hortense J. Spillers (1987: 80) argues, the mark of a slave could be found in his exclusion from the patrilineal "social fiction of the Father's name, the Father's law" that was granted as a privilege only to free members of society, then Me's dual losses, particularly that of his father, can be read as a further testament to white America's refusal to recognize black people as legitimate members of the polis even in the twenty-first century's supposedly postracial landscape.

Reimagining Segregation and Slavery as Structures of Black Agency

Unwilling to accept Dickens's erasure, Me endeavors to reinstate slavery and segregation in his hometown as a way to reaffirm the existence of its black residents. This move draws ironic attention to the fact that the racist US nation refuses to recognize black people as members of the polis except in terms of their exclusion from civic society. In attempting to bring back these institutions, Me reaches for an absurd solution to the problem of black people's present-day social death. The absurdity lies in the tautology of the solution's logic: if, as the reasoning goes, black people can be recognized as bare life only under the terms of the white supremacist racial contract, then it would seem that black people must embrace their categorization as such in order to gain recognition by the government. For Me, one way to remind the US nation of the existence and value of Dickens is to reimagine it as a twenty-first-century hub of slavery and segregation, since this move co-opts the racist logic of the state by declaring Dickens's legitimacy through an embrace of its illegitimacy. If black people are relegated to a state of exception in which their lives are "included in the juridical order solely in the form of [their] exclusion" (Agamben 1998: 12), then Me's actions make visible an otherwise invisible population by reengaging the logic of historically necropolitical power structures that are designed to affirm black people's inclusion in US society only in terms of their exclusion.

Me decides to reinstate slavery and segregation after developing a relationship with another Dickens resident named Hominy Jenkins, who is the last surviving actor from the television show *Our Gang* and who was celebrated in the heyday of his acting career for performing racist tropes as the understudy to the main black member of the Little Rascals, Buckwheat. After the erasure of Dickens, Hominy becomes suicidal because fans of *Our Gang* no longer know where to find him, given that his address no longer appears on city maps. These circumstances are psychologically debilitating for Hominy, who laments to Me, "When Dickens disappeared, I disappeared. I don't get fan mail anymore. I haven't had a visitor in ten years, 'cause don't nobody know where to find me. I just want to feel relevant" (Beatty 2015: 77). In the desperate throes of this existential crisis, Hominy attempts to kill himself by "self-lynching" (75) but is saved just in time by Me's intervention, which prompts Hominy to declare himself Me's slave. When Me attempts to reject being a slave owner, Hominy tells him, "Massa, . . . sometimes we just have to accept who we are and act accordingly. I'm a slave. That's who I am. It's the role I was born to play" (77). Hominy's frank acceptance of his slavelike status helps Me understand that the most effective way to make Dickens relevant again is to emphasize how it has been rendered irrelevant. Just as Hominy can feel legitimate only by occupying the position of a slave, Me reasons that Dickens can gain recognition again only by reprising the traditionally racist power structures embedded in slavery and segregation. This discovery prompts Me to accept his nominal status as Hominy's slave owner and initiate efforts to segregate Dickens's public spaces.

In an ironic twist of events, reintroducing slavery and segregation back into Dickens has the unexpected effect of unifying the residents and giving them a feeling of purpose. After Me places a sign on a city bus that reads "PRIORITY SEATING FOR SENIORS, DISABLED, AND WHITES" (128), the bus driver Marpessa reports that the sign's presence increases civility among her passengers. She tells Me: "It's the signs. People grouse at first, but the racism takes them back. Makes them humble. Makes them realize how far we've come and, more important, how far we have to go. On that bus it's like the specter of segregation has brought Dickens together" (163). A similarly surprising outcome occurs when Me segregates the local middle school by placing a sign across the street that advertises the impending construction of a whites-only school. After only six weeks of segregated schooling, Me learns that "grades are up and behavioral problems are down" (208). Me theorizes that these acts of segregation produce the powerful effect of unifying Dickens because they remind residents of the "domineering white presence" (208) in the backdrop of their lives. As he puts it, the reinstitution of segregation "brings out our need to impress, to behave, to tuck in our shirts, do our homework, show up on time, make our free throws, teach, and prove our self-worth in hopes that we won't be fired, arrested, or trucked away and shot" (208). The satirical premise of this response hinges not only on the residents' lack of outrage at the return of segregation to their neighborhood (which reveals their acute awareness that white America has dismissed them as socially dead) but also on their self-conscious attempts at self-improvement in the hopes of being accepted by the white majority. This strategy finds origins in the ideology of black uplift that gained popularity during the post-Reconstruction era, which called for the adoption of bourgeois values like thrift, chastity, and patriarchal familial structures as a means of gaining civil rights. According to Kevin K. Gaines (1996), racial uplift ultimately failed as a political strategy because it was built on black people's "unconscious internalized racism" (6) that "implicitly faulted African Americans for their lowly status" (4) and ignored the systemic structures that made social mobility largely unattainable for black people. In reverting to an accommodationist strategy that is already—and always has been—doomed to failure, the Dickens residents reveal that there are few productive modes of resistance for black people in the twenty-first century. This rather nihilistic message takes shape in the reductio ad absurdum of the black community's seemingly positive response to the specter of segregation, which absurdly suggests that the best way to manage the social death of black people is to accept it—not because this strategy will eventually overturn white America's insistence on categorizing black people as bare life but because there may be few other ways to survive within the limited confines of a necropolitical white supremacist racial order.

Just as segregation brings the people of Dickens closer together, Me's embrace of his titular status as a slave owner becomes a catalyst for strengthening the community. This process begins at the symbolic site of slavery, the "farm in the middle of the ghetto" (Beatty 2015: 53) that Me grew up on and inherited after his father's passing. This farm can be read as a modern-day slave plantation, given that Me recalls laboring in the fields throughout his childhood to help his father grow a variety of crops, including cotton. However, unlike its antebellum predecessors, Me's farm is reimagined not as a space of black oppression but as a space of black unification. In this way, Me's farm invokes what George Lipsitz (2011: 19) terms the "Black spatial imaginary," a worldview emerging out of the black community that contests "the oppressions of race by imagining strategic realignments of place." Indeed, Me's farm can be understood as a strategic realignment of the space of the slave plantation, given that it stands as a site of community building rather than degradation. The farm's power to build community stems from its production of crops that possess an almost magical ability to soothe and unify.

Perhaps the clearest example of this phenomenon can be found in the power of the Japanese satsuma mandarin tree to bring much-needed relief to the Dickens community on a particularly pungent day, when an overwhelming stench dubbed "The Stank" permeates the neighborhood. In search of relief from this overpowering smell, hundreds of local residents flock to Me's farm, attracted to the refreshing scent of the tree, which is "perfuming the grounds like some ten-foot-tall air freshener" (Beatty 2015: 187). This gathering ends up turning into a community affair in which Me distributes a free breakfast of milk and satsuma mandarins to each resident in attendance. This tree, then, stands as a pillar of life-giving sustenance to the community, offering the people nutrition and relief from the dehumanizing stench of pollution. Unlike the antebellum slave plantations on which Me's farm is modeled, this modern-day plantation is reimagined as an oasis that can offer people a critical space of rejuvenation. The specter of slavery invoked by the physical site of Me's modern-day plantation thus functions much like the specter of segregation to bring life back to the socially dead community of Dickens. Yet this victory is overshadowed by the satirical premise of this scenario, which lies in the original reason for the residents' congregation. The very fact that they are gathering at this modern-day plantation to escape an oppressive stench just beyond the farm's borders gestures to the inescapable presence of the necropolitical state, which continues to subject them to toxic conditions.

Although reinstating slavery and segregation succeeds in unifying and nourishing the community (even as it continues to reinforce the socially dead status of its residents), the wider public insists on condemning Me as a sellout. This fact is rather ironic, given that this same public originally had no qualms about wiping Dickens off the map. In exposing the public's hypocrisy, *The Sellout* unapologetically satirizes a mainstream US society that preaches racial equality while dismissing whole communities of color as socially dead. Like Gunnar's establishment as a race leader, then, Me's categorization as a race traitor exposes the insidious nature of the necropolitics of black exceptionalism. What the outraged public fails to realize is that Me is far from a race traitor; in contrast, every action he takes strives to affirm, rather than erase, black lives. Me's devotion to his community is so significant, in fact, that he is willing to be tried and possibly punished as a criminal if doing so will grant his fellow townspeople a sense of worth. The extent of Me's commitment becomes fully apparent at the end of the novel, when the weather channel accurately reports the temperature of Dickens at 88 degrees (284). This institutional acknowledgment of Dickens's existence moves Me to tears, revealing his sense of relief that his hometown has been brought back into the fold of the Los Angeles community. With Dickens back on the map and the residents unified, Me's "selling out" reads more as a radical act of antiracist protest than a self-hating act of racial betrayal.

Conclusion

Beatty's satire bites because it exposes a disturbing truth: the various political strategies that black people have engaged throughout US history to achieve liberation, from abolition to racial uplift to civil rights, have all ultimately failed. This failure is inevitable in a necropolitical state so threatened by black organizing that it relentlessly weaponizes the full might of its laws, criminal justice system, and militarized police force to suppress movements for black liberation. This suppression manifests in the systematic criminalization, exile, and murder of major black leaders throughout US history, such as W. E. B. Du Bois, Martin Luther King Jr., Malcolm X, Assata Shakur, and Angela Davis. By exploring the absurd experiences of two seemingly oppositional black figures, the race leader Gunnar and the race traitor Me, *The White Boy Shuffle* and *The Sellout* call attention to the need to interrogate the crisis of black leadership in the post–civil rights era and to question how black people might achieve civic inclusion in a necropolitical state that insists on treating them as bare life. By calling for rather nihilistic strategies for achieving black liberation, specifically suicide, slavery, and segregation, both Gunnar and Me seem to suggest that one possible answer to addressing the crisis of black leadership and community can be found in seeking liberation through nihilism; after all, as Paul Gilroy (1994: 68) explains, nihilism can take on a social quality that "generates community and specifies the fortified boundaries of racial particularity." This message is captured by Me's observation at the end of *The Sellout*, "As fucked up and meaningless as it all is, sometimes it's the nihilism that makes life worth living"

(Beatty 2015: 277). Yet Beatty complicates this message by establishing Gunnar and Me as problematic leaders, whose nihilistic strategies for black liberation ultimately yield a greater loss of black lives and agency. By problematizing Gunnar's and Me's positioning as figures of black exception and leadership, Beatty suggests that black organizing should not revolve around a single leader but should emerge from stratified modes of resistance dispersed throughout the black community. We might look to the Black Lives Matter movement as a model for this type of nonhierarchical organizing, given its diversified leadership structure and lack of headquarters. With such nonhierarchical organizing comes the potential for black communities to bear the weight of radical transformation collectively and to imagine new modes of black agency and resilience.

Roberta Wolfson is an assistant professor in the English Department at California State Polytechnic University, San Luis Obispo, where she specializes in twentieth- and twenty-first-century US literature, with particular emphases on multiethnic US literatures (African American, Asian American, and Latinx). She earned her PhD in English from the University of California, Santa Barbara, where she held an American Cultures and Global Contexts Center Graduate Fellowship, a Eugene Cota-Robles Fellowship, and a Chicano Studies Institute Dissertation Research Grant. Her research interests include comparative race studies, mixed-race studies, and risk studies. Her scholarly work is published in *MELUS* (*Multi-Ethnic Literature of the United States*), and she is currently working on a monograph that considers how writers of color use antiracist literature to challenge the racism of the modern US security state.

Notes

1   My use of the term *color-blind* here builds on Eduardo Bonilla-Silva's (2006: 2) concept of color-blind racism, a racist ideology that "explains contemporary racial inequality as the outcome of nonracial dynamics." By "neoliberal multiculturalism," I am using Jodi Melamed's (2011) sense of the term, which she defines as a contemporary ideology that sees global capitalism as inherently antiracist. Like color-blind racism, neoliberal multiculturalism reinforces structural inequities caused by the uneven distribution of resources and therefore perpetuates racist, sexist, and heteronormative structures, despite purporting to be antiracist in philosophy.

2   For an in-depth analysis of the prison-industrial complex, see Davis 2003, DuVernay 2016, and Alexander 2010. Michelle Alexander (2010: 13) argues that mass incarceration relegates black people to "an *undercaste—*

a lower caste of individuals who are permanently barred by law and custom from mainstream society."

3 For a comprehensive review of the legal history that has entrenched the connection between whiteness and citizenship, see Ngai 2004 and Smith 2003.

4 See Rushdy 1999 for a further exploration of the neo-slave narrative genre.

5 In an interview with the *Paris Review*, Beatty remarked that being a writer of satire "would limit what I could do, how I could write about something. I'm just writing. Some of it's funny" (C. Jackson 2015). However, his edited collection, *Hokum: An Anthology of African-American Humor* (2006a), has earned him recognition as a contemporary theorist of African American humor.

6 Here I am building on Rolland Murray's (2008) and Eva Cherniavsky's (2017) interpretations of Gunnar's advocacy for suicide as a source of empowerment for his black community.

7 Throughout US history, violence committed against black bodies has often served as a source of spectacle and entertainment for white audiences, most notably in the form of spectacle lynchings. See Hale 1998 and Wood 2009.

8 In a macabre projection of the consequences of Gunnar's call for mass suicide in *The White Boy Shuffle*, suicide attempts are disturbingly frequent in Dickens. As the town's resident psychologist, Me's father is often called on to talk suicidal residents out of killing themselves.

9 The death of Me's father mirrors many police killings of black people that have attracted national attention in recent years. These cases include Eric Garner (July 17, 2014), Michael Brown (August 9, 2014), Tamir Rice (November 22, 2014), Freddie Gray (April 12, 2015), Sandra Bland (July 13, 2015), Samuel DuBose (July 19, 2015), Alton Sterling (July 5, 2016), Philando Castile (July 6, 2016), and Botham Shem Jean (September 6, 2018). On the rare occasions when the police officers responsible for these deaths are indicted or charged with a criminal conviction, they are disproportionately acquitted. A *New York Times* study found that out of fifteen high-profile cases in which black people were killed by police from 2014 to 2016, only three officers were convicted of a criminal charge (Lee and Park 2018).

References

Agamben, Giorgio. 1998. *Homo Sacer: Sovereign Power and Bare Life*. Translated by Daniel Heller-Roazen. Stanford, CA: Stanford Univ. Press.

Alexander, Michelle. 2010. *The New Jim Crow: Mass Incarceration in the Age of Colorblindness*. New York: New Press.

Allewaert, Monique. 2013. *Ariel's Ecology: Plantations, Personhood, and Colonialism in the American Tropics*. Minneapolis: Univ. of Minnesota Press.

Anderson, Elijah. 2011. *The Cosmopolitan Canopy: Race and Civility in Everyday Life*. New York: Norton.

Beatty, Paul. 1996. *The White Boy Shuffle*. New York: Picador.

Beatty, Paul, ed. 2006a. *Hokum: An Anthology of African-American Humor*. New York: Bloomsbury.

Beatty, Paul. 2006b. Introduction to Beatty 2006a: 1–12.

Beatty, Paul. 2015. *The Sellout*. New York: Picador.

Bonilla-Silva, Eduardo. 2006. *Racism without Racists: Color-Blind Racism and the Persistence of Racial Inequality in the United States*. Lanham, MD: Rowman and Littlefield.

Butler, Judith. 2004. *Precarious Life: The Power of Mourning and Violence*. San Francisco: Verso.

Caponi, Gena Dagel. 1999. "Introduction: The Case for an African American Aesthetic." In *Signifyin(g), Sanctifyin', and Slam Dunking: A Reader in African American Expressive Culture*, edited by Gena Dagel Caponi, 1–41. Amherst: Univ. of Massachusetts Press.

Carpio, Glenda. 2008. *Laughing Fit to Kill: Black Humor in the Fictions of Slavery*. New York: Oxford Univ. Press.

Cashmore, Ellis. 2012. *Beyond Black: Celebrity and Race in Obama's America*. New York: Bloomsbury.

Cherniavsky, Eva. 2017. *Neocitizenship: Political Culture after Democracy*. New York: New York Univ. Press.

Davis, Angela Y. 2003. *Are Prisons Obsolete?* New York: Seven Stories Press.

DiAngelo, Robin. 2018. *White Fragility: Why It's So Hard for White People to Talk about Racism*. Boston: Beacon.

Dickson-Carr, Darryl. 2001. *African American Satire: The Sacredly Profane Novel*. Columbia: Univ. of Missouri Press.

Dubey, Madhu. 2003. *Signs and Cities: Black Literary Postmodernism*. Chicago: Univ. of Chicago Press.

DuVernay, Ava, dir. 2016. *13th*. Los Angeles: Kandoo Films.

Gaines, Kevin K. 1996. *Uplifting the Race: Black Leadership, Politics, and Culture in the Twentieth Century*. Chapel Hill: Univ. of North Carolina Press.

Gilroy, Paul. 1994. "'After the Love Has Gone': Bio-Politics and Etho-Poetics in the Black Public Sphere." *Public Culture* 7, no. 1: 49–76.

Grassian, Daniel. 2009. *Writing the Future of Black America: Literature of the Hip-Hop Generation*. Columbia: Univ. of South Carolina Press.

Hale, Grace Elizabeth. 1998. *Making Whiteness: The Culture of Segregation in the South, 1890–1940*. New York: Pantheon.

Hartman, Saidiya V. 1997. *Scenes of Subjection: Terror, Slavery, and Self-Making in Nineteenth-Century America*. New York: Oxford Univ. Press.

Hayakawa, S. I. 1957. "Suicide as a Communicative Act." *ETC: A Review of General Semantics* 15, no. 1: 46–51.

Ikard, David H. 2013. *Blinded by the Whites: Why Race Still Matters in 21st-Century America.* Bloomington: Indiana Univ. Press.

Jackson, Chris. 2015. "Our Thing: An Interview with Paul Beatty." *Paris Review,* May 7. www.theparisreview.org/blog/2015/05/07/our-thing-an-interview-with-paul-beatty/.

Jackson, Zakiyyah Iman. 2015. "Outer Worlds: The Persistence of Race in Movement 'Beyond the Human.'" *GLQ: A Journal of Lesbian and Gay Studies* 21, no. 2–3: 215–18.

Kelley, Robin D. G. 1997. *Yo' Mama's Disfunktional! Fighting the Culture Wars in Urban America.* Boston: Beacon.

Lee, Jasmine, and Haeyoun Park. 2018. "15 Black Lives Ended in Confrontations with Police: 3 Officers Convicted." *New York Times,* October 5. www.nytimes.com/interactive/2017/05/17/us/black-deaths-police.html.

Lipsitz, George. 2011. *How Racism Takes Place.* Philadelphia: Temple Univ. Press.

May, Reuben A. Buford. 2008. *Living through the Hoop: High School Basketball, Race, and the American Dream.* New York: New York Univ. Press.

McKnight, Utz. 2013. *Race and the Politics of the Exception: Equality, Sovereignty, and American Democracy.* New York: Routledge.

Melamed, Jodi. 2011. *Represent and Destroy: Rationalizing Violence in the New Capitalism.* Minneapolis: Univ. of Minnesota Press.

Mills, Charles W. 1997. *The Racial Contract.* Ithaca, NY: Cornell Univ. Press.

Murray, Rolland. 2008. "Black Crisis Shuffle: Fiction, Race, and Simulation." *African American Review* 42, no. 2: 215–33.

Ngai, Mae. 2004. *Impossible Subjects: Illegal Aliens and the Making of Modern America.* Princeton, NJ: Princeton Univ. Press.

Patterson, Orlando. 1982. *Slavery and Social Death: A Comparative Study.* Cambridge, MA: Harvard Univ. Press.

Pickens, Therí A. 2014. *New Body Politics: Narrating Arab and Black Identity in the Contemporary United States.* New York: Routledge.

Rankin, Andrew. 2011. *Seppuku: A History of Samurai Suicide.* New York: Kodansha.

Rushdy, Ashraf H. A. 1999. *Neo-Slave Narratives: Studies in the Social Logic of a Literary Form.* Oxford: Oxford Univ. Press.

Scott, Daryl Michael. 1997. *Contempt and Pity: Social Policy and the Image of the Damaged Black Psyche, 1880–1996.* Chapel Hill: Univ. of North Carolina Press.

Smith, Llewellyn M., dir. 2003. "The House We Live in." Episode 3 of *Race: The Power of an Illusion.* San Francisco: California Newsreel.

Snyder, Terri L. 2015. *The Power to Die: Slavery and Suicide in British North America.* Chicago: Univ. of Chicago Press.

Spillers, Hortense J. 1987. "Mama's Baby, Papa's Maybe: An American Grammar Book." *Diacritics* 17, no. 2: 64–81.

Stewart, Anthony. 2011. "Giving the People What They Want: The African American Exception as Racial Cliché in Percival Everett's *Erasure*." In *American Exceptionalisms: From Winthrop to Winfrey*, edited by Sylvia Söderlind and James Taylor Carson, 167–89. Albany: SUNY Press.

Weheliye, Alexander G. 2014. *Habeas Viscus: Racializing Assemblages, Biopolitics, and Black Feminist Theories of the Human*. Durham, NC: Duke Univ. Press.

Wise, Tim. 2009. *Between Barack and a Hard Place: Racism and White Denial in the Age of Obama*. San Francisco: City Lights.

Wood, Amy Louise. 2009. *Lynching and Spectacle: Witnessing Racial Violence in America, 1890–1940*. Chapel Hill: Univ. of North Carolina Press.

Zita Cristina Nunes · Epilogue

T he untitled cover image and the image on the following page, *How My Grandfather Survived* (2015) by Cedrick Tamasala, as well as the conditions that gave rise to their display, perfectly
illustrate the concerns and tensions of the essays in this collection,
linking all of them together in a global network.

Tamasala's works were part of a 2017 exhibition at the Sculpture-
Center in Long Island City, New York. The exhibit enacted the entangled
and fraught relationships that characterize the postplantation by displaying the engagement of a group of artists with their environment
and materials, slavery and colonialism, and the circulation of commodities as art and activism. Produced by the Cercle d'Art des Travailleurs de Plantation Congolaise (Congolese Plantation Workers Art
League)—a laborers' collective that includes Michel Ekeba, Eléonore
Hellio, Mathieu Kilapi Kasiama, Mananga Kibuila, Mbuku Kimpala,
Thomas Leba, Mega Mingeidi, in addition to Tamasala—the works
contribute to the larger vision Dutch artist Renzo Martens manifested
in the Lusanga International Research Centre for Art and Economic
Inequality.[1] The research center, an arm of the Institute for Human
Activities, is housed in the White Cube building designed by Rem
Koolhaas on the former Anglo-Dutch Unilever palm oil plantation in
Lusanga, Republic of Congo. The Institute for Human Activities web-
site states: "With the establishment of the White Cube, the mecha-
nisms through which plantations underwrite the art world are reversed.
It attracts the capital and visibility needed to invent a new ecological

American Literature, Volume 91, Number 3, September 2019
DOI 10.1215/00029831-7722164 © 2019 by Duke University Press

Figure 1   Cedrick Tamasala, *How My Grandfather Survived*, 2015, installation view, *Cercle d'Art des Travailleurs de Plantation Congolaise*, SculptureCenter, New York, 2017. Chocolate. 15 by 8.3 by 9.4 inches (38 by 21 by 24 cm). Courtesy the Cercle d'Art des Travailleurs de Plantation Congolaise; Galerie Fons Welters, Amsterdam; and KOW, Berlin. Photo by Kyle Knodell

and economic model on site: the post-plantation. Former plantation workers develop this new model for landscape restoration."

The artists are involved in the landscape restoration by planting shared experimental gardens to produce cacao. The artist-farmers thereby shift the scale of agricultural production from the vast extractive cultivation of palms for oil that enriched multinational corporations to the small-scale and sustainable cultivation of cacao. As mapped out in the cover image by Tamasala, cultivating and working with cacao also references the growth of the colonial enterprise under King Leopold of Belgium, as well as the invention of Dutch mechanical methods to process the chocolate consumed as a luxury throughout the world since its introduction by the Aztecs to Spanish colonizers, the branding of Belgian chocolate, and the establishment of legal regulations and commercial networks that transferred the wealth generated in Africa to Europe and North America. Much as the fabrication of chocolate required transport north to gain value, so too do these sculptures produced by the farmer-artists. Initially formed in clay in Lusanga and digitized, the molds were sent to Amsterdam to be three-dimensionally printed, cast in chocolate, and then exhibited in prestigious venues like the Tate Modern. The resulting organic sculptures carry with them not only the history of this movement away from their producers but also an aesthetic of ephemerality and decay. The smell that emanates from the sculptures and attaches to visitors long after they leave is a powerful reminder of the uneven visible and invisible ways we—and no less those of us writing at our desks in universities that owe their financial, if not physical, location to the plantation—are imbricated in the afterlife of plantation slavery.

Zita Cristina Nunes is associate professor of comparative literature and English at the University of Maryland, College Park.

Note

1   Renzo Martens is an acknowledged provocateur, and perhaps as a result, response to his collaboration with the Cercle has been mixed. Many reviewers discuss this collaboration in relation to his *Enjoy Poverty* project, for which he urged Congolese photographers to themselves capitalize on the global north's appetite for disturbing images of "African" poverty, disease, and violence rather than cede this ground to profiteering American and European journalists and filmmakers. See, for example, Okeke-Ogulu 2017; Bishop 2017; and Institute for Human Activities 2017.

References

Bishop, Claire. 2017. Review of Cercle d'Art des Travailleurs de Plantation Congolaise. *Artforum* 55, no. 9. www.artforum.com/print/reviews/201705/cercle-d-art-des-travailleurs-de-plantation-congolaise-67939.

Institute for Human Activities. 2017. "Matter of Critique, Part 4." January 29. www.humanactivities.org/en/matter-of-critique-part-iv/.

Institute for Human Activities. n.d. www.humanactivities.org/en/ (accessed March 20, 2019).

Okeke-Agulu, Chika. 2017. Review of Cercle d'Art des Travailleurs de Plantation Congolaise. *Artforum* 55, no. 9. www.artforum.com/print/reviews /201705/cercle-d-art-des-travailleurs-de-plantation-congolaise-67938.

Book Reviews

The Difficult Art of Giving: Patronage, Philanthropy, and the American Literary Market. By Francesca Sawaya. Philadelphia: Univ. of Pennsylvania Press. 2014. ix, 264 pp. Cloth, $55.00; e-book available.

Captains of Charity: The Writing and Wages of Postrevolutionary Atlantic Benevolence. By Mary Kathleen Eyring. Durham: Univ. of New Hampshire Press. 2017. xii, 280 pp. Paper, $45.00; e-book, $44.99.

Francesca Sawaya's *The Difficult Art of Giving* and Mary Kathleen Eyring's *Captains of Charity*, two recent additions to the ongoing analysis of American attitudes toward charitable giving, offer compelling readings of both prominent and lesser-known authors. While each addresses different periods of American history, they share some key insights regarding the intersection of philanthropy, literature, and a rapidly changing economic landscape, even as they differ rather dramatically in their interpretations. More importantly, they are a welcome reminder that recent critiques of the nonprofit sector, including of corporate and family foundations, are not new; writers have been exploring, exposing, and taking advantage of the fraught intersection between the marketplace and charitable organizations since the days when they began gaining prominence in the United States.

Sawaya focuses on the late nineteenth and early twentieth centuries and extends more familiar notions of philanthropy to include not only the emerging corporate foundations that now dominate the nonprofit landscape, but also patronage. She argues that the former emerged, in part, from the latter. Complex networks of friendships and influence, including personal relationships between authors and corporate benefactors, were fostered by elite private clubs and literary associations like the Authors Club, which welcomed Andrew Carnegie as a member. One of the book's particular strengths is the

American Literature, Volume 91, Number 3, September 2019
DOI 10.1215/00029831-7722176 © 2019 by Duke University Press

way that Sawaya traces Carnegie's influence on both the rhetoric and the practice of philanthropy. His famous essay, "The Gospel of Wealth" (1889), promoted a "business" model that sought to corporatize philanthropy even as it
refused to criticize the economic system that contributed to the very problems wealthy donors ostensibly sought to address.

The authors in Sawaya's study, which include Mark Twain, Henry James,
William Dean Howells, Charles W. Chesnutt, and Theodore Dreiser, benefited from the friendship and patronage of wealthy benefactors, or their institutions, even as they employed their fiction to interrogate how such relationships could compromise artistic independence. Such connections could be
personal, as in the case of Twain's friendship with Standard Oil executive
Henry H. Rogers, or at a further remove, as in the case of Chesnutt's education, which was supported by a wealthy Northern banker. Sawaya provides
intriguing readings of key texts by these authors: one example that feels quite
timely given the rise of donor-funded journalism is Sawaya's discussion of
Howells's novel *A Hazard of New Fortunes* (1890). She argues that Carnegie
and John D. Rockefeller served as models for the millionaire Jacob Dryfoos,
who sponsors a literary magazine and then hopes to influence its contents:
"In Howells's fictional exploration of the dilemma of print media," Sawaya
writes, " . . . the market challenges artistic and intellectual creativity and integ-
rity, but a newer challenge is the capitalist sponsor, the philanthropist, who
mediates the relation of the intellectual to the market and who *seems* to allow
her/him to bypass the market" (77). Philanthropy may appear to offer the artist an escape from economic entanglements, but for writers like those Sawaya
discusses, such evasions were illusory.

Eyring also sees philanthropy as intricately linked to capitalism. While
Sawaya examines how corporate philanthropy at the end of the nineteenth
century tended to spring from and perpetuate elite networks of white male
privilege, however, Eyring argues that the integration of charity and industry
in the postrevolutionary period meant that working in the emergent field
offered members of marginalized groups, including free African Americans
and women, a degree of economic and social agency. She analyzes both the
writings and careers of authors including Sarah Pogson Smith, Nancy Prince,
and Sarah Josepha Hale, arguing that their decisions to connect their written work with charitable causes provided them with tangible rewards. Eyring
sees Hale's founding of the Seaman's Aid Society, for example, as helping
to pave the way to her editorship of the magazine *Godey's Lady's Book*. The
social and religious approval that came from working to help others, Eyring
argues—and the audience one reached in writing to support such efforts—
were nonmonetary benefits charity offered to those who practiced it.

Hale's work on behalf of sailors and their families is particularly significant to Eyring's analysis, as she contends the Atlantic maritime industry provided the foundation for the rise of the nonprofit sector. The harsh conditions
accompanying maritime trade meant there were always people in need, and

the profits from the very same enterprises that contributed to people's hardship simultaneously provided funds sought by charitable workers like Hale or Smith. Eyring's discussion of Smith, who donated the proceeds from the sale of her book *Daughters of Eve* (1826) to the New York Institution for the Instruction of the Deaf and Dumb (founded in 1818), illustrates the kind of intersection Eyring sees as a fundamental part of the nascent nonprofit sector. Smith's personal interests (Eyring reads Smith's donation in part as a marketing tactic), industry needs (the institute featured a curriculum that prepared its students to pursue trades valued in maritime commerce), and the needs of the students and their families were all served by Smith's philanthropic enterprise.

Both Sawaya and Eyring ably demonstrate the social and economic forces that shaped philanthropy at distinct moments in US history and the ways that writers contributed to, reflected, and interrogated these forces. What remains less clear, perhaps inevitably so, is the role that personal conviction may have played in the benevolent actions of many of the subjects of these texts. Sawaya notes, "I hope to avoid the Scylla and Charybdis that plague analyses of philanthropy: on the one hand, the naturalization of it as an expression of the benevolent progressivism of corporate capitalism, or more simply of the good intentions of individual capitalists; on the other hand, its reduction to an easy and unchallenged capitalist hegemony" (3). This is a laudable aim, and difficult to achieve. In arguing persuasively for the benefits her subjects accrued through their philanthropic actions—benefits rendering them "captains of charity"—Eyring at times glances over these more personal commitments. If, as Eyring argues, Prince's missionary work in Haiti was likely driven by economic necessity, for instance, it certainly remains the case that she may have been equally moved by religious or altruistic sentiments, just as Hale may have been moved by the plight of sailors and their families. True to her aim, Sawaya goes further in examining the entanglement of self-interest and altruism, attending to the role that emotions like loyalty and gratitude played in the friendship between Twain and Rogers, for example. It is difficult not to read her text and be reminded of a question she asks early on, "Could or did philanthropy ever exist?" (8), and answer in the negative: capitalist hegemony often lurks on the edge of the discussion. Still, given the myriad intentions that motivate charitable action, and the social and economic forces behind it, both of these authors have done remarkable work in tracing the development of philanthropy in American literature and culture during two key periods in the nation's history.

Martin T. Buinicki is the Walter G. Friedrich Professor of American Literature at Valparaiso University and author of *Negotiating Copyright* (2006) and *Walt Whitman's Reconstruction* (2011). He currently serves on the faculty advisory committee of the Learning by Giving Foundation, which provides grants to support experiential philanthropy in university courses.

Weapons of Democracy: Propaganda, Progressivism, and American Public Opinion. By Jonathan Auerbach. Baltimore: Johns Hopkins Univ. Press. 2015. ix, 232 pp. Cloth, $49.95.

Untimely Democracy: The Politics of Progress after Slavery. By Gregory Laski. New York: Oxford Univ. Press. 2018. xv, 288 pp. Cloth, $74.00; e-book available.

Direct Democracy: Collective Power, the Swarm, and the Literatures of the Americas. By Scott Henkel. Jackson: Univ. Press of Mississippi. 2017. xii, 224 pp. Cloth, $65.00; paper, $35.00.

Is there such a thing as the common good? Since Aristotle, Western political theorists have argued that the function of government is to promote the general welfare. Since the Enlightenment, they have often credited democracy as the form of government best suited to do so. Both ideas seem antiquated when considering American democracy today. A reality television star holds the White House, elected by Russian bots on Twitter; slavery's structural legacy persists in police brutality against unarmed black men; and even a catastrophic threat to civilization itself—global warming—provides insufficient ground for cooperation or consensus. Some hope can be found in insurgent and decentralized movements like Occupy Wall Street and #MeToo, but traditional democracy, at least, seems to have ceased to function in some fundamental way.

In light of such concerns three recent books in American studies take up the urgent project of reimagining and rethinking democracy by returning to debates about public opinion, racial progress, and the power of the multitude in the long nineteenth century. Reading canonical and lesser-known novels alongside works of sociology, philosophy, oratory, and political and educational theory, Jonathan Auerbach, Gregory Laski, and Scott Henkel challenge the field's reductive drive to periodize by century, uncovering a long and rich history of writing about democracy on either side of 1900. Their studies offer insight into the origins of some of the salient issues of our present nadir—the manipulation of opinion through the media, the untimely persistence of slavery in attitude and effect, and the power and potential of a decentralized, networked resistance. All three authors are committed to exploring the complexity of the attitudes to democracy found within their archive, rather than rehearsing now-familiar critiques of their blind spots regarding race, gender, and exceptionalism. They point out that nineteenth- and early twentieth-century American writers not only championed American democracy's successes, they also responded in interesting and important ways to its failures.

American Literature, Volume 91, Number 3, September 2019
DOI 10.1215/00029831-7722188   © 2019 by Duke University Press

As Laski and Henkel in particular show, those failures often called on writers to imagine alternative forms of democratic power and governance.

Auerbach's *Weapons of Democracy*, as Bill Brown notes in his blurb, is an "unnerving and chilling book." Five chapters, moving from the 1880s to the 1930s, track an increasing crisis of confidence within US institutions in the idea of government, journalism, and education as forces for the common good. Examining writing by Walter Lippmann, John Dewey, Mark Twain, Theodore Roosevelt, Woodrow Wilson, Julia Lathrop, Randolph Bourne, and many others, Auerbach tells the dispiriting story of the gradual transfer of the skills and tactics of publicity (invented by the muckrakers to push for labor rights, women's rights, and industrial reform) to the business of corporate publicity and public relations bureaus, which sought to shape public opinion in their own interests. The book begins at the close of the nineteenth century, in a chapter exploring utopian fiction, the emergence of muckraking, and the rise of the first corporate publicity bureaus. It ends with a chapter on former journalist–turned–corporate publicist Ivy Lee, who, in the 1930s, advised the German firm Farben on the best ways to influence American public opinion in favor of the Nazis.

Auerbach's title comes from George Creel, who receives extensive treatment in chapters 2 and 3. A former muckraker and the head of Woodrow Wilson's Committee on Public Information, the propaganda bureau of the US government during World War I, Creel, in 1914, praised as "weapons of democracy" the publicity tactics used by the government to sway public opinion against corporate malfeasance. But "weapons of democracy" could equally well describe Creel's attitude toward his own war propaganda tactics for Wilson (66), and the phrase was later used by Adolf Hitler, in 1933, to describe his aspirations to destroy democracy by its own weapons—by getting elected. It aptly captures the book's central but largely unarticulated question: is the common good, or even democracy itself, anything more than a convenient lie by the few to seize power over the many?

Laski's *Untimely Democracy* is a study of how African American writers during the same period confronted this question when they were forced to reckon with the contradiction between the ideology of American democratic, spiritual, and technological progress and the untimely persistence of slavery in the form of Jim Crow segregation. Their answer, Laski shows, was not to renounce democracy but to rethink its temporal assumptions. For black writers and thinkers during the oft-cited nadir of race relations circa 1900, temporal repetition and recursivity, rather than linear ascent, became a locus of black political and democratic possibility. Laski begins with a reading of W. E. B. Du Bois's *The Souls of Black Folk* (1903) and of Du Bois's term "present-past," which he coined to describe slavery's legacy. Chapter 2 reads narrative recursivity and repetition in *Life and Times of Frederick Douglass* (1881) as well as in Douglass's later revisions and speeches as an index of his perception of failed progress in the nadir. The book then turns, in chapter 3, to a fascinating lesser-known nineteenth-century archive of efforts to attain reparations for slavery and explores Stephen Crane's novella *The Monster* (1898) as a response to this context. In a revolutionary reading, *The Monster* emerges as a sophisticated analysis of black "hereditary social degradation" (127) and as a novella that makes the case for reparations thirty years on.

Chapter 4 shows how the novels of Charles W. Chesnutt and the nonfiction writing of Sutton Griggs anticipate current critical trends—Afropessimism (Chesnutt) and black optimism (Griggs)—and argues that the prophetic modes of thought found in the work of both writers are a means of sustaining untimely democratic hope. *Untimely Democracy* closes with a chapter on the uncanny connections between present and past in Pauline E. Hopkins's novels. In *Contending Forces* (1900), Laski sees an illustration of Jacques Rancière's notion of "dissensus"—a challenge to the sensible order that determines the inclusion or exclusion of particular groups in politics—in the stillness of the audience and the swooning collapse of the protagonist Sappho Clark, in a scene set at an American Colored League meeting. For Hopkins, *Untimely Democracy*'s hero, slavery's present-past motivates both a strategy of narrative representation and a mode of political protest.

While *Untimely Democracy* speaks to the temporal turn in American studies, Henkel's *Direct Democracy* speaks to its spatial turn, examining how sympathetic and critical observers in Haiti, Mexico, and the US mainland during the long nineteenth century represented the power of groups and multitudes engaged in revolution and other challenges to constituted powers. The book's two main interventions are to bring a discussion of race, slavery, and the multitude to the conversation about democratic power found in thinkers such as Carl Schmitt, Walter Benjamin, and Giorgio Agamben and to show that the common nineteenth- and early twentieth-century metaphor of "the swarm" anticipated contemporary theories about the agency of assemblages and networks. The Haitian slave rebellion, Henkel argues, was the most influential example of swarm power for nineteenth- and early twentieth-century thinkers; it forms the context for the first and last chapters, which concern, respectively, C. L. R. James's *The Black Jacobins* (1938) and Marie Vieux Chauvet's novella *Love* (1968). In between, Henkel examines the metaphor of the swarm in Thomas Carlyle, Walt Whitman, and Lucy Parsons; in William Styron's *The Confessions of Nat Turner* (1967); and in the novels of B. Traven, which treat the Mexican Revolution of 1910–19.

Of the three books reviewed here, *Direct Democracy* is the most infused with political hope, because it examines actually successful challenges to unjust political and social regimes. Henkel is largely sanguine about the violence necessary for the swarm to overthrow constituted power and the difficulty of maintaining collective agency and decision-making both during and after. Yet he has an important reminder: "The only way to threaten a systematized injustice credibly is to present a collective challenge to it" (105). In a time of such social and political division, perhaps this is a lesson that we would do well to take to heart.

Katherine Biers is a visiting associate professor in the Department of English at New York University and the author of *Virtual Modernism: Writing and Technology in the Progressive Era* (2013).

The Transmutation of Love and Avant-Garde Poetics. By Jeanne Heuving.
Tuscaloosa: Univ. of Alabama Press. 2016. xv, 240 pp. Paper, $34.95;
e-book available.

The Marriage Plot: Or, How Jews Fell in Love with Love, and with Literature.
By Naomi Seidman. Stanford, CA: Stanford Univ. Press. 2016. x, 368 pp.
Cloth, $90.00; paper, $29.95; e-book available.

What's love got to do with *lit*? Very little, scholarship might lead us to believe.
Even work shaped by affect theory's return of emotions to literary study
leaves love, forlorn and unrequited, largely alone. Sianne Ngai focuses on the
"uglier" feelings (envy, anxiety), Rita Felski on the ways literature enchants
and shocks, and Deidre Lynch on the love *of* literature, not the literature of
love. This absence doesn't reflect love's prominence as literary motive and
subject matter. Enter Jeanne Heuving and Naomi Seidman, who, working
from different fields (American avant-garde poetics and modern Jewish literatures, respectively), suggest it is time we stop being embarrassed and start
talking about love. They reveal that, far from a sentimental flaw, love is actually a catalyst to literary innovation.

The difficulty of effective biographical criticism presents a primary obsta-
cle to scholarship's engagement with love. Among Heuving's most important
contributions in *The Transmutation of Love* is, then, her modeling of a new
and useful approach to biographical criticism, one that reunites it with studies
of formal poetics. Avoiding both literary gossip and armchair psychoanalysis,
she begins from the simple observation that the ways we express love will
affect how we write it. Through readings of the poetry of Ezra Pound and
H.D., Heuving shows that the modernist imperative to "make it new" included
a long-overlooked reimagining of love poetry. The major formal innovations
of Pound's *Cantos* (1925) and H.D.'s *Sea Garden* (1916), we learn, emerge
directly from the poets' search for alternatives to the traditional format in
which a lover writes to or about his beloved. Grounding the development of
imagism within Pound's and H.D.'s (entangled) love lives, Heuving shows
how the imagist creation of poetry "in which an egoistic poetic speaker no longer serves as the primary locus of the poem" (52) forms a new love poetry by
displacing the lover and redirecting the poem's energy "onto their poems' others and languages" (64). Chapters focused on these poets enable Heuving to
craft a compelling case for H.D.'s centrality to the histories of modernist and
avant-garde poetics.

As a bisexual woman, H.D. cannot map herself onto earlier love poetry's
standard heterosexual lover-beloved patterns. The transmutation of love is, in

American Literature, Volume 91, Number 3, September 2019
DOI 10.1215/00029831-7722200   © 2019 by Duke University Press

part, the consequence of this, a revision that results in an opening up of who can write love poetry across lines of gender, sexual orientation, and race. These afterlives and influences of H.D.'s and Pound's innovations are traced across the book's final chapters, which turn to the postwar avant-garde of Robert Duncan, Kathleen Fraser, and Nathaniel Mackey. Mackey and Duncan, for instance, both face personal and societal restrictions on the ability, as gay men, to say, "I love." Duncan, whose extensive commentaries on his own poetic process reveal that "for him the experience of love and the writing of love are inseparable" (116), eventually develops a way to name the kind of love he experiences. Things are more complicated for Mackey. "For African American men," Heuving notes, "the legacy of lynching, especially given its message of sexual punishment, hardly makes questing after an unavailable beloved an attractive literary genre" (158). The options available to Duncan as a *white* gay poet, even as he grapples with the melancholy of an unavailable, unnameable love object, are far broader than those available to Mackey. By observing the ways in which American racial dynamics ultimately limit the expansion of love poetry begun by Pound's and H.D.'s transmutations, Heuving adds an important final turn to her discussion of avant-garde love poetry.

Naomi Seidman fixes her sights on romantic, rather than sexual, love. *The Marriage Plot* takes up modern Jewish literature across language (Hebrew, Yiddish, English) and genre (novel, short story, theater, film). On this broad canvas, Seidman shows not just how poetry transmutes love but how love first changes Jewish life and culture—and how Jewish cultural productions then change American and European ideas of love. Literature, Seidman argues, played a central role, as Jewish marriage was secularized and modernized over the course of the nineteenth and twentieth centuries. Beyond reading novels as reflections of changing attitudes, Seidman argues that literature was pivotal in introducing Jews to Christian concepts of romantic love and, ultimately, in transforming these into "a modern sexual counter-narrative to the Christian chivalric models of love" (69), one that continues to shape how Americans think about sex.

These transformations take place on the level of genre. The Hebrew novels of the mid-nineteenth-century Haskalah, or Jewish Enlightenment, were shaped by the conventions of novelistic romance in European languages: romantic love and love marriages enter the Jewish imagination less through observation of people than in the act of reading, which, in turn, opens Jews to new modes of courtship, marriage, kinship, and community. Yet, she insists, "the Jewish adoption of European literary and sexual conventions was always partial and ambivalent" (68), leading to the production of "Jewish sexual heresies" (302) by Sigmund Freud, Philip Roth, Erica Jong, and Lenny Bruce, which counter, often in satirical, deflating ways, "the romantic sublime" (303).

The presence of existing Jewish literary genres and conventions enable this shift: courtship letters between the betrothed; *yihus brifs* (accounts of family pedigree); extended, nonnuclear family (*makhotonim*); and the figure of the matchmaker. Literary practices with roots in the language and culture of European Jewry permeate twentieth-century American Jewish writing, revealing a portrait of a transnational American literary heritage: makhotonim reappear in the aunts, grandmothers, and nonbiological maternal figures of Grace Paley's fiction, whereas Tony Kushner's *Angels in America* (1991, 1993) can be recognized as a play of and about yihus brifs. Kushner's play opens with a genealogical recitation (as do the nineteenth-century memoirs of the Haskalah), framing Louis Ironson as one cousin among many in a nonnuclear kinship network later mimicked by the dream visitation of Prior Walter's illustrious namesakes. Such conventions, when they reemerge in American Jewish literature, satirize and undermine the assumption that *only* the two lovers have perspectives that merit inclusion in narratives of young love. "Modern Jewish narrative," Seidman observes, "so dedicated at its outset to expelling the intrusive families that stood in the way of modern romance, finally became a stage on which these cousins and aunts could crowd and on which their voices could resound" (252).

In this, perhaps, Seidman's and Heuving's approaches are at their most divergent. Where Seidman follows modern Jewish writers beyond a "focus on the psychosexual individual, sexual couple, and nuclear family" (252), the first two are very much the spaces in which Heuving's readings reside. In this and their differentiation of romantic and sexual love, both scholars begin to demonstrate the multifarious nature of love literature. Far from limiting writers to formulas and clichés, love writing enables the embedding of difference.

Joshua Logan Wall is a postdoctoral fellow in English at the University of Michigan. He is at work on a book project, "Situating Poetry: Performance and Covenant in American Literature."

Black Power TV. By Devorah Heitner. Durham, NC: Duke Univ. Press. 2013. xiii, 190 pp. Cloth, $89.95; paper, $23.95; e-book, $22.95.

Race News: Black Journalists and the Fight for Racial Justice in the Twentieth Century. By Fred Carroll. Urbana: Univ. of Illinois Press. 2017. viii, 264 pp. Cloth, $95.00; paper, $27.95; e-book, $25.16.

The 1960s were a turbulent time in US history. Racism and discrimination pervaded every aspect of American society, including the television and publishing industries. Years of activism by African Americans and their allies resulted in the passage of the Civil Rights Act (1964) and Voting Rights Act (1965). While these landmark decisions lifted barriers that prohibited African Americans full access to public spaces, employment, and the constitutional right to vote, this legislature could not mandate social change. Racial discrimination continued to hinder the educational, housing, employment, and social opportunities of African Americans. Feelings of disillusionment and outrage continued to rise alongside poverty levels within African American communities. These racial tensions reached a boiling point during the 1960s and 1970s as African American journalists, activists, and artists took to the streets, the printing press, and the emerging black media to fight for black liberation. Devorah Heitner's *Black Power TV* and Fred Carroll's *Race News* offer a richly detailed glimpse into this chapter of US history, recovering the efforts of local black television programs and historically black newspapers to disseminate black power politics and Black Arts movement theory and performance to a much wider audience.

Black Power TV and *Race News* emerge out of a growing field of scholarship on the black power era. Indeed, the past decade has witnessed a dramatic increase in book-length studies about the black power era, including efforts to consider black women's leadership within the movement. Heitner's interdisciplinary study contributes to this body of knowledge by situating television activism as a vital component of the black power movement and by attending to the intersectional concerns within black power ideology. I especially appreciate that Heitner includes not only well-known activists and public intellectuals in her discussion but also the activism of staff members whose off-camera labor helped sustain the programs and their black-focused mission. Carroll provides an in-depth account of how journalists and editors—from the 1880s to the black power movement of the 1960s and 1970s—used their agency to promote black liberation politics from within both commercial and alternative black presses. Written during an era of "hashtag activism," both books offer valuable insights into how activists of the past used

American Literature, Volume 91, Number 3, September 2019
DOI 10.1215/00029831-7722212   © 2019 by Duke University Press

television and print media to promote racial justice and discuss the need to continue these efforts in our digital age.

Despite the limitations of archival evidence—due, in part, to the formerly common practice of taping over previously aired programs—Heitner offers a thoroughly researched, accessible, and well-written book. *Black Power TV* is divided into four case studies that examine how television programs helped circulate black power politics and Black Arts movement performance among everyday black audiences. In so doing, Heitner recuperates the "invisibility" of black audiences within traditional rating systems of the past, noting that "African Americans made up significant portions of viewing audiences in many cities" (18). Chapters 1 and 2 explore the circumstances that impacted the emergence of local black programing. Heitner persuasively argues that Brooklyn's *Inside Bedford-Stuyvesant* (1968) was "an important discursive and cultural center" of "homegrown talent and political organizing" (25). She then analyzes how *Say Brother* staff members promoted revolutionary politics by revealing the pervasiveness of institutionalized racism within Boston's supposedly "racially progressive community" (21). Chapters 3 and 4 investigate two nationally broadcast television programs: the "newsmagazine style" *Black Journal* and the "arts-focused" *Soul!* (21). Heitner first considers how *Black Journal*'s coverage of political struggle on the African continent provided audiences with a diasporic view of black empowerment. She then examines how *Soul!* promoted the Black Arts ethos, writing that the program "unabashedly posited musicians, actors, and poets as experts on the state of Black people, of Black liberation, and of the political and aesthetic contribution of new cultural forms of Black identity and to the world at large" (22). *Black Power TV* concludes with a discussion of the decline of black television programing.

Race News is an incredibly insightful and well-written book that offers both a broad history of black journalism in the United States and a deeply nuanced investigation of black power politics in the newsroom. Carroll begins his study by inviting those unfamiliar with early black journalism practices to consider the fluid nature of journalism during segregation. Carroll writes: "The boundaries of the commercial and alternative presses were never rigid, and the definition of journalist was broad. Segregation restrained black writers' careers and earnings and often compelled authors, poets, scholars, and activists to publish alongside working reporters, infusing black journalism with an unexpected cultural vibrancy and cosmopolitan character" (3). Throughout the seven chapters, Carroll offers a compelling analysis of how reporters, editors, and publishers used their agency to engage with issues of integration and black radicalism at home and anticolonialism abroad while also combatting "surveillance, censorship, and ridicule" from the federal government and white press (9). Chapter 1 uses Robert Abbott's newspaper *Chicago Defender* and W. E. B. Du Bois's magazine *Crisis* as a lens to explore how the Great Migration (1916–70) and censorship during World War I impacted black journalism and editorial practices. Chapter 2 considers the more radical editors of the 1920s and 1930s, whose activism resulted in the formation of alternative black presses. Chapter 3 reveals how alternative black presses of the 1930s advanced "Marxist-inspired critiques of capitalism, colonialism, and racial exploitation" (10). Chapter 5 investigates how Cold War politics of the 1940s and 1950s hindered the proliferation of left-leaning journalism. Chapter 6 documents how alternative publications such as the Black Panther party's *Black Panther* and the Nation of Islam's *Muhammad Speaks* gained widespread readership and ultimately challenged the commercial press's conservative views by endorsing a more radical black power politics. Carroll completes his study with an examination of how black journalists continued to resist institutional racism from within the white-dominated newsroom.

Works such as *Race News* and *Black Power TV* are long overdue, and both deserve praise for their contribution to the fields of African American history and media, communication, and gender studies. Carroll offers the first scholarly monograph of the political and professional development of black journalism in the twentieth-century United States while Heitner reclaims a vital but heretofore marginalized aspect of the black power movement. Graduate students and scholars interested in the history of black journalism, the black power movement, early black programing, and the Black Arts movement will find these books invaluable. The interdisciplinary content, accessible language, and structure of the books (i.e., chronological and case studies, respectively) will also appeal to undergraduates enrolled in upper division seminars.

La Donna L. Forsgren is an assistant professor of film, television, and theater at the University of Notre Dame. She is the author of *In Search of Our Warrior Mothers: Women Dramatists of the Black Arts Movement* (2018). She has also published articles on writers James Baldwin, Ben Caldwell, Lydia R. Diamond, Barbara Ann Teer, J. e. Franklin, Sonia Sanchez, Carlton Molette, and Barbara Molette.

Ghostly Figures: Memory and Belatedness in Postwar American Poetry. By
Ann Keniston. Iowa City: Univ. of Iowa Press. 2015. xii, 240 pp. Paper,
$49.95; e-book, $49.95.

Indirect Action: Schizophrenia, Epilepsy, AIDS, and the Course of Health Activism.
By Lisa Diedrich. Minneapolis: Univ. of Minnesota Press. 2016. 290 pp. Cloth,
$98.00; paper, $28.00.

How do studies of the belated and the indirect offer insight into a culture that
values the present and the direct? Two books transcend typical readings both
of belatedness as mere melancholy and of indirection as pure apathy. Ann
Keniston's *Ghostly Figures* connects how we look back at the past and its legacies with the fundamental premises (and limits) of close reading, whereas
Lisa Diedrich's *Indirect Action* advocates for a nonlinear approach that prob-
lematizes narratives of health activism.

Ghostly Figures explores how "postwar poems often depict speakers who
remember the past only partially, in ways that reveal that memory is itself
obstructed" (1–2). For Keniston, belatedness is as psychological as it is formal: a breaching of the standard rules of tropes, the literary structures that
keep us in the present and separate us from past and future. Because speakers
of belatedness can do so only from the spectatorship of their present, their
poems dwell uneasily and incompletely in the events that generated them.
Thus it becomes difficult for both the speaker and the reader of the poem to
clearly differentiate between past and present, literal and figural. Throughout
the book, Keniston studies how these poems' speakers are "drawn back and
forth across the line of mortality, at once asserting their similarity to and difference from the dead" (38).

The effect of this is ghostly, and Keniston studies this ghostliness adeptly.
The speaker of Sylvia Plath's infamous poem "Daddy" (1965) both utters,
"Daddy, I have had to kill you," and either mourns or is relieved that Daddy
"died before I had time" to do so (39). The speaker of Adrienne Rich's *Dark
Fields of the Republic* (1995) "occupies a position of frustrated watching,"
which creates an asymmetrical relationship between the speaker and what
she sees, an asymmetry that complicates the bonds of "you" and "I" that are
basic assumptions of the lyric (70). In her third chapter, Keniston reads a clus-
ter of gay male poets who experience the belatedness of witnessing the AIDS
epidemic "by describing scenes in which the dead return in ghostly form"
(94). Such ghostly presences show the persistence of intimacy even during a
time in which intimacy is seen as a contagion that "confuse[s] the positions
of lamenter and lamented" (96). Keniston studies Jorie Graham's *Region of*

American Literature, Volume 91, Number 3, September 2019
DOI 10.1215/00029831-7722224 © 2019 by Duke University Press

Unlikeness (1991) as a struggle in the basic meanings of poetic tropes, where metaphors, similes, and synecdoche seem to not do their work, where speakers are "impelled to dismantle their own poetics even as they yearn to make actual experiences meaningful and whole" (152). Susan Howe's *The Midnight* (2003) consists of poems that "look *at*" language, rather than attempt to "look *through*" it (162). Belatedness for Howe is "to reuse what already existed and thus to remake older texts" (170); thus the poems are "fragments that remain adjacent to one another in a poem that exposes the randomness of its own assemblage" (175). Memory is, as Keniston notes in the book's coda, exposed for its artificiality in such poetry. Belatedness, then, is a sort of artifice that exposes the careful construction of the confessional, the structure of the ephemeral. The poet's presence constructs the very absence that gives way to prolepsis and prosopopoeia. The very stuff of poetry, Keniston lucidly reminds us, is predicated on belatedness.

If Keniston provides a guide to how belatedness informs contemporary poetry, Diedrich offers, in *Indirect Action*, a guide to problematize contemporary narratives of medicine. Diedrich uses the trope of indirection to get at the ways in which illness cannot be wholly understood "through discrete disciplines and categories" (3). For her, indirection is also a method, a way of reading discrete texts—and what she calls "snapshots"—that complicate the linear story we tell about medicine.

Her first chapter, "Doing Queer Love," explores how the presumed linear narrative of AIDS conceals how AIDS activists—mostly conceived of as gay men—were influenced by earlier waves of feminism. In particular, Diedrich emphasizes how AIDS activism was predicated on the successes of the lesbian movement of the 1970s, a way of showing how the relationship between lesbians and gay men forms a broader "network of allegiances" (32). The second chapter explores the space of the clinic, given the rise of feminist self-care movements in the 1970s. Examining a variety of pamphlets circulated among feminist groups on matters such as how to perform a pelvic exam, Diedrich not only shows how women became more empowered about their own health through feminism but how "medicine appropriates one of health feminism's key tenets—that our relationship to our bodies and health must be an active, even vigilant one" (64). Staying with the site of the clinic in her third chapter, Diedrich explores John Berger and Jean Mohr's *A Fortunate Man* (1967), a narrative of a country doctor in the United Kingdom in the early 1960s. Diedrich finds political implications in the work of a general practitioner: the one who attends not only to the microscopic emergencies that punctuate a patient's life but develops macroscopic long-term relationships in a community, which require a different "temporality of doctoring" (97). The fourth chapter traces how Rachel Carson's *Silent Spring* (1962) "is an early call for interdisciplinary and collaborative methods in approaching socioscientific problems" through tracing Carson's letters between herself and Frank Egler, the author of the "biopsychosocial" model of medicine (119). Her fifth chapter on David Beauchard's *Epileptic* (1996) reveals that "the difficulty in telling is not only in the stigma associated with epilepsy but also about the failure of language to adequately capture the experience of epilepsy" (155). And her closing chapter on Susan Smiley's documentary *Out of the Shadow* (2004) complicates the act of witnessing as daughters experience their mother's schizophrenia not only as a medical condition they must help her manage but also as a shadow they grow up in, one that conceals "the structural violence of a broken health system" (193). In sum, Diedrich explores the possibility of a different story to tell about medicine: one of the generalist instead of the specialist, of the fraught and peculiar narratives of patients rather than the seemingly clean and tidy narratives of specialist practitioners. This premise could have been articulated without copious references to Michel Foucault, Gilles Deleuze, and Félix Guattari, which tend to clog Diedrich's otherwise incisive writing style and who, though they enable Diedrich to illuminate a valuable archive of texts, seem to occasionally function as a panacea to the complex social and cultural issues she examines.

The belated and the indirect—in the texts so well studied by Keniston and Diedrich—offer crucial perspectives about who we are: how we grapple with our memories, how we negotiate the terrain of our bodies. They remind us that we are as foreign to ourselves as we are connected to others. *Ghostly Figures* and *Indirect Action* return us to the necessity of figurative language and cultural theory so that we may better negotiate the strangeness that is part of being human.

Douglas Dowland is associate professor of English at Ohio Northern University. His book, *Weak Nationalisms: Affect and Nonfiction in Postwar America*, is forthcoming with the University of Nebraska Press.

If God Meant to Interfere: American Literature and the Rise of the Christian Right.
**By Christopher Douglas. Ithaca, NY: Cornell Univ. Press. 2016. viii, 367 pp.
Cloth, $39.95.**

The Production of American Religious Freedom. **By Finbarr Curtis. New York:
New York Univ. Press. 2016. x, 209 pp. Cloth, $89.00; paper, $28.00; e-book
available.**

It has been more than a decade since the publication of Charles Taylor's *A Secular Age* in 2007. Along with equally pathbreaking works like Talal Asad's *Formations of the Secular* (2003), Taylor's magnum opus forced scholars in the humanities and social sciences to address more rigorously the categories of "the religious" and "the secular" and their relation to each other. In Taylor's account, secularity named not what was opposed to religiosity but the very conditions for belief—religious and otherwise—in modernity. A secular age, therefore, did not herald the twilight of religion but made possible the rapid pluralization of nominally religious and nonreligious belief systems. Two recent books reveal the stark differences in method yielded by writing about religion after Taylor: Christopher Douglas's *If God Meant to Interfere: American Literature and the Rise of the Christian Right* and Finbarr Curtis's *The Production of American Religious Freedom.*

Douglas's volume is a lively, sprawling study of the "entanglements" between what Douglas calls the Christian resurgence of the 1970s and the rise of multiculturalism and postmodernism. That these occurred in tandem is more than mere coincidence in Douglas's account. Coming on the heels of the postwar conviction of an Abrahamic consensus on religious matters (itself something of a fiction), Douglas contends, "multiculturalism and postmodernism became complexly intertwined with the [Christian] resurgence" (4). For Douglas, Taylor's understanding of secularity as the grounds for the conditions of belief provides fertile conceptual ground for understanding these entanglements.

The first part of the book, "Multicultural Entanglements," argues that both conservative Christians and multiculturalists alike have uncritically embraced a view of religion that conflates it with cultural identity. "Multicultural religion," Douglas writes, "is figured as the imperative to be true to one's familial, ancestral, and sometimes even racial religious culture" (104). In bracing and perceptive readings of novels by Barbara Kingsolver, Ishmael Reed, Marilynne Robinson, and many others, Douglas shows how literary authors have used narratives of Christian hegemony as a springboard for recovering religious traditions (as forms of cultural identity) that had been erased by American

American Literature, Volume 91, Number 3, September 2019
DOI 10.1215/00029831-7722236   © 2019 by Duke University Press

imperialism. Writers of the Christian resurgence then adopt many of the same strategies and assumptions of progressive multiculturalism to assert Christianity itself as a genuine identity as well as a vital and valid cultural force.

"Postmodern Entanglements," the book's second part, grapples with the postmodern skepticism toward expertise and objectivity. Douglas perceptively notes how vital historicity has been to the formation and resilience of religious identity in the late twentieth century, especially in its skepticism about expertise. In readings of Philip Roth and Christian authors Francis Schaeffer and Tim LaHaye, Douglas demonstrates that as expert consensus on issues like evolution and the historical-critical method of biblical scholarship has posed an increasingly dire existential threat to Christian fundamentalism, postmodernism serves not as one more "threat to be beaten back, but a resource to be embraced in its struggle against modern knowledge" (279).

Douglas's approach to his topic is first and foremost as a literary critic, which encompasses a passion for explication but also the adoption of a normative lens. At its best, this approach yields original readings of modern canonical texts like Robinson's *Gilead* (2004), which Douglas takes to task for Robinson's deliberate repression of antebellum pro-slavery Christianity. At other times, however, it can feel myopic, so close to individual texts and authors that one loses track of the underlying historical narrative. Taken as a whole, however, *If God Meant to Interfere* demands that literary critics pay attention to a form of religiosity—conservative Christianity—that in its doctrinal rigidity and unapologetic universalism sits outside most paradigms for postsecular or postmodern religion (as either belief without content or a "weak" persistent force). It represents a vital and necessary intervention into American literary studies.

Whereas Douglas's book builds on the foundation established by Taylor and others, Curtis's *The Production of American Religious Freedom* is an ambitious work of history that aims to expose the underlying incoherence of a keystone of modern religiosity: religious freedom. The book's governing claim is that "there is no such thing as religious freedom, or at least no one thing" (2). This, Curtis argues, is a challenge to "the commonsensical" notion that "religion is an interior, individual concern in need of political and legal safeguards" (3). As a way of puncturing this American common sense, Curtis interrogates how an economy of religious freedom actually operates. In this, he challenges the free-market economic model of religious choice popularized by Roger Finke and Rodney Stark in *The Churching of America, 1776–2005* (2005). Curtis's religious actors are a far cry from Finke and Stark's rational religious consumers; they are subject to the influence of a host of private institutions and forces that "define, produce, and distribute contested social resources in American life" (3). At its best, *The Production of American Religious Freedom* astutely diagnoses the often-troubling realities of how free-market economics impacts and shapes religious choice but is shortchanged by Curtis's allergy to overarching historical narratives.

Curtis approaches his hefty task by presenting a series of case studies intended to reveal how rhetorics of religious freedom have been harnessed. The chapters, which cover everything from D. W. Griffith's *Birth of a Nation* to the intelligent design movement to the 2014 Supreme Court case *Burwell v. Hobby Lobby Stores*, are admirable for their breadth. The best of these, in this reader's opinion, is the first chapter, on Charles Grandison Finney's science of revivalism, which presents a persuasive counternarrative to a historiographical tradition of religious democratization. The other chapters, however, do not always capitalize on the promise of the first. At times, Curtis's initial economic analysis recedes as he explores forms of religious nationalism. These chapters are not unrelated to the book's themes, but Curtis neglects to do the necessary signposting and narrative stitching that would bring them into coherence.

Curtis's reluctance to weave a broader narrative thus frustrates the lofty claims he wants to make about privatization, free-market economics, and religious freedom. Additionally, even in a work eager to sidestep myopic attention on how state and federal governments conceptualize and regulate religion, it is surprising how little attention is paid, for instance, to the long history of Supreme Court decisions on religious freedom. Some genealogy of the concept would have gone a long way toward making Curtis's sweeping assertion that there is "no such thing as religious freedom"—and his collection of case studies—potentially far more palatable and persuasive. Even in our supposedly postsecular age, *The Production of American Religious Freedom* asks for perhaps too much of a reader's faith. Nevertheless, both this book and *If God to Meant to Interfere* evidence how dynamic understandings of the relationship between the religious and the secular remain more than a decade after the publication of *A Secular Age*.

Grant Shreve is an independent scholar and professional writer living in Baltimore. He holds a PhD in American literature from Johns Hopkins University.

A Literature of Questions: Nonfiction for the Critical Child. By Joe Sutliff Sanders.
Minneapolis: Univ. of Minnesota Press. 2018. 274 pp. Cloth, $100.00; paper,
$25.00; e-book, $23.75.

*Was the Cat in the Hat Black? The Hidden Racism of Children's Literature, and the
Need for Diverse Books.* By Philip Nel. New York: Oxford Univ. Press. 2017.
x, 290 pp. Cloth, $29.95; paper, $19.95; e-book, $9.99.

Is Anglophone children's literature a literature of questions or a questionable
literature? Both, apparently, if we take cue from these two strong studies. Joe
Sutliff Sanders's *A Literature of Questions* refers more specifically to nonfiction for children, historically understood as a literature of facts or answers.
The best such material, Sanders avers, invites interrogative reading rather
than insisting on its own authority and sufficiency. Whereas Sanders emphasizes the progressive energies of nonfiction, Nel pushes in the other direction,
calling out structural racism in and around children's literature and in solidarity with initiatives like Black Lives Matter.

A Literature of Questions is the first long study of children's nonfiction and
quite timely in our moment of alternative facts. It's terrific scholarship. Sanders isn't content to argue that good nonfiction invites questions more than
answers; rather, he asserts that nonfiction does this *especially* well, perhaps
better than other genres. Theorizing from various sources, Sanders proposes
that good nonfiction models "punctuated plurality," a dialectical process
of meaning making. I'm not persuaded of nonfiction's specialness in this
regard—or of the advantages of a formalist rather than a historical account of
the genre—but I learned much from Sanders's analysis of the literary and
rhetorical devices he sees at work. Using a rich variety of contemporary and
historical texts, Sanders demonstrates how voice (chap. 2), "character" (chap. 3),
peritexts (chap. 4), and photographs (chap. 5) all complicate textual authority
and amplify as much as satisfy reader curiosity. Sanders is quick to acknowledge that matters can be complicated, noting that some invitations to engagement may not be as unconditional as they seem. This is conveyed in chapter
6, a case study of Tanya Lee Stone's 2009 picture book *Almost Astronauts*,
about a group of women almost chosen to be astronauts in the early years
of the US space program. Here, Sanders suggests, we can see the tension
between the encouragement of critical thinking and the desire for "reliability"
(the delivery of clear facts). Even "the best nonfiction should never ask its
readers to depend on it with full confidence" (198), he remarks, as *Almost
Astronauts* ultimately does. Chapter 7 considers the place of sentimentality
and empathy, while the conclusion turns to the question of children's capacity

American Literature, Volume 91, Number 3, September 2019
DOI 10.1215/00029831-7722248   © 2019 by Duke University Press

for critical engagement. Sanders saves that question for last, he says, because it annoys him so, but he patiently works through the relevant research to affirm that, yes, children are active and savvy little critics.

Nel is no stranger to the fact that children's literature can be progressive. He wrote a biography of Crockett Johnson and Ruth Krauss (2012) and coedited an anthology titled *Tales for Little Rebels: A Collection of Radical Children's Literature* (2010). In *Was the Cat in the Hat Black?*, however, his focus is the racism that children's literature both hides and combats. Not much has changed for the better since Nancy Larrick first spotlighted "The All-White World of Children's Books" in her 1965 article for the *Saturday Review*. While children of color now make up about half of the school population, Nel notes, the percentage of children's books featuring people of color has never topped 15 percent (and the percentage of books *by* people of color is even lower). Nel sets about discussing where racism persists and what to do about it, and in this work he writes for general readers as much as for specialists.

Nel's title may sound familiar as it echoes Shelley Fisher Fishkin's *Was Huck Black?* (1993), which proposes that Mark Twain's Huck Finn is modeled on an African American child, to the general credit of Twain. Nel's book begins with a similar and more skeptical account of Dr. Seuss, arguing that the iconic Cat in the Hat likewise had mixed racial ancestry, modeled in part on an elevator operator named Annie Williams but also drawn from blackface and caricature. The Cat in the Hat thus links gloved hands with Mickey Mouse, Bugs Bunny, Raggedy Ann, and other such figures. Like Twain, Seuss was a complicated figure, prone to unconscious racism while committed to progressive causes. The answer to Nel's titular question seems to be "sort of, in messed-up ways," whereas Fishkin reads Huck's "blackness" more positively.

Subsequent chapters track racism in children's classics, including "revised" versions (chap. 2); in William Joyce's multimodal *The Fantastic Flying Books of Mr. Morris Lessmore* (2012), ostensibly about Hurricane Katrina but more an evasion of its complexity (chap. 3); in the practice of whitewashing covers of young adult novels featuring characters of color (chap. 4); and in the function of genre as "the new Jim Crow" (169, chap. 5). Throughout, Nel builds on existing conversations in the popular press as well as relevant scholarship on racism and white privilege in children's literature by such scholars as Robin Bernstein, Michelle Martin, and Katharine Capshaw. I take minor issue with the classics chapter, in which Nel concludes—reluctantly—that we should teach racist classics critically; I think there's a stronger argument for ignoring those books altogether. But I agree that some aren't going away anytime soon and that it's better to teach the problems than to pretend they've been fixed through minor language changes.

The Seuss chapter is fascinating and the best researched (Nel is a Seuss biographer too), but I found the final chapter the most provocative. I could see an argument for reading it first. There Nel points out that resistance to books by and about people of color is anything but new in the publishing world, such that writers of color have been forced to self-publish or establish small presses. Furthermore, publishing is a self-selecting line of work in that salaries remain low and typically the only people who can afford such work are people who don't have to rely solely on those incomes. Finally, when it comes to texts written or illustrated by people of color, mainstream publishers prefer historical fiction and realism to science fiction and fantasy, thereby reinforcing the notion that racism is a thing of the past and limiting engagement with racism to the narrowly mimetic. Against such segregation, suggests Nel, we need diverse *genres* as well as diverse books and authors (and publishers and editors).

Nel concludes the volume with a nineteen-point "Manifesto for Anti-Racist Children's Literature," recommending not only expansion on the literary side of things but also involvement with organizations like Black Lives Matter, Rich in Color, and the Zinn Education Project. *Was the Cat in the Hat Black?* is more a call to action than *A Literature of Questions*, but both make significant contributions to scholarship while underscoring the role children's literature plays in mindful education and ethical citizenship.

Kenneth Kidd is professor of English at the University of Florida and author of *Making American Boys: Boyology and the Feral Tale* (2004), *Freud in Oz: At the Intersections of Psychoanalysis and Children's Literature* (2011), and the forthcoming *Theory for Beginners, or Children's Literature Otherwise*.

Mere Reading: The Poetics of Wonder in Modern American Novels. By Lee Clark Mitchell. New York: Bloomsbury Academic. 2017. x, 262 pp. Cloth, $90.00; paper, $26.96; e-book, $21.56.

Anti-Book: On the Art and Politics of Radical Publishing. By Nicholas Thoburn. Minneapolis: Univ. of Minnesota Press. 2016. xiii, 372 pp. Cloth, $105.00; paper, $30.00.

Making Literature Now. By Amy Hungerford. Stanford, CA: Stanford Univ. Press. 2016. xiii, 199 pp. Cloth, $75.00; paper, $22.95; e-book available.

To read or not to read seems to be the great question for literary studies of our time. More specifically, in a world of abundant literary production, how can we decide what to read and how to read it? Three recent books by Amy Hungerford, Lee Clark Mitchell, and Nicholas Thoburn have, in their own ways, turned to this problem. Certainly, these are not the only titles to pursue this question of reading in the digital age. Other works on this theme from just within the past couple of years include David Letzler's excellent *The Cruft of Fiction* (2017); Zara Dinnen's astute *The Digital Banal* (2018); a host of fascinating work in the digital/distant reading field, including Andrew Piper's *Enumerations* (2018) and Ted Underwood's *Distant Horizons* (2019); and surely many others. Yet the triad of titles under review showcases the distinctively different approaches that are being adopted in the face of "literary overproduction," as Hungerford calls it (142).

Specifically, these books turn to a type of antimimetic formalism in which a tension is observed between a literary work's form and its representational subject matter. For Mitchell, the answer to the challenges of our age is close reading, returning to the sense of wonder we might find in the attention to the language of prose as described by Tony Tanner, which should be considered as tightly crafted as poetry (5); for Thoburn we can respond by interrogating those book-works that critically examine their own media forms within a framework of material texts (1); and for Hungerford we need to think through the labor forms and hidden narratives of emergent contemporary literature but also, perhaps now infamously, to adopt paradigms of "critical not-reading" that more thoroughly, and perhaps politically, rationalize our still underremarked-upon cultures of the great unread, as Margaret Cohen termed them (148–63).

Each of these books works very differently. Mitchell's approach turns to Willa Cather, Vladimir Nabokov, Marilynne Robinson, Cormac McCarthy, and Junot Díaz in its exemplary demonstration of the power of close textual

American Literature, Volume 91, Number 3, September 2019
DOI 10.1215/00029831-7722260   © 2019 by Duke University Press

attention. While it was not clear to me why Mitchell's work needed to be particularly focused on the "modern American novels" of his subtitle, the Barthesian "bliss" that his book extracts from its chosen works more than pays off. For not only do Mitchell's close readings succeed—perhaps none more so than in his demonstration of the disjunction and oscillation of the form and content of Nabokov's *Lolita* (1955)—but the work is also prefaced by a brilliant history of close reading that should find its way into undergraduate syllabi worldwide. Certainly, there were instances in this book where I wanted to interject with a more intertextual approach. For instance, Mitchell's citation of McCarthy's reference in *The Road* (2006) to a man who appears "like an animal inside a skull looking out the eyeholes" (184) is surely a reference to Russell Hoban's seminal dystopia, *Riddley Walker* (1980), in which there is "some kind of thing it aint us but yet its in us. Its looking out thru our eye hoals" (6), a fact that is here left without comment. Yet this is the challenge of balancing content and context with which Mitchell's work grapples and, on its own terms, nonetheless succeeds.

By contrast, Thoburn offers a dense and rich theoretical account of what he calls a "communism of text" drawing on Theodor Adorno, Antonin Artaud, Walter Benjamin, André Breton, Gilles Deleuze and Félix Guattari, Michel Foucault, and, of course, Karl Marx for his wide-ranging analysis. Thoburn's premise is that the materiality of the book—not, that is, solely the codex—can speak to us in ways that could work against the text's literary or formal content, as a reflexive critical commentary. The most superficial example of this is the commodification of Marx's *Capital* (1867), packaged and sold on loop ever since its authorship. However, in its conjunction of politics, aesthetics, and materiality, what I found most compelling in Thoburn's work was his astute understanding of the manifesto. Thoburn does not put forward a manifesto for the postdigital book, but he does analyze how manifestos work "in the future perfect," a mode in which their "claim to authority in the present *will have been* sanctioned by the actualization of its subject in the future" (27). It is this performative loop to which the materiality of the book might gesture, and so, even while Thoburn reads the bookishness of books against their content, his work resonates with the sense of "oscillation" one finds in Mitchell. The authority of form forever struggles against the power of content, unfolding temporal lines in our experiences of reading.

Finally, Hungerford's book, by now itself well established as an important text in the field of contemporary literary studies, straddles these divides of close reading and material textuality, of aesthetics and politics. With her carefully documented histories of underground literary institutions, such as McSweeney's, through digital experiments such as the Small Demons project, up to her provocative final chapter in which she refuses to read any more David Foster Wallace, Hungerford's book is a well-crafted tour de force of its genre. What works so well in this text is that the objections one might raise to it are already rebuffed by the final page. Why, for instance, focus on the case studies that Hungerford chooses? Well, the text asks back, why do we focus on anything? The "refusal to read . . . is not radical," as Hungerford notes, "it is normal" (162). It is what we all do every day in our selection processes for where we spend our limited lifetimes of reading. And being *honest* about such procedures of selection is the critical feature to which we should draw attention, Hungerford's work seems to imply. Hungerford suggests that this selectiveness is merely another part of our reading practice, a habit we should make explicit and attempt to rationalize.

While these three texts take differing approaches to reading in the digital age, I was most surprised at the connections I forged among these books. Why should works on the material form of the book and its production in the present day find themselves sitting alongside a text that so forcefully argues for a return to close reading? Perhaps the answer is attention: how we pay it, where we spend it, and the ways in which we monetarily metaphorize it within paradigms of scarcity. Each of these books asks us to evaluate critically that most slippery of terms: the *form* of literature, in whatever form that might take.

Martin Paul Eve is professor of literature, technology, and publishing at Birkbeck College, University of London. He holds a PhD from the University of Sussex and is the author of five books, most recently *Close Reading with Computers* (2019). In 2017 Martin was named as one of the *Guardian's* five finalists for higher education's most inspiring leader award, and in 2018 he was awarded the KU Leuven Honorary Medal in the Humanities and Social Sciences.

Brief Mention

General

In the Neighborhood: Women's Publication in Early America. By Caroline Wigginton.
Amherst: Univ. of Massachusetts Press. 2016. xi, 223 pp. Paper, $25.95.

Informed by archival research, this monograph examines early American publics through the lens of women's quotidian exchanges. Shifting the conversation away from a traditional focus on male-authored republican print culture, Wigginton directs her readers to what she calls women's "relational publication," or how a variety of technologies—material, scriptive, print, or performative—could dynamically shape public and private worlds. Through close readings, Wigginton attends to the particularity of the works of Creek diplomat Coosaponakeesa, African American poet Phillis Wheatley, and Quaker poet Milcah Martha Moore, illustrating how these women conceptualized community and even shifted the balance of power.

Mark Twain among the Indians and Other Indigenous Peoples. By Kerry Driscoll.
Oakland: Univ. of California Press. 2018. xvi, 448 pp. Cloth, $95.00; paper, $34.95; e-book, $95.00.

Drawing from a vast archive of letters, sketches, marginalia, and manuscripts, Driscoll examines Twain's "vexingly erratic and paradoxical" views on native peoples—both in the Northern and Southern Hemispheres. Informed by cultural studies, the monograph charts the author's quixotic opinions across a span of nearly sixty years, ranging from those expressed in well-known works such as *The Adventures of Tom Sawyer* (1876) and *Following the Equator* (1897) to more obscure essays. This book will be of special interest to scholars both of Twain and of indigenous studies.

American Literature, Volume 91, Number 3, September 2019
DOI 10.1215/00029831-7722292   © 2019 by Duke University Press

The Life of Mark Twain: The Middle Years, 1871–1891. By Gary Scharnhorst. Columbia: Univ. of Missouri Press. 2019. xii, 622 pp. Paper, $36.95.

In this second book of a multivolume biography, Scharnhorst continues his highly detailed exploration of Twain's life, including his family life in Elmira, New York, and Hartford, Connecticut, his writing aspirations and routines, his relationships with editors, and his monetary ventures, literary reception, and travels. This book covers Twain as most people know him, authoring in these years such works as *Roughing It* (1872), *The Adventures of Tom Sawyer* (1876), *A Tramp Abroad* (1880), *The Prince and the Pauper* (1881), *Life on the Mississippi* (1883), *Adventures of Huckleberry Finn* (1884), and *A Connecticut Yankee in King Arthur's Court* (1889).

Reading Reconstruction: Sherwood Bonner and the Literature of the Post–Civil War South. By Kathryn B. McKee. Baton Rouge: Louisiana State Univ. Press. 2019. xii, 354 pp. Cloth, $49.95; e-book available.

Katharine Sherwood Bonner McDowell (1849–83) is often cast as a merely regional author whose output was meager due to her early death. Yet her travel sketches, poems, and one completed novel reveal how closely she observed the Reconstruction era and how her writings embody the fraught relationship between postbellum white feminism and racism. Rather than merely functioning as a biography, this book places Bonner within the context of Reconstruction literature, arguing "that the bulk of Bonner's work actively resists seamless incorporation into a falsely limited range of expectations for 'southern' writing and artistic production by women in the postbellum era."

Finding Thoreau: The Meaning of Nature in the Making of an Environmental Icon. By Richard W. Judd. Amherst: Univ. of Massachusetts Press. 2018. xii, 217 pp. Paper, $27.95.

Everyone tries to find the "real" Henry David Thoreau. Rather than arguing for a real Thoreau, Judd details the many studies of the transcendentalist. Using a historiographical approach, this book begins with a short biography before examining how Thoreau was a window into certain periods: from being a "prophet without honor" during his lifetime (1817–62) to becoming an environmental icon in the late twentieth century. Judd approaches this study decade by decade, including such periods as 1920 to 1960, when Thoreau's "reputation as a nature writer was eclipsed by his timeliness as a social critic."

A Liberal Education in Late Emerson: Readings in the Rhetoric of Mind. By Sean Ross Meehan. Rochester, NY: Camden House. 2019. xii, 176 pp. Cloth, $90.00.

As scholars increasingly reconsider the vitality of Ralph Waldo Emerson's later works, this study extends that reconsideration to the educational contexts of his 1860s writings. In his addresses and lectures at colleges, Emerson espouses a view of the mind aligned with the rhetorical ideas of classical colleges. He was doing this at a time when colleges were transforming into modern universities by becoming more scientifically specialized. The book argues that this transformative period in education illuminates Emerson's "interest in the mind's cultivation" and impacted other thinkers engaged with this topic, including Walt Whitman, Charles W. Eliot, William James, and W. E. B. Du Bois.

Thinking in Search of a Language: Essays on American Intellect and Intuition. By Herwig Friedl. New York: Bloomsbury Academic. 2019. x, 400 pp. Cloth, $130.00; paper, $34.95.

Delving into modernist, postmetaphysical thinking strategies, the goal of these essays is to "critically appreciate and testify to the continuing, unceasing productive openness of Emerson's and of pragmatist thinking." The first section of essays focuses on Emerson's engagement with philosophy, especially the way he approaches Being as preverbal. Such topics include Emerson's relation to, among others, the pre-Socratic philosophers, mysticism, Persian literature, G. W. F. Hegel, and Stoic philosophy. The second section analyzes the experimental and constraint-escaping inquiries of William James and John Dewey, including such topics as ontological skepticism and the impact of James's radical empiricism on the Kyoto school.

Henry James's Feminist Afterlives: Annie Fields, Emily Dickinson, Marguerite Duras. By Kathryn Wichelns. Cham, Switzerland: Palgrave Macmillan. 2018. xi, 178 pp. Paper, $27.99; e-book, $79.99.

This monograph is a selective study of the ways in which three women engaged with James's "gender-transgressive" aesthetics. Drawing from both queer and feminist theory, Wichelns analyzes James's correspondence with writer and women's rights activist Fields, and then she examines Dickinson's and Duras's revisions of his fiction. The book makes the case that across continents, centuries, and languages these women perceived in James's work a shared ambivalence about class- and nation-specific gender expectations.

Chicago and the Making of American Modernism: Cather, Hemingway, Faulkner, and Fitzgerald in Conflict. By Michelle E. Moore. London: Bloomsbury Academic. 2019. x, 247 pp. Cloth, $114.00; e-book, $102.60.

In the history of American modernism, certain cities—such as New York, Paris, and New Orleans—eclipse others as sites of importance. In this monograph, Moore argues that Chicago also deserves recognition for its influence on American modernists, who were, in fact, defining themselves in opposition to its "small-town" literary realism, evangelical movements, and business "boosterism." Drawing from archival research, the book examines how a single metropolis left its mark on the literature of Willa Cather, William Faulkner, Ernest Hemingway, and F. Scott Fitzgerald.

Rufus: James Agee in Tennessee. By Paul F. Brown. Knoxville: Univ. of Tennessee Press. 2018. xviii, 422 pp. Cloth, $34.95; e-book, $34.95.

Agee (1909–55) wrote the Pulitzer Prize–winning novel *A Death in the Family* (1957) and the screenplay for *The African Queen* (1951). Because his literary achievements occurred when he was living in the north, his hometown of Knoxville, Tennessee, is often overlooked within his life's story. As the first literary biography focusing on Agee's connection to Tennessee, this study examines how his ancestors migrated to East Tennessee, the story of his parents meeting in Knoxville, and the impact of his father's tragic death in a car accident on Agee's writing life. While focusing on how locations in Tennessee inspired him, the book also includes Agee's influences on the area.

American Small-Town Fiction, 1940–1960: A Critical Study. By Nathanael T. Booth. Jefferson, NC: McFarland. 2019. vii, 209 pp. Paper, $39.95.

Picking up on Ima Honaker Herron's *The Small Town in American Literature* (1939), the last major study of small-town fiction, Booth extends the analysis into postwar fiction. Although small towns are often seen as pivotal to America as a concept, the texts substantiating this claim are often overlooked. Each chapter is organized around a small-town landmark, such as the train station, schoolhouse, malt shop, and movie theater, analyzing such works as Ellery Queen's *Calamity Town* (1942), Ray Bradbury's *Dandelion Wine* (1957), Henry Bellamann's *Kings Row* (1940), and Toshio Mori's *Yokohama, California* (1949). Booth argues, "The small town offered writers the opportunity to examine, to critique, and to explore the tensions facing America."

Robert Duncan and the Pragmatist Sublime. By James Maynard. Albuquerque: Univ. of New Mexico Press. 2018. xviii, 211 pp. Cloth, $65.00.

The term "pragmatist sublime" refers to the sublime as pluralistic and rela-tional. Duncan therefore contributes to the history of the sublime, as this study argues, because he viewed the poem as a "multiphasic" experience of language. Connecting Duncan to the pragmatists William James, John Dewey, and Alfred North Whitehead, each chapter analyzes a development within Duncan's view of excess within his poetry. Such topics include the way surrealism impacted his poetics of process, how his mature poetics emerged alongside his engagement with Whitehead's metaphysics, and the influence of Dante Alighieri and Walt Whitman on his conception of divine humanism.

Affect, Psychoanalysis, and American Poetry: This Feeling of Exaltation. By John Steen. London: Bloomsbury Academic. 2018. ix, 212 pp. Cloth, $114.00; e-book, $102.60.

Drawing on object relations, queer theory, and psychoanalysis, this mono-graph investigates the nuanced relationship between affect and American poetics in the wake of modernism. Building on these critical frameworks, Steen argues that these poems do not contain but instead grapple with uncon-tainable negative feelings such as anxiety, mourning, rage, and shame. The works of Wallace Stevens, Randall Jarrell, Robert Creeley, and Claudia Ran-kine are among Steen's objects of study.

Reading the Novels of John Williams: A Flaw of Light. By Mark Asquith. Lanham, MD: Lexington Books. 2018. vii, 181 pp. Cloth, $90.00; e-book, $85.50.

The poet Stanley Miller Williams called John Williams "one of the finest fic-tion writers of the twentieth century." This book is a critical introduction to the novelist, who served in World War II, came of age as a writer during the heyday of New Criticism, dabbled in poetry, and taught creative writing at the University of Denver. Each chapter analyzes the context, themes, and recep-tion history of Williams's three major novels: *Butcher's Crossing* (1960), *Stoner* (1965), and *Augustus* (1971). From westerns to academic novels, Williams, as this study shows, "was fascinated by the way that our plans and sense of who we are is shaped by life's accidents."

The Man Who Wrote the Perfect Novel: John Williams, Stoner, and the Writing Life. By Charles J. Shields. Austin: Univ. of Texas Press. 2018. xii, 305 pp. Cloth, $29.95.

John Williams was an award-winning novelist, and yet American readers largely forgot him after his death in 1994. Despite being underappreciated, his masterpiece *Stoner* (1965), a novel about a farm boy turned professor, became a bestseller in Europe in 2013. The *New York Times* called the book "the perfect novel," and the *Sunday Times* called it "the greatest novel you have never read." This biography presents both Williams and his works, from his childhood in rural Texas during the Great Depression to his academic life and literary achievements, which include winning the National Book Award for *Augustus* (1971).

John Ashbery and Anglo-American Exchange: The Minor Eras. By Oli Hazzard. Oxford: Oxford Univ. Press. 2018. 209 pp. Cloth, $74.00.

To frame postwar poet John Ashbery as distinctly American would be a mistake, Hazzard argues. Taking a predominantly biographical approach, this monograph demonstrates the significance of Anglo-American contexts to Ashbery's poetry, especially in regard to his conception of national imaginaries. Hazzard shows that this transatlantic literary influence was reciprocal and that the American writer in turn helps us better understand four English poets: W. H. Auden, F. T. Prince, Lee Harwood, and Mark Ford.

A Theology of Sense: John Updike, Embodiment, and Late Twentieth-Century American Literature. By Scott Dill. Columbus: Ohio State Univ. Press. 2018. xv, 204 pp. Cloth, $64.95; e-book, $19.95.

This monograph advances the argument that in spite of the secular appearance of Updike's work, a theological conviction grounds his exploration of the body's sensory knowledge. Accordingly, each chapter analyzes the author's essays, novels, and poems through one of the five senses—touch, sight, taste, sound, and smell—and its relation to broader theological, philosophical, and ethical concerns. Dill's book will be of interest to scholars of religious studies, postsecularism, philosophy, and post-1945 US literature.

Shreds of Matter: Cormac McCarthy and the Concept of Nature. By Julius Greve. Hanover, NH: Dartmouth College Press. 2018. xii, 333 pp. Cloth, $95.00; paper, $45.00, e-book, $44.99.

This monograph advocates for a critical framework of McCarthy's work that is grounded in geocriticism, speculative realism, and philosophies of nature— namely Schellingian *Naturphilosophie*. Taking a transatlantic approach, Greve traces the concept of nature from nineteenth-century American and German transcendentalism to the literary present, contextualizing his close readings of works such as *Blood Meridian* (1985), *Suttree* (1979), and *No Country for Old Men* (2005). The aim of McCarthy's project, he argues, is to "present nature as thinking itself in literature" or, in other words, to enlist novels to speculate about nature's identity.

T. E. D. Klein and the Rupture of Civilization: A Study in Critical Horror. By Thomas Phillips. Jefferson, NC: McFarland. 2017. vi, 188 pp. Paper, $35.00.

This book situates Klein's slender oeuvre in the domain of what Phillips terms "critical horror," a subgenre of horror fiction aligned, either explicitly or implicitly, with critical theory. Through close readings of works such as *The Ceremonies* (1984), Phillips illuminates critical horror's engagement with themes of injustice, ethics, phantasmagoria, and cultural complacency. An exclusive interview with Klein supplements the book's critical analysis.

Edwidge Danticat: The Haitian Diasporic Imaginary. By Nadège T. Clitandre. Charlottesville: Univ. of Virginia Press. 2018. xx, 249 pp. Cloth, $65.00; paper, $29.50; e-book, $65.00.

Clitandre argues that Danticat's works—which include short stories, novels, and essays—articulate a diasporic consciousness that illustrates a global displacement reified in localized spaces. Enlisting the trope of the echo, the monograph analyzes the ways in which the Haitian-born writer's oeuvre navigates the diasporic imaginary and the dialogic relationships of local/global and nation/diaspora. Clitandre's scholarship advances the practice of "globalectical" reading that is rooted in social, political, and cultural transformation.

None of This Is Normal: The Fiction of Jeff VanderMeer. By Benjamin J. Robertson. Minneapolis: Univ. of Minnesota Press. 2018. 207 pp. Cloth, $80.00; paper, $19.95.

The Anthropocene, speculative realism, and new materialism are among the frameworks with which this monograph considers works such as *Annihilation* (2014) and *Borne* (2017). As a mode of analysis, Robertson advances the idea of "fantastic materiality," or what he defines as a materiality manifest in horror, fiction, or fantasy—as opposed to mimetic representations often found in literary realism. This study contends that a sustained consideration of the "alien norms" in VanderMeer's weird fiction can help us imagine possibilities for both humans and nonhumans in the age of the Anthropocene.

The American Writer: Literary Life in the United States from the 1920s to the Present. By Lawrence R. Samuel. Jefferson, NC: McFarland. 2018. v, 164 pp. Paper, $39.95.

Focusing on agents, editors, and readers, this book argues, "those who have used language as their creative medium have held a unique and special place in our collective imagination, making the writer a fascinating character in the real-life American narrative." The study discerns five general archetypes defining the American writer: modernists (1920–39), realists, (1940–59), intellectuals (1960–79), individualists (1980–99), and nomads (2000–present). Across this historical arc, the book analyzes key themes such as the making of money and the question of whether there is ever an authentic American literature.

American Gothic Literature: A Thematic Study from Mary Rowlandson to Colson Whitehead. By Ruth Bienstock Anolik. Jefferson, NC: McFarland. 2019. vii, 306 pp. Paper, $55.00.

As a follow-up to her previous book, *Property and Power in English Gothic Literature* (2015), Anolik's new study analyzes how America changed the English gothic mode. Focusing on the themes of property and power, she argues, "the flexible and constantly evolving gothic mode remains both popular and culturally important, as the terms of power and possession that haunt Western culture continue to evolve." The book examines how the gothic allowed women writers such as Louisa May Alcott and Charlotte Perkins Gilman to respond to society's constrictions on women; how Edgar Allan Poe and Harriet Jacobs used the gothic to think about chattel slavery; and how the gothic gave voice to a variety of American anxieties, such as the dispossession of Native Americans.

Pivotal Voices, Era of Transition: Toward a Twenty-First Century Poetics. By Rigoberto González. Ann Arbor: Univ. of Michigan Press. 2017. 223 pp. Paper, $34.95.

This collection of essays and book reviews seeks to remap the coordinates of American poetry scholarship by focusing on writers of color, especially those from intersectional communities. Alongside his project of looking ahead to new directions of US poetry, González also meditates on the legacy of literary figures such as Alurista and Francisco X. Alarcón. The collection features essays on the works of Natalie Diaz, Carmen Giménez Smith, Kamilah Aisha Moon, and Ocean Vuong, among others.

Announcements

**Call for Papers—Special Issue of *American Literature*:
The Infrastructure of Emergency**

American Literature and *Resilience: A Journal of the Environmental Humanities* invite submissions for a joint special issue titled "The Infrastructure of Emergency," coedited by John Levi Barnard, Stephanie Foote, Jessica Hurley, and Jeffrey Insko. This joint special issue aims to draw together scholars of American literary and cultural studies with others working across the environmental humanities to trace the long histories and possible futures of infrastructure under conditions of planetary ecological emergency, with a particular focus on the infrastructures of empire and capital and the local and global environmental ramifications of their historical unfolding. Areas of interest include but are not limited to energy and resource extraction, delivery, and consumption; shipping, air traffic, roads, canals, railroads, highways, and the networks of commerce; agriculture, food production, and the rendering of animal capital; waste management, garbage, and recycling; the infrastructures of global health, epidemics, and epidemiology; infrastructures of urban spaces, including public transit and housing, water provision, sewage and sanitation, gentrification, dislocation, and neglect; information technology, communication networks, and "the cloud"; precarious infrastructures threatened by rising sea levels, hurricanes, wildfires, and heat waves; and projections of imperial power, the military-industrial complex, and the logistics of war. These are only a few. More broadly, we invite submissions that take an expansive view of the concept of infrastructure, its representations in literature and other media, its history and historical contexts, and its implications for environmental justice at local, regional, and planetary scales.

Submissions of 11,000 words or fewer (including endnotes and references) should be submitted electronically at www.editorialmanager.com/al/default
.asp or www.resiliencejournal.org/publishing-in-resilience/submission-form/

American Literature, Volume 91, Number 3, September 2019
DOI 10.1215/00029831-7890244   © 2019 by Duke University Press

by **March 1, 2020.** Editors may sort the essays between the two journals based on their focus and methodology, and in accordance with the larger design of the joint issue. Editors will read and provide feedback on 400-word abstracts if they are submitted by August 1, 2019. Send abstracts directly to John Levi Barnard (jlb@tragos.org). Please feel free to email any of the editors with questions: John Levi Barnard (jlb@tragos.org), Stephanie Foote (stephanie .foote@mail.wvu.edu), Jessica Hurley (hurleyj@uchicago.edu), and Jeffrey Insko (insko@oakland.edu).

Call for Papers—Special Issue of *American Literature*:
How Literature Understands Poverty

This special issue examines the role of literature and criticism in addressing poverty and dispossession. In a 2009 *Inside Higher Ed* op-ed, Keith Gandal predicted that the economic crisis would lead to literary studies finally putting "poverty near the top of the agenda and the center of the field." Ten years later, poverty has become a focus of scholarship in the social sciences, particularly geography, anthropology, sociology, and critical legal studies. Yet the topic remains stubbornly marginal to literary studies, even though qualitative social scientific methods have been taken up in the discipline as never before. This special issue addresses this oversight by asking what literature and criticism distinctively have to offer to an understanding of poverty and impoverished communities in the United States and abroad. What theories and methods of reading does literature about poverty demand? What language for talking about poverty does literature provide? In turn, what kinds of demands and pressures do efforts to address poverty, dispossession, and extreme economic inequality place on literary form and language?

In the United States, the contradictions of poverty are especially acute: while the nation has the world's highest GDP, a 2018 United Nations report found that more than 40 million Americans live in poverty, almost half of those in "extreme poverty." More than 50 million more live in near poverty. As a settler colonial state, the United States was founded on the material dispossession of whole populations. More recently, mechanisms of asset stripping among already beleaguered communities have expanded under the neoliberal logics of development and accumulation. State governments have subjected the most vulnerable populations to more extractive and less accountable schemes of privatized exploitation, as economic disparities have dovetailed with racial, ethnic, and gender hierarchies. In the face of these exacerbating conditions of impoverishment, Americanist literary scholarship has retrenched somewhat. Class representation feels less urgent than other issues, and where class is addressed at all, it is often treated as a static category of analysis, separated from dynamics of dispossession along lines of race, gender, and nationality. Elsewhere, scholarship on racial capitalism, settler colonialism, neoliberalism, and necropolitics has shed valuable light on socioeconomic and geopolitical structures whose operative effects produce impoverishment. Yet much of this work remains silent about poverty as a lived and represented experience and as a category of aesthetic production and interpretation. Bucking that trend, this special issue foregrounds poverty as a primary category of literary study. We seek articles that model a range of approaches to probing economic, racial, and social contradictions endemic to capitalist accumulation as a special problem of representation as such.

Fifty years since Oscar Lewis popularized the term "culture of poverty," we ask what it would mean for literary scholars to treat poverty not as an object of sociological examination but as a subject of artistic and cultural inquiry in its own right. In what ways does our discomfort with this subject invite us to reflect on our own prevailing methodological assumptions and thematic avoidances? In other words, what can be gained from revisiting poverty in the literary imagination, both in terms of generating an understanding beyond its social scientific definition and as a site for self-inquiry into the practice of literary scholarship?

In the spirit of that pivot, this special issue seeks to revise and reimagine the category of poverty itself. It follows recent work that attends to the productive dilemmas of representation that this category highlights. Gavin Jones's *American Hungers: The Problem of Poverty in U.S. Literature, 1840–1945* (2007) suggests that poverty has not been more widely represented in literary criticism because the treatment of material deprivation as having cultural and aesthetic value poses ethical and representational dilemmas. Keith Gandal, author of *The Virtues of the Vicious: Jacob Riis, Stephen Crane and the Spectacle of the Slum* (1997) and *Class Representation in Modern Fiction and Film* (2007), and Walter Benn Michaels, author of *The Trouble with Diversity: How We Learned to Love Identity and Ignore Inequality* (2006), agree with Jones that the problem of economic privation in American literature has been subsumed by the language of identity. Michael Denning argues in "Representing Global Labor" (2007) and "Wageless Life" (2010) for reassessing the categories of labor and class to account for global poverty, precarity, and unemployment. In this special issue, we seek articles that will contribute to these reassessments. What counts as the literature of "poverty"? How can analyses of literary and other aesthetic representations of poverty complement, complicate, and even challenge social scientific approaches? How might we extend poverty as an analytic to incorporate dispossession more broadly and to connect poverty to other forms of imperial and economic displacement, conquest, and exploitation?

Submissions of 11,000 words or fewer (including endnotes and references) should be submitted electronically at www.editorialmanager.com/al/default.asp by **October 1, 2020.** When choosing a submission type, select "Submission-Special Issue-Poverty." For assistance with the submission process, please contact the office of *American Literature* at am-lit@duke.edu or (919) 684–3396. For inquiries about the content of the issue, please contact the coeditors: Clare Callahan (callahanc5@sacredheart.edu), Joseph Entin (jentin@brooklyn .cuny.edu), Irvin Hunt (ijh@illinois.edu), and Kinohi Nishikawa (kinohin@ princeton.edu).

Printed and bound by CPI Group (UK) Ltd, Croydon, CR0 4YY

13/04/2025

14656478-0001